Radical Relationships

New Perspectives on the Civil War Era

SERIES EDITORS
Judkin Browning, Appalachian State University
Susanna Lee, North Carolina State University

SERIES ADVISORY BOARD
Stephen Berry, University of Georgia
Jane Turner Censer, George Mason University
Paul Escott, Wake Forest University
Lorien Foote, Texas A&M University
Anne Marshall, Mississippi State University
Barton Myers, Washington & Lee University
Michael Thomas Smith, McNeese State University
Susannah Ural, University of Southern Mississippi
Heather Andrea Williams, University of Pennsylvania
Kidada Williams, Wayne State University

Radical Relationships

The Civil War–Era Correspondence
of Mathilde Franziska Anneke

Translated by Viktorija Bilić

Edited by Alison Clark Efford
and Viktorija Bilić

The University of Georgia Press
ATHENS

© 2021 by the University of Georgia Press
Athens, Georgia 30602
www.ugapress.org
All rights reserved
Set in by 9.75/13.5 Baskerville 10 Pro Regular
by Kaelin Chappell Broaddus

Most University of Georgia Press titles are
available from popular e-book vendors.

Printed digitally

Library of Congress Cataloging-in-Publication Data

Names: Anneke, Mathilde Franziska Giesler,
   1817–1884, author. | Bilić, Viktorija, translator,
   editor. | Efford, Alison Clark, 1979– editor.
Title: Radical relationships : the Civil War–era correspondence
   of Mathilde Franziska Anneke / translated by Viktorija
   Bilić ; edited by Alison Clark Efford and Viktorija Bilić.
Description: Athens : The University of Georgia Press,
   [2021] | Series: New perspectives on the Civil War era
   | Includes bibliographical references and index.
Identifiers: LCCN 2021006471 | ISBN 9780820360225
   (hardback) | ISBN 9780820360232 (paperback)
   | ISBN 9780820360249 (ebook)
Subjects: LCSH: Anneke, Mathilde Franziska Giesler,
   1817–1884—Correspondence. | Feminists—United
   States—Correspondence. | Women abolitionists—United
   States—Correspondence. | Women authors, German—
   Correspondence. | Forty-Eighters (American immigrants)—
   Wisconsin—Milwaukee—Correspondence. | Women—
   United States—Social conditions—19th century. | United
   States—History—Civil War, 1861–1865—Social aspects.
Classification: LCC HQ1413.A52 A335 2021 | DDC 305.420973—dc23
LC record available at https://lccn.loc.gov/2021006471

Contents

List of Illustrations vii

Acknowledgments ix

Maps xi

INTRODUCTION
by Alison Clark Efford 1

EDITORIAL AND TRANSLATION METHOD
by Viktorija Bilić 13

CHAPTER 1. Old Ties Tested, New Bonds Formed,
February–August 1859 21

CHAPTER 2. Europe Bound,
September 1859–August 1860 62

CHAPTER 3. Radical Refuge in the Alps,
August 1860–March 1862 96

CHAPTER 4. Transatlantic Struggles,
April 1862–February 1863 130

CHAPTER 5. An Impetuous Colonel,
April–October 1863 164

CHAPTER 6. Separation,
February 1864–January 1865 197

CHAPTER 7. Endings and Beginnings,
February–August 1865 223

Select Bibliography 245

Index 251

Illustrations

Mathilde Franziska Anneke on horseback in Baden 2
First page of letter from Mathilde to Fritz 15
First page of letter from Fritz to Mathilde 16
Milwaukee in the 1850s 26
Postcard ca. 1864 of the hotel "zum Tiefen Brunnen" in Zürich 40
Zürich in the 1860s 105
The Beust School (Erziehungsanstalt von F. Beust) in Zürich 105
Mathilde Anneke standing next to Mary Booth 135
Mary Booth to Mathilde Franziska Anneke, Zürich, December 24, 1862 156
Drawing by Lillian Booth for her sister Ella 175

Acknowledgments

AS THIS BOOK DEVELOPED INTO A MORE CHALLENGING AND rewarding project than either of us originally envisioned, we found ourselves relying on many people in the United States, Germany, and Switzerland. It would have been impossible to present the lives of Mathilde Franziska Anneke, Fritz Anneke, and Mary Booth if it were not for the work of skilled archivists. Thanks go to the staff of the Wisconsin Historical Society, which holds the Anneke and Booth collections from which we drew the letters. Archivists at the society's Milwaukee Area Research Center, housed at the University of Wisconsin–Milwaukee (UWM), made research a pleasure. We are also grateful to archivists in Zürich, Switzerland, at the Stadtarchiv, Amt für Stadtbau, Zentralbibliothek, and Staatsarchiv Kanton Zürich, especially Karin Beck and Rudolf Vögele. In Sprockhövel, Germany, Karin Hockamp and Winfried Korngiebel at the Stadtarchiv Sprockhövel went out of their way to introduce Viktorija to Mathilde's hometown and share indispensable biographical information. In Rastatt, Germany, Irmgard Stamm gave Viktorija a tour of the city in light of its role in the Revolutions of 1848.

We were fortunate to receive support from our respective universities. Viktorija's research in Germany and Switzerland was made possible by a Research and Creative Activities (RACAS) grant awarded for the project "Translating the Civil War–Era Letters of Mathilde Franziska Anneke." She is grateful to the Office of Research at UWM for supporting the project. Marquette's Center for Transnational Justice provided a grant to commission maps from Christopher Archuleta in the University of Wisconsin–Madison Cartography Lab. Catherine Kirchman, who was then working on a Master of Library and Information Sciences at UWM, helped to scan some of the original German letters, and graduate research assistants William Denzer, Olga Shchennikova, and Christian Krueger in Marquette's History Department helped to transcribe some of the English-language letters and format the bibliography. Melanie Lorenz stood out among the research assistants for contributing a Swiss perspective and working on supplemental materials.

Within our wider circle of colleagues, we must first recognize Walter Kamphoefner, who introduced us to each other and provided ongoing support. Antje Petty at the Max Kade Institute for German-American Studies, University of Wisconsin–Madison, has been a wonderful resource, solving some of the most intractable puzzles we encountered in transcribing old German handwriting. Margo Anderson (UWM) and Renny Harrigan shared their collection of material about Mathilde, and Peter Staudenmaier (Marquette) commented on the introduction. A special thank you goes to Martha Kornelius for feedback on the English translations and for offering valuable advice throughout this project.

Series editors Judkin Browning and Susannah Lee have been unusually generous in encouragement and criticism. As this was the first time we have ventured into publishing documentary sources, we needed more guidance and feedback than we or they expected. At the University of Georgia Press, executive editor Mick Gusinde-Duffy has been exemplary in his shepherding of the project.

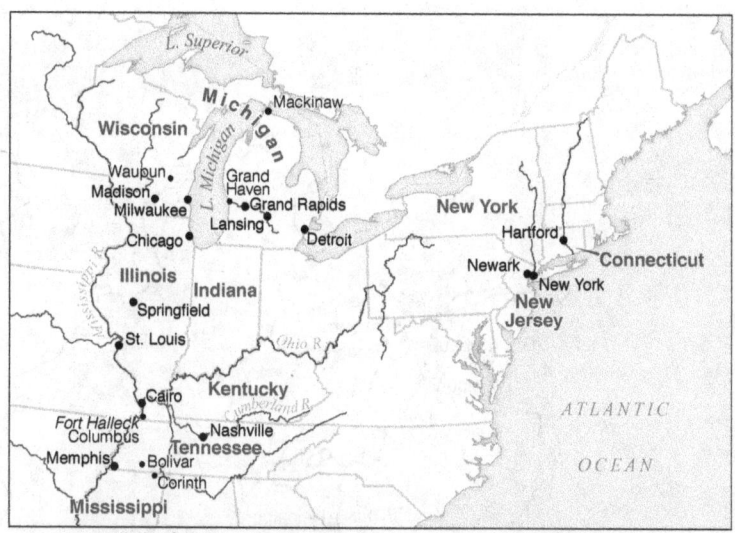

The northeastern United States during the Civil War with select locations mentioned in the correspondence.
Christopher Archuleta, University of Wisconsin–Madison Cartography Lab.

Central Europe in 1860 with select locations mentioned in the correspondence.
Christopher Archuleta, University of Wisconsin—Madison Cartography Lab.

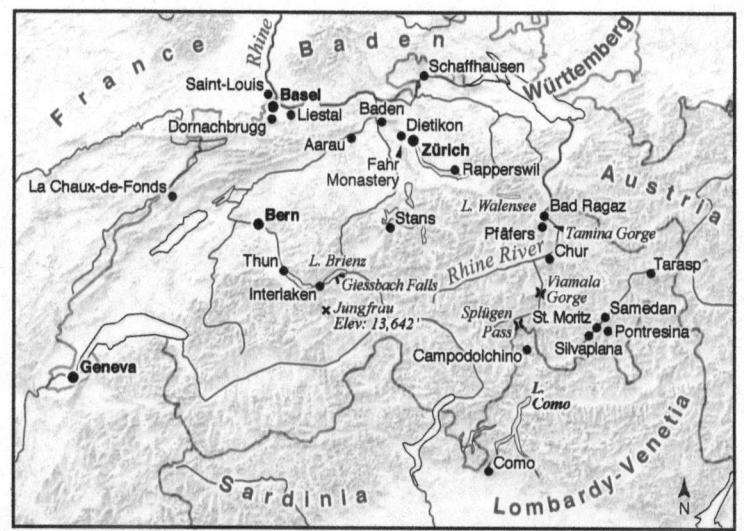

Switzerland in 1860 with select locations mentioned in the correspondence.
Christopher Archuleta, University of Wisconsin—Madison Cartography Lab.

Radical Relationships

Introduction

Alison Clark Efford

MATHILDE FRANZISKA ANNEKE'S CONTEMPORARIES PROBABLY thought of her as a trousered thirty-two-year-old on horseback flanked by other revolutionary soldiers. In 1849, Mathilde joined her husband Fritz in the southern state of Baden to fight for a Germany united under a constitutional government.[1] She was already known as a democrat, a socialist, and a feminist, but military action sealed her credentials as a "Forty-Eighter," a participant in the unsuccessful German Revolutions of 1848–1849. When the Annekes fled to the United States, Mathilde's reputation as a woman who defied convention in the pursuit of justice launched her into a new life. She published a memoir of the Baden campaign,[2] gave lectures before German American crowds, wrote for German American periodicals, and briefly published her own newspaper. Her experiences as a Forty-Eighter informed the work that filled the second half of her life: educating girls and agitating to end slavery and enfranchise women.

Historian Anke Ortlepp has written, "Making Anneke's writings available to English-speaking readers would introduce them to a fascinating woman and grant her the attention that she deserves as one of the German[-American] community's most prolific writers, women's rights activists, and political radicals."[3] The translations in this volume begin that task with a selection of personal letters covering the period from 1859 to 1865. In addition to encompassing the Civil War, these

---

1. We use the first names of Mathilde, Fritz, and Mary Booth to reflect the familiar tone of their letters and avoid confusing the two Annekes. Like them, we refer to Sherman Booth, who fell outside the circle of intimacy, as "Booth."

2. Mathilde Franziska Anneke, *Memoiren einer Frau aus dem badisch-pfälzischen Feldzuge* (Newark, N.J.: Buchdruckerei von F. Anneke, 1853).

3. Anke Ortlepp, "Deutsch-Athen Revisited: Writing the History of Germans in Milwaukee," in *Perspectives on Milwaukee's Past*, ed. Margo Anderson and Victor Greene (Champaign, Ill.: University of Illinois Press, 2009), 124.

Colored lithograph of Mathilde Franziska Anneke on horseback in Baden in 1849. Fr. Nöldeke, "[Mathilde Franziska] Anneke," 1849.
Courtesy of Landesarchiv Baden-Württemberg, Generallandesarchiv Karlsruhe, Germany.

years bracketed Mathilde's passionate relationship to Anglo-American abolitionist and writer Mary Booth. A breathless series of dramatic events filled Mathilde and Mary's time together. Soon after they met in Milwaukee, Mathilde moved into Mary's home to support her through the trials of Mary's famous husband Sherman Booth, first for the "seduction" of a fourteen-year-old and then for engineering the jailbreak of a man who had fled slavery. With Booth still imprisoned, the two women took three of their children and left for Switzerland, where they collaborated on antislavery stories, debated the U.S. Civil War with individuals ranging from American abolitionist Gerrit Smith to German socialist Ferdinand Lassalle, and followed Fritz's career in the Union army—until it was cut short by a court martial. In 1865, six tumultuous years ended when the Confederacy capitulated, Mary died, and Mathilde returned to Milwaukee.

As Ortlepp suggested, the letters reveal the drama of Mathilde's intertwined personal and political lives. They provide especially rich material in two areas. First, they showcase the global dimensions of the Civil War, detailing a dense web of interactions among American opponents of slavery and European radicals. Mathilde, Fritz, and Mary tried to influence European views of the war in the United States, while Europe affected how they approached slavery, the subordination of women, and other forms of injustice. Second, the letters provide a case study of an emotionally intense relationship between women. Mathilde and Mary pooled their resources, raised their children together, collaborated professionally, and pursued a politics that critiqued existing social structures. Mathilde and Mary's unusually well-documented partnership highlights the interplay between same-sex passion and heterosexual norms.

Mathilde's early life in German Europe shaped the woman she had become by the time she met Mary at age forty-one. Mathilde Franziska Giesler was born on April 3, 1817, in Hiddinghausen, Prussian Westphalia, into a wealthy family with connections to both the educated middle classes and the landed gentry. Her mother, Elisabeth Hülswitt, had previously been married to an aristocrat who died, and her father, Karl Giesler, held senior civil service positions and managed his investments. After attending a public elementary school, Mathilde and her siblings received their education from private tutors and, doubtless, the conversations of politically active family friends.[4]

Hers was a privileged childhood, but Mathilde's fortunes changed abruptly when she married Alfred von Tabouillot in 1836. The nineteen-year-old Mathilde agreed to the match because the wealthy wine merchant promised to pay off debts that her father had accrued in a disastrous railroad investment. Although she was optimistic about finding love, her husband drank to excess and treated her "horrifically."[5] Mathilde left within a year and spent several more years trying to extricate herself and her daughter Johanna ("Fanny," 1837–1877) from the violent marriage. Initially, a Prussian court ordered her to return to her husband. Fearing for her safety, she refused, which cost her the chance of alimony and child support. In 1841, she finally won a divorce, but not before she had learned devastating lessons in how law and social convention endangered, impoverished, and constrained women.[6]

Mathilde became politically active as a struggling single mother living in Münster in the 1840s. Supporting herself and Fanny by writing plays, short stories, and articles, she gravitated toward people who were challenging social, economic, and political injustice.[7] After exhibiting early religiosity, Mathilde became particularly critical of the ways that religious traditions and institutions subjugated women. In 1847, she articulated her position in a pamphlet defending Louise Aston, a divorced woman whom Berlin authorities had exiled from the city for her outspoken feminism and frankness about sex. In *Woman in Conflict with Society* (Das Weib im Conflict mit den socialen Verhältnissen), Mathilde argued that "society," embodied especially in the Catholic

---

4. The most reliable source for Mathilde's early life is Karin Hockamp, *"Von vielem Geist und großer Herzensgüte": Mathilde Franziska Anneke, 1817–1884* (Bochum: Brockmeyer, 2012), 11–16. Researchers should be aware that there are many errors in biographies of Mathilde, including the often-cited Maria Wagner, *Mathilde Franziska Anneke in Selbstzeugnissen und Dokumenten* (Frankfurt am Main: Fischer, 1980). For coverage of the 1850s and 1860s, we recommend Mischa Honeck, *We Are the Revolutionists: German-Speaking Immigrants and American Abolitionists after 1848* (Athens, Ga.: University of Georgia Press, 2011), 104–36.

5. Quoted in Hockamp, *Von vielem Geist und großer Herzensgüte*, 15. On the marriage, see also Wilhelm Schulte, "Die Gieslers aus Blankenstein: Ein Beitrag zur märkischen Kultur- und Familiengeschichte," *Der Märker* 9, no. 5 (1960): 127.

6. Annette Hanschke, "Frauen und Scheidung im Vormärz: Mathilde Franziska Anneke. Ein Beitrag zum Scheidungsrecht und zur Scheidungswirklichkeit von Frauen im landrechtlichen Preußen," *Geschichte in Köln* 34 (1993): 70–75.

7. Hockamp, *Von vielem Geist und großer Herzensgüte*, 16–18.

Church's interpretation of marriage, had enslaved women. She maintained that women should free themselves from its irrational restraints and raise independent daughters.[8]

For Mathilde, it seemed obvious that sexism was inseparable from economic barriers and political oppression, which were the subject of more widespread protest. By the 1840s, serfdom and guild restrictions had disappeared from most of German Europe, but German monarchs, the landed gentry, and well-connected capitalists manipulated markets in goods and labor. Anger at what historian Jonathan Sperber calls "unfree market economies" was mounting at the same time that an agricultural crisis gathered across the continent and British industrial production squeezed German craftspeople and small manufacturers.[9] Many critics thought that if all men could vote, and their elected representatives wielded meaningful power, German states would implement fairer economic policies. Liberals and radicals lobbied for a press free from censorship and the right to protest their governments. In German Europe, such ideas could not be separated from the diplomatic relationships among states. Mathilde and others on the Left thought that creating a unified Germany would sweep away the inequitable practices that had grown up within the patchwork of separate kingdoms, duchies, and principalities. Some favored a constitutional monarchy, but she came to advocate a republic.[10]

In the political ferment of the 1840s, it became clear how important

---

8. Mathilde Franziska Tabouillot, "Das Weib im Conflict mit den socialen Verhältnissen," self-published pamphlet, [1846–1847], Box 6, Folder 7, Fritz Anneke and Mathilde Franziska Anneke Papers, Wisconsin Historical Society, Madison (hereafter simply "Anneke Papers"). For excerpts, see also Mathilde Franziska Anneke, "Das Weib im Konflikt mit den sozialen Verhältnissen," in *Frauenemanzipation im deutschen Vormärz: Texte und Documente*, ed. Renate Möhrmann (Stuttgart: Philipp Reclam, 1978), 82–87.

9. Jonathan Sperber, *Rhineland Radicals: The Democratic Movement and the Revolutions of 1848–1849* (Princeton, N.J.: Princeton University Press, 1991), 63. See also Bruce Levine, *The Spirit of 1848: German Immigrants, Labor Conflict, and the Coming of the Civil War* (Urbana, Ill.: University of Illinois Press, 1992), 19–41; James J. Sheehan, *German History, 1770–1866* (Oxford: Clarendon, 1989), 451–524.

10. James Sheehan, "The German States and the European Revolution," in *Revolution and the Meanings of Freedom in the Nineteenth Century*, ed. Isser Woloch (Stanford, Calif.: Stanford University Press, 1996), 259–60; Sperber, *Rhineland Radicals*, 92–94; James Sheehan, *German Liberalism in the Nineteenth Century* (Chicago: University of Chicago Press, 1978); Brian E. Vick, *Defining Germany: The 1848 Frankfurt Parliamentarians and National Identity* (Cambridge, Mass.: Harvard University Press, 2002).

personal relationships were to Mathilde's radical politics. While living in Münster, she met her second husband, the fiery communist Fritz Anneke, at a democratic debating society. Fritz was born Carl Friedrich Theodor Anneke in 1818 in the nearby city of Dortmund to the family of a senior civil servant with military experience. Fritz himself became an artillery lieutenant in the Prussian army, but by 1842 he was also spending time with the people involved in Cologne's famous *Rheinische Zeitung*, including Karl Marx. Fritz met Mathilde after he was finally expelled from the army in 1845 for a duel related to his communist affiliations. They married in 1847 and moved to Cologne in Prussia's Rhine Province.[11] In Münster and Cologne, Mathilde made lifelong friends and mingled with notable figures including the important author Annette von Droste-Hülshoff, Russian anarchist Mikhail Bakunin, and future Civil War general August Willich.[12]

Cologne played a key role in the momentous year of 1848. After the French deposed their king in February, a wave of protests spread across Europe. Germans took to the streets in Berlin, Vienna, and dozens of smaller towns and cities; they brandished weapons outside rural manor houses. In Cologne, Fritz helped to organize demonstrations of thousands of workers who demanded economic concessions and local political power as well as constitutional government. As Prussian rulers hesitated and a national German parliament met in Frankfurt, Karl Marx rushed back to Cologne from exile.[13] On July 3, the scrambling authorities decided to arrest Fritz, leaving Mathilde in a precarious situation. Without Fritz's income and about to give birth, she feared she too would be detained. But her son (Fritz, 1848–1858) arrived on July 21, and within two months she started publishing a new "social-democratic" newspaper, the *Neue Kölnische Zeitung*, out of her apartment. Important Cologne radicals, including Marx, supported the ven-

---

11. Wilhelm Schulte, *Fritz Anneke: Ein Leben für die Freiheit in Deutschland und in den USA* (Dortmund: Historischer Verein Dortmund, 1961), 10–11; Dieter Dowe, *Aktion und Organisation: Arbeiterbewegung, sozialistische und kommunistische Bewegung in der preußischen Rheinprovinz, 1820–1852* (Hannover: Verlag für Literatur und Zeitgeschehen, 1970), 69–74, 113–29.

12. Schulte, *Fritz Anneke*, 23–24.

13. David McLellan, *Karl Marx: A Biography* (New York: Palgrave Macmillan, 2006), 177–81; Levine, *Spirit of 1848*, 41–42.

ture in various ways, and Fritz pitched in once he was released from jail on December 23.[14]

Although the forces of reaction had regrouped by spring 1849, the Annekes held out hope. In May, Fritz, along with poet and revolutionary Gottfried Kinkel and twenty-year-old future U.S. general and senator Carl Schurz, marched with a small group of Westphalian volunteers to Baden's Palatinate region where republican troops hung onto power.[15] After leaving the children in care of her mother, Mathilde also traveled to Baden, serving in battle as an unarmed *Ordonnanzoffizierin* (orderly officer or aide-de-camp).[16] The campaign constituted a formative experience for the European Left, but it did not create a united Germany. Prussia assisted Baden in defeating the uprising in July, forcing Fritz and Mathilde to flee via Strasbourg to Zürich.

Before 1849 was out, the Annekes had decided to move to the United States, settling in the Milwaukee area with several other members of the Giesler and Anneke families. Milwaukee had just over twenty thousand residents in 1850, but the city on Lake Michigan was growing fast. German-born residents made up about 36 percent of the population, and their U.S.-born children swelled the German community.[17] Although German immigrants were politically and religiously divided, the majority supported the broad aims of the Revolutions of 1848.[18] A smaller contingent formed an eager audience for radical books, articles, and lectures. Mathilde addressed local audiences on the Revolutions of 1848 and toured the Midwest advocating "the uplift of women" and "demanding" the "improvement of their social position, the right to work, and above all, the right to vote."[19] In March 1852, she pub-

---

14. Schulte, *Fritz Anneke*, 27, 31. See also Wilfried Korngiebel, "Die *Neue Rheinische Zeitung* und die *Neue Kölnische Zeitung*, 1848/49," in *"Die Vernunft befiehlt uns frei zu sein!" Mathilde Franziska Anneke: Demokratin, Frauenrechtlerin, Schriftstellerin*, ed. Karin Hockamp, Wilfried Korngiebel, and Susanne Slobodzian (Münster: Westfälisches Dampfboot, 2018), 59–84.

15. Schulte, *Fritz Anneke*, 36–38.

16. Anneke, *Memoiren einer Frau aus dem badisch-pfälzischen Feldzuge*.

17. Kathleen Neils Conzen, *Immigrant Milwaukee: Accommodation and Community in a Frontier City* (Cambridge, Mass.: Harvard University Press, 1976), 14.

18. Alison Clark Efford, *German Immigrants, Race, and Citizenship in the Civil War Era* (New York: Cambridge University Press, 2013), 17–51.

19. Mathilde to Alexander Jonas, April 26, 1877. Gerhard K. Friesen, "A Letter from M. F. Anneke: A Forgotten German American Pioneer in Women's Rights," *Journal of German-American Studies*, 12, no. 2 (1977): 36.

lished the inaugural issue of the monthly *Deutsche Frauen-Zeitung*, the first woman-owned feminist periodical in the United States.[20] But Mathilde faced a boycott from male printers in Milwaukee, and when an opportunity for Fritz opened up in Newark, New Jersey, she moved the *Frauen-Zeitung* to the New York area before it languished a few years later. In Newark, Mathilde continued to write, but the six years the family spent on the East Coast were extremely difficult ones. Fritz and Mathilde lost four of their children, including their son Fritz, two three-year-old daughters, and an infant.[21] The grieving parents returned to Milwaukee with Percy (1850–1928) and Hertha (1855–1945) in 1858.

It was on arriving back in Milwaukee that Mathilde met Mary. Like most white abolitionists in Wisconsin, Mary and Sherman Booth hailed from New England and the New York area. Mary Humphrey Corss had been born in New Haven, Connecticut, where Sherman had also spent time as a student at Yale. Sherman Booth was a temperance advocate and abolitionist who in 1839 taught English to the Africans imprisoned for taking over the slave ship *Amistad*. He did not meet Mary until 1849, when she visited a friend in Milwaukee. By that time, Booth was publisher of the *Wisconsin Freeman* and one of Wisconsin's leading abolitionists.[22] The Anglo-American abolitionist movement was inspired by the words and actions of African Americans and had deep roots in transatlantic exchange, but it was culturally distinct from German American antislavery politics. Anglo-American abolitionism bore the imprint of New England and mid-Atlantic Protestantism and had strong ties to temperance.[23] Despite their differences, Mathilde found common cause with the Booths.

Grappling with the nuances of Mathilde, Mary, and Fritz's actions and interactions between 1859 and 1865 will draw readers into debates over the transatlantic dimensions of the Civil War and the nature of same-sex relationships in the nineteenth century. In recent decades, research placing the Civil War in the context of worldwide developments has

---

20. Efford, *German Immigrants, Race, and Citizenship*, 49–50.
21. Honeck, *We Are the Revolutionists*, 107, 105.
22. Diane S. Butler, "The Public Life and Private Affairs of Sherman M. Booth," *Wisconsin Magazine of History* 82, no 3 (1999): 169.
23. Manisha Sinha, *The Slave's Cause: A History of Abolition* (New Haven, Conn.: Yale University Press, 2016); Efford, *German Immigrants, Race, and Citizenship*, 53–85.

changed how historians have approached the conflict. It is not news to historians that the foreign-born made up about 25 percent of Union troops or that the U.S. and Confederate governments worked hard to win the backing of other countries.[24] In the twenty-first century, however, historians have rededicated themselves to exploring interconnections between the United States and events abroad, questioning the extent to which the history of the United States was self-contained and exceptional.

Although some studies emphasize that Europeans saw the United States as a beacon of progress, most transnational histories of the Civil War have shown that its struggles resembled others around the world.[25] The American republic was building an empire, beating back challenges to government power, and facing fierce demands for freedom and equality from those it violently repressed.[26] These trends were global ones in part because of international networks. Several groundbreaking works have demonstrated that the supporters and opponents of slavery depended on transnational cooperation.[27] There is more research on English speakers than German speakers, but many historians have studied the German Forty-Eighters.[28] In the thoroughly researched *We Are the Revolutionists: German-Speaking Immigrants and American Abolitionists after 1848* (2011), Mischa Honeck notably features

---

24. Ella Lonn, *Foreigners in the Union Army and Navy* (Baton Rouge, La.: Louisiana State University Press, 1951), 581–82.

25. On the United States as an ideal, see Don H. Doyle, *The Cause of All Nations: An International History of the American Civil War* (New York: Basic Books, 2014).

26. For overviews, see Thomas Bender, *A Nation among Nations: America's Place in World History* (New York: Hill and Wang, 2006); Steven Hahn, *A Nation without Borders: The United States and Its World in an Age of Civil Wars, 1830–1910* (New York: Penguin, 2016); Jörg Nagler, Don H. Doyle, and Marcus Gräser, eds., *The Transnational Significance of the American Civil War* (Cham: Palgrave Macmillan, 2016).

27. See for example Edward Bartlett Rugemer, *The Problem of Emancipation: The Caribbean Roots of the American Civil War* (Baton Rouge, La.: Louisiana State University Press, 2008); W. Caleb McDaniel, *The Problem of Democracy in the Age of Slavery: Garrisonian Abolitionists and Transatlantic Reform* (Baton Rouge, La.: Louisiana State University Press, 2013).

28. Along with numerous biographies and older works, see Levine, *Spirit of 1848*; Efford, *German Immigrants, Race, and Citizenship*; Kristen Layne Anderson, *Abolitionizing Missouri: German Immigrants and Racial Ideology in Nineteenth-Century America* (Baton Rouge, La.: Louisiana State University Press, 2017); Andrew Zimmerman, "From the Second American Revolution to the First International and Back Again: Marxism, the Popular Front, and the American Civil War," in *The World the Civil War Made*, ed. Gregory P. Downs and Kate Masur (Chapel Hill, N.C.: University of North Carolina Press, 2015), 304–37.

Mary and Mathilde in his argument that cross-cultural relationships fueled antislavery activism.[29]

Mathilde's relationship with Mary merits attention in its own right.[30] Mary told Mathilde that she was the "morning-star of my soul, the beautiful auroral glow of my heart, the saintly lilly [sic] of my dream"; Mathilde's described Mary as "the scent that fill[ed] the air" in the Swiss mountains.[31] It is understandable that twenty-first-century readers might be curious whether they were sexual partners. Since the early twentieth century, genital contact has been the dominant criterion for categorizing relationships between people of the same gender. Around 1900, sexologists and psychologists popularized a definition of "lesbian" based on "deviant" sexual activity.[32] Women who later sought to reclaim lesbian identity also focused on sex, searching for women in the past who had desired other women as they did.[33] Yet scholarship on the erotically charged "romantic friendships" in the nineteenth century shows that they did not fit neatly into twentieth-century categories.[34] It would be anachronistic to call romantic friends lesbians. They did not identify as such, since the category had yet to take on its modern form, and we do not know what they did in bed. It would be equally anachronistic, however, to call them straight. That category did not exist yet either, and romantic friends related to other women with a passion unknown to straight-identified women today.[35] Romantic friendships did

---

29. Honeck, *We Are the Revolutionists*. An important book on transatlantic feminism also mentions Mathilde repeatedly. Bonnie S. Anderson, *Joyous Greetings: The First International Women's Movement, 1830–1860* (New York: Oxford University Press, 2000).

30. Although it reproduces transcription errors, the best account is Joey Horsley, "A German-American Feminist and her Female Marriages: Mathilde Franziska Anneke, 1817–1884," *Fembio*, accessed July 30, 2020, http://www.fembio.org/english/biography.php/woman/biography_extra/mathilde-franziska-anneke.

31. Mary to Mathilde, 1862, p. 214; Mathilde to Mary, 1864, p. 283.

32. Lillian Faderman, *Surpassing the Love of Men: Romantic Friendship and Love between Women from the Renaissance to the Present* (New York: William Morrow and Company, 1981), 239–331.

33. Martha Vicinus, "The History of Lesbian History," *Feminist Studies* 38 (2012): 566–96.

34. The two pioneering works were Carroll Smith-Rosenberg, "The Female World of Love and Ritual: Relations between Women in Nineteenth-Century America," *Signs* 1 (1975): 1–29; Faderman, *Surpassing the Love of Men*.

35. Lesbian historians worry that setting a scrupulously high bar for lesbianism not only denies it a history, but also ignores the historical role of sexuality. See especially Terry Castle, *The Apparitional Lesbian: Female Homosexuality and Modern Culture* (New York: Columbia University Press, 1993); Judith M. Bennett, "The L-Word in Women's History," in

not necessarily involve genital contact and bore relatively little stigma, but they demonstrate the significance of same-sex desire and its subversive potential.[36] The approaches of queer studies, which attend to the spectrum of behaviors and desires that exist in conversation with heterosexual norms, are well suited to Mathilde and Mary's letters.[37]

Taking Mathilde and Mary's relationship on its own terms means recognizing that the two women adored each other and that their partnership offered appealing alternatives to heterosexual marriage. When Mary first met Mathilde, she was in awe. In a letter to her sister, Mary glowingly compared Mathilde to Joan of Arc, the French saint who had gone into battle dressed as a man.[38] Mary, who had also lost a baby, helped Mathilde survive her grief over the deaths of her four children. Mathilde helped Mary endure both illness and the ignominy of her husband's seduction trial. The decision to move to Switzerland grew out of their emotional and practical dependence on each other. Together, they could raise their children while experiencing adventure and a renewed sense of purpose. Instead of living with a rapist who belittled her, Mary had an attentive partner who introduced her to witty, elegant, and educated Europeans. For her part, Mathilde threw herself into caring for a lighthearted younger woman and gained a collaborator and coparent. Mathilde appreciated Mary's talent and independent accomplishments, but she assumed a somewhat parental role in the partnership because of Mary's relative youth, her illness, and her unfamiliarity with Europe.

Mathilde's joyous and profound love for Mary connected her feelings and her principles. With her critique of marriage already public record, her personal letters show how much she valued intense human

---

History Matters: Patriarchy and the Challenge of Feminism (Philadelphia: University of Pennsylvania Press, 2006), 108–27; Martha Vicinus, "Lesbian History: All Theory and No Facts or All Facts and No Theory?" *Radical History Review* 60 (1994): 57–75.

36. See Marylynne Diggs, "Romantic Friends or a 'Different Race of Creatures'? The Representation of Lesbian Pathology in Nineteenth-Century America," *Feminist Studies* 21 (1995): 317–40; Lisa Moore, "'Something More Tender Still than Friendship': Romantic Friendship in Early-Nineteenth-Century England," *Feminist Studies* 18 (1992): 499–520.

37. Dáša Frančíková, "Romantic Friendship: Exploring Modern Categories of Sexuality, Love, and Desire between Women," in *Understanding and Teaching U.S. Lesbian, Gay, Bisexual, and Transgender History*, ed. Leila J. Rupp and Susan K. Freeman, 2nd ed. (Madison, Wisc.: University of Wisconsin Press, 2017), 143–52. For an example of such analysis, see Martha Vicinus, *Intimate Friends: Women Who Loved Women, 1778–1928* (Chicago: University of Chicago Press, 2004).

38. Mary to Jane Corss, February 15, 1859, p. 33.

connection. It seems that Mathilde was committed to promoting equal relationships in part because she believed that passion and intimacy were essential for humans to thrive. Her rather untraditional marriage to Fritz had for a time fulfilled her, but in 1859 she told him that although she cared for him as the father of their children, they no longer loved each other "like lovers."[39] After they separated for good in 1861, Mathilde did not show any romantic interest in men. Mary, on the other hand, did. She and Lassalle flirted with each other, for example, and on one trip away, she wrote playfully to Mathilde, "I wish you could be here with us, & me especially, but until I have you again I must content myself with Lassalle."[40] Mary's letters hint that Mathilde was somewhat jealous, but Mathilde's understanding of love generally elided distinctions between the platonic and the sexual. Mathilde's relationships did not shock her contemporaries, but they were radical because they enacted her vision of a transformed world.

Mathilde's life did not end with Mary's death in 1865. She went on to run a private girls' school in Milwaukee called the Töchter-Institut (Daughters' Institute) and to become Wisconsin's foremost proponent of woman suffrage.[41] When Elizabeth Cady Stanton and Susan B. Anthony formed the National Woman Suffrage Association in 1869, Mathilde served as one of its vice presidents.[42] As might be expected, historians have not completely ignored this remarkable woman, but Anglophone readers lack a full-length biography and professional translations of her writing. We hope these letters introduce more people to the trousered woman on horseback who infused her American activism with the spirit of 1848.

---

39. Mathilde to Fritz, [June or July] 1859, p. 44.
40. Mary to Mathilde, [July 1863], Box 5, Folder 1, Anneke Papers.
41. On the school, see Anke Ortlepp, "*Auf denn, Ihr Schwestern!*": *Deutschamerikanische Frauenvereine in Milwaukee, Wisconsin, 1844–1914* (Stuttgart: Franz Steiner, 2004), 153–59.
42. Annette P. Bus, "Mathilde Anneke and the Suffrage Movement," in *German Forty-Eighters in the United States*, ed. Charlotte L. Brancaforte (New York: Peter Lang, 1989), 79–92.

Editorial and Translation Method

Viktorija Bilić

THE WORK OF SELECTING LETTERS AND DETERMINING AND IMplementing translation strategy heavily affected this collection of sources on the Civil War. The letters that appear in this book represent only a fraction of the contents of two large archival collections. The Fritz Anneke and Mathilde Anneke Papers at the Wisconsin Historical Society in Madison span the years between 1791 and 1884, containing over six thousand individual document pages. Both prolific writers, Mathilde and Fritz produced about two thousand personal letters and several speech drafts, notebook entries, poem and essay collections, as well as newspaper clippings. Donated by their daughter Hertha Anneke Sanne in 1940, these documents form the main source on the family's history.[1] While most of the letters in this volume are translated from Fritz's or Mathilde's German, a smaller number were written in English originally by Mary Booth. The Booth letters come from the Sherman M. Booth Family Papers, owned by the Wisconsin Historical Society and housed at the University of Wisconsin–Milwaukee.

The selected letters illustrate the correspondents' personal lives against the backdrop of the historical events of the years 1859 to 1865. We balanced several goals in the selection process: providing an engaging narrative that tracked the physical movements of the "characters," including revealing information about their relationships with each other and their children, showing how they were involved in the Civil War and in public activism, and capturing transnational interactions. With some exceptions, the letters were exchanged among the three protagonists—Mathilde, Fritz, and Mary. The letters included in *Radical Relationships* make up about 10 percent of the letters in the Anneke collection and about 3 percent of the letters in the Booth collection for the

---

1. Finding Aid, Anneke Papers, Wisconsin Historical Society, accessed July 30, 2020, http://digital.library.wisc.edu/1711.dl/wiarchives.uw-whs-wis000lw.

years we cover. In general, we tried to avoid making too many cuts to the letters in order to convey the texture of the originals.

During the transcription and editing phase, we sought to preserve the authenticity of the original letters. We kept all misspellings such as "carraige" and "does'nt" in Mary Booth's letters. We strove to maintain all capitalization and punctuation as it appears in the letters, although it was often difficult to distinguish between Mary's periods and dashes. We did make minor changes, such as replacing Mary's "xc" with "&c" and plus signs with ampersands for ease of reading, as indicated in the first footnote in chapter 1, so that the formatting has been adapted and interpolations added to the relevant sentences. Ellipses (". . .") indicate the few places where text has been cut.

Mathilde and Fritz wrote most of their letters in *Kurrentschrift*, an old form of German handwriting that can be difficult to decipher and daunts even experienced German scholars.[2] Our transcription of the German letters followed the same editorial guidelines as those of the English letters, preserving the originals precisely. We initially expected that Maria Wagner's *Mathilde Franziska Anneke in Selbstzeugnissen und Dokumenten* (1980) might prove a useful transcription aid, as it includes several paragraphs of the German letters selected for this volume. Wagner did not, however, make her selection and editing process clear, and her transcriptions contain numerous mistakes, omissions, additions, and other errors.

The process of translation has obviously affected most of the letters in this collection, so it is important to describe the decisions that have shaped the texts. Two broad theories in translation studies underpin my choice of translation strategy: the notion of *domestication/foreignization* and the *skopos* theory. An introduction to these two fundamental theories will help the reader understand the decisions involved in rendering a text in a new language.[3]

---

2. Harald Süß, *Deutsche Schreibschrift: Lehrbuch* (Munich: Knaur, 2004), 1–80.

3. Other schools of thought in translation studies that have influenced my approach to historical translation include hermeneutic approaches to translation (George Steiner, Larisa Cercel), descriptive translation studies and cultural translation (Susan Bassnett, André Lefevere), and the theory of translatorial action (Justa Holz-Mänttäri). See Holger Siever, *Übersetzungswissenschaft: Eine Einführung* (Tübingen: Narr, 2015); Mary Snell-Hornby, Hans G. Hönig, Paul Kußmaul, and Peter A. Schmitt, eds., *Handbuch Translation* (Tübingen: Stauffenburg, 1998); Lawrence Venuti, ed., *The Translation Studies Reader* (London and New York: Routledge, 2012).

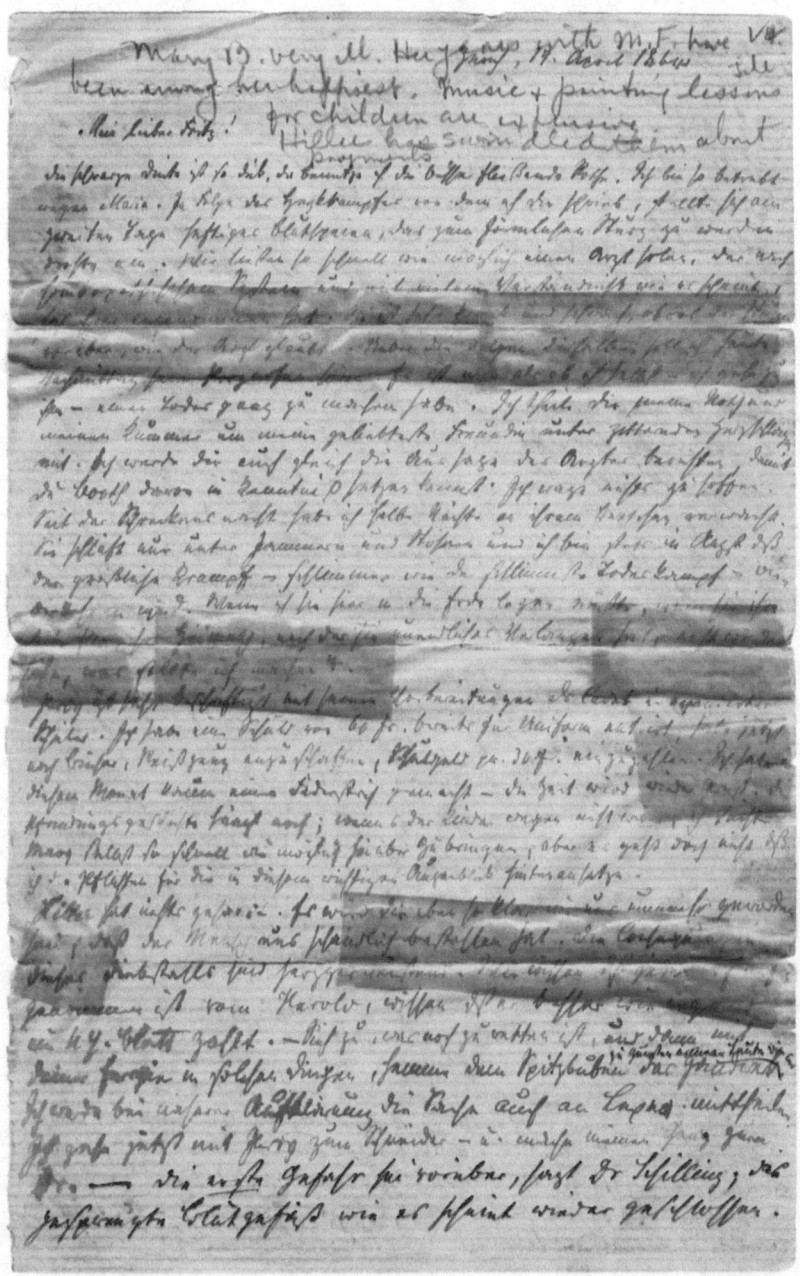

First page of Mathilde Franziska Anneke to Fritz Anneke, Zürich, April 19, 1864. The English comments in pencil were likely added by the Annekes' daughter Hertha Sanne and her collaborator Henriette M. Heinzen, who transcribed and translated some of the letters shortly before Sanne donated the collection to the Wisconsin Historical Society in the early 1940s.
Courtesy of Wisconsin Historical Society, Madison.

First page of Fritz Anneke to Mathilde Franziska Anneke.
Fort Halleck, Columbus, Kentucky, September 9, 1863.
Courtesy of Wisconsin Historical Society, Madison.

Friedrich Schleiermacher articulated the distinction between domestication and foreignization back in the nineteenth century. In 1813, Schleiermacher introduced two paths a translator can take in his well-known lecture "On the Different Methods of Translating" ("Über die verschiedenen Methoden des Übersetzens"): "Either the translator leaves the writer in peace as much as possible and moves the reader toward him; or he leaves the reader in peace as much as possible and moves the writer toward him."[4]

One path, *domestication*, intends to bring the author closer to the reader by making her speak as a domestic author would speak to people in her own language. The second path, *foreignization*, aims at bringing the reader closer to the author and stresses the foreignness of the original and source text culture. The methods of domestication ("Einbürgern") and foreignization ("Verfremden") are entirely different and have been debated in translation studies for hundreds of years. Several translation scholars have taken up the issue and further developed these basic approaches to translation practice. German translation scholar Juliane House distinguishes between overt translation and covert translation. Overt translations (foreignization) are obviously translations that are to be recognized as such. Covert translations (domestication), as the name implies, are not to be recognized as translations. Instead, covert translations enjoy "the status of an original text in the receiving lingua-culture."[5] If translators are cultural "bridge-builders," an overt translation takes the reader "over the bridge" to learn about different cultures. In covert translation, the reader stays "on his or her side of the bridge," and when the text has been translated well, the reader is unaware that the target text at hand is a translation.

More recently, in the 1970s and 1980s, German translation scholar Hans J. Vermeer established a strategy that is based on the aim or purpose (*skopos*) of a translation. According to Vermeer, there are different ways of translating a text depending on its function and the target au-

---

4. "Entweder der Uebersezer läßt den Schriftsteller möglichst in Ruhe, und bewegt den Leser ihm entgegen; oder er läßt den Leser möglichst in Ruhe und bewegt den Schriftsteller ihm entgegen." Friedrich Schleiermacher, "Ueber die verschiedenen Methoden des Uebersetzens (1813)," in *Das Problem des Übersetzens*, ed. Hans Joachim Störig (Stuttgart: Goverts, 1963), 5; trans. Susan Bernofsky, as "On the Different Methods of Translating," in Venuti, *The Translation Studies Reader*, 49.

5. Juliane House, "Overt and Covert Translation," in *Handbook of Translation Studies*, ed. Yves Gambier and Luc van Doorslaer (Amsterdam: John Benjamins, 2010), 245–46.

dience. He declares the function to be the main factor influencing the translation process.[6]

I was mainly guided by a foreignizing translation approach, although there are elements of domesticating translation as well. I endeavored to approximate the style of the source material by using American English that was common in the nineteenth century. My intention has been to remain faithful to the tone of the original text. The function or *skopos* of the source text is distinctive in the case of personal letters. Fritz and Mathilde exchanged the originals with no intention of publishing them. The translations inform readers about this correspondence by making it available in English. My goal was to translate the historical letters for a general audience who may or may not be familiar with the Annekes. For this reason, historical footnotes inform our audience about various references in the letters. The historian and the translator are coauthors who fill in knowledge gaps and contextualize the letter contents for a modern audience. In places, long German sentence structures needed to be changed, and in other places culture-specific elements (*realia*) needed to be explained either in the target text or in a footnote. In-text explanations were inserted subtly. For example, in 1859, Mathilde wrote to Fritz, "The *Gradaus* is now published under the name *Volksblatt*" ("Gradaus ist zum Volksblatt geworden").[7] In German, "Volksblatt" could also mean "a people's paper" or "a paper for the people." Since in this case the newspaper was in fact renamed, however, I chose a translation that reflected this meaning and was as stylistically smooth as the original but included additional explanatory words.

My overarching approach to foreignization and *skopos* guided my response to specific translation challenges in Mathilde and Fritz's letters. The unique writing styles of Mathilde and Fritz presented several translation challenges. The letter writers occasionally mixed German and English, for example, a common phenomenon in immigrant letters. In such cases, as an element of foreignization, I kept the Annekes' English words and German-English word creations, italicizing them in the English translations to highlight that Mathilde or Fritz were using

---

6. Katharina Reiß and Hans Josef Vermeer, *Grundlegung einer allgemeinen Translationstheorie* (Tübingen: Niemeyer, 1984).

7. Mathilde to Fritz, July 15, 1859, Box 3, Folder 5, Anneke Papers, p. 48.

these English words in the German original.[8] For example, in a letter dated September 23, 1859, Mathilde wrote to Fritz about events in Milwaukee: "These things always provide interesting material for my *papers*. Maria has written you all about the political *affairs*."[9] Other translation challenges included stylistic elements such as irony, sarcasm, and literary references. I attempted to preserve all instances of irony and sarcasm in the target text. One of many examples is Mathilde Anneke's sarcastic tone when referring to men who had disappointed her. Mathilde, who had published Catholic prayer books in 1837 but rejected religion by the mid-1840s, frequently used the German abbreviation "Hl" (*Heiliger, der Heilige*) to mock sanctimonious men who wielded some sort of power. I translated "Hl" as "St." (Saint). She referred to Mary's husband in this disparaging way on March 16, 1862: "The noble St. Booth, who had promised Mary to send money around this time, says he can't send anything but that she should not *despair* and should trust the heavens instead."[10] In their letters, both Mathilde and Fritz frequently made references to German-speaking poets and philosophers. For literary quotations, whenever the Annekes quoted a German poet like Heinrich Heine, I cited a prominent English translation if such a translation exists, and in other cases, I translated the quotation myself. Footnotes inform the reader about such literary references and their translations.

In line with the notion that one can only translate a text when fully understanding its (historical) context, researching not only the main letter protagonists but also all persons and events referenced in the letter corpus has been an invaluable step in ensuring a high-quality translation.[11] Archival research in the Zürich-based Beust-Lipka col-

---

8. When Mathilde and Fritz wanted to emphasize something themselves, they used underlining. We replicate the originals in that regard.

9. "Diese Sachen geben mir immer interessanten Stoff für meine Päpers. Ueber die polit. Affaires hat Maria Dir geschrieben. . . ." Mathilde to Fritz, September 23, 1859, Box 3, Folder 5, Anneke Papers, p. 67.

10. "Der edle Hl Booth, der wie Mary erwartete nach seinem Versprechen, Geld in diese Zeit senden werde, sagt er kann nicht—aber sie solle nicht in Dispair dort gerathen sondern auf den Himmel bauen." Mathilde to Fritz, March 16, 1862, Box 3, Folder 5, Anneke Papers, p. 127.

11. Viktorija Bilić, *Historische amerikanische und deutsche Briefsammlungen: Alltagstexte als Gegenstand des Kooperativen Übersetzens* (Trier: Wissenschaftlicher Verlag Trier, 2014), 154–60.

lection at the Stadtarchiv (City Archives) and the Staatsarchiv (Canton Archives), for example, provided invaluable background information. The literary works published by the Annekes can be considered helpful parallel texts in the translation process as well. Mathilde published German novels and plays, for example, while Fritz contributed numerous articles to German American newspapers. These texts serve as background texts and provide a deeper understanding of the content discussed in the letters. An important part of this research prior to translating was consulting with and collaborating with an expert historian who provided the historical introduction and explanatory footnotes for the letter translations. In general, the translation process was influenced by productive debates between a translator and a historian. From start to finish, the historical challenge influenced my translation process.

Interested readers can find translation exercises—along with supplemental information and assignments suitable for German, history, and gender studies classrooms—online. An open-access website offers digital resources for students and scholars to interact with the primary material included in the volume. Search for this book on www.ugapress.org.

CHAPTER 1

Old Ties Tested, New Bonds Formed

February–August 1859

THE BOOTH AND ANNEKE FAMILIES BECAME ENTWINED IN 1859 as each recovered from a domestic trauma. In 1858, the deaths of the four children on the East Coast had prompted Fritz and Mathilde Anneke to move back to Milwaukee, home to numerous members of their extended families, including Mathilde's mother, Elisabeth Giesler; Mathilde's sister Johanna Weiskirch; and Fritz's brother Carl Anneke. Yet the Annekes did not stay together in Milwaukee for long. Seeing conflict brewing on the Italian Peninsula, Fritz persuaded three Milwaukee editors to engage him as a war correspondent. Reporting on what would become known as the Second War for Italian Independence promised Fritz meaningful work and the possibility of mixing with nationalists and revolutionaries who shared the ideals he and Mathilde had fought for in 1848 and 1849.

By the time Fritz left for Europe in May 1859, Mathilde had established a firm bond with Mary Booth, whose life was also in turmoil. Mary's husband Sherman was famous for his abolitionism, especially his part in instigating the 1854 jailbreak of Joshua Glover, who had escaped slavery in Missouri. In March 1859, however, Sherman Booth was arrested for another reason, for "seducing" a fourteen-year-old girl who had cared for his daughters. Mary, convinced that Booth was guilty of rape, depended increasingly on Mathilde. Their growing affection was evident in the fact that they addressed each other by names no one else used. Mary began calling her older friend "Franziska Maria" because she considered Mathilde an ugly name,[1] while Mathilde used the German form of Mary's name, Maria. In addition to providing emotional support, Mathilde gave Mary money, nursed her when

---

1. Mathilde to Franziska Hammacher, April 4, 1861, in *"Ich gestehe, die Herrschaft der fluchwürdigen 'Demokratie' dieses Landes macht mich betrübt . . .": Mathilde Franziska Annekes Briefe an Franziska und Friedrich Hammacher, 1860–1884*, ed. Erhard Kiehnbaum (Hamburg: Argument Verlag mit Ariadne, 2017), 70.

she was sick, and helped to manage Booth's lawyers. In fact, Mathilde moved into the Booth home with her son Percy (nine) and daughter Hertha (four). The Booths' daughter Lillian May or Lili (four) lived there too, but their older daughter Mary Ella (nine) left to stay with Mary's mother, Adeline P. Corss, in Hartford, Connecticut. Unsurprisingly, Mary corresponded regularly with Ella (as everyone called Mary Ella), her mother, and also her sister Jane Corss. The letters in this chapter cover the period from Mary and Mathilde's meeting until Booth's trial ended with a hung jury.

Mary Booth to her sister Jane Corss
Milwaukee, February 15, 1859
(English original)

My dear Jane:

I was very happy to hear from you & and glad that you are now able to wear nice dresses. I will send you what you wish with the greatest pleasure as soon as I am able to sew. I have not been very well of late, but now I am better.

I send you a very beautiful mereno dress by Salsman,[2] who will start for the East to-morrow. Abby, and the twins[3] will go with him. The twins have grown very pretty.—I will make your pink mereno loose dress, as you wished, the first thing I do.

I received a box of most beautiful flowers, among which were a white calla, and orange flowers, from Mrs. Mitchel,[4] yesterday—and from Madam Anneke, a pot of mingionette in blossom.

Madam Anneke is the beautiful German woman whom we heard lecture at Treat's hall,[5] when Ella was a baby. She was in battle, like "Joan

---

2. Thomas Salsman was a friend of the Corss family who was taking the dress to Jane Corss. U.S. Census, Population Schedules (1860), 4th Ward, Milwaukee, Wisc., p. 41, dwelling 315, family 329.

3. Salsman and his wife Abby had three-year-old twins. Ibid.

4. Possibly philanthropist Martha Mitchell, the wife of railroad magnate and financier Alexander Mitchell. Frances E. Willard and Mary A. Livermore, eds., *A Woman of the Century* (Buffalo: Charles Wells Mouton, 1893), 510–11.

5. A venue in central Milwaukee. *Milwaukee Daily Sentinel*, March 18, 1852.

of Arc." You admired her very much then, and perhaps you remember her. She has lived in New York[6] since then, until within a few months.

Her whole life has been devoted to literature, and she has published about fifty books, poetry, novels, and scientific, and revolutionary works.[7]—Her mother[8] is a splendid old lady. She sent me some "soup" a few days ago, *which* <u>shows her to be very good</u>! She was the most intimate friend of Madam Ida Pfiffer.[9]

Madam Anneke speaks but very little English, but I mannage to understand her. She has been celebrated by <u>Heine</u>, <u>Freiliheurt</u>, <u>Sallet</u>,[10] and all the modern German Poets. Mr. Richmond[11] is in raptures over her—and thinks there are few such living women, and is happy that she is my friend. She spends part of every day here, now since I have not been well—but I am nearly well now—and the first thing I do will be to make your pink loose dress. Mr. & Mrs. Spalding,[12] and Mrs. Faxon ("<u>She that was Josephene Hood</u>")[13] send their love to you.

Write as often as you can
  With much love I am as ever
  aff.[14] Mary

---

6. Mathilde had actually lived in Newark, N.J.

7. Mary apparently means to include individual articles and poems in the count.

8. Elisabeth Giesler.

9. The adventures of Austrian travel writer Ida Pfeiffer (1797–1858) were famous enough for Henry Thoreau to mention in *Walden*. *Encyclopædia Britannica*, 11th ed. (New York: The Encyclopædia Britannica Company, 1911), 21:340; Henry Thoreau, *Walden* (Boston: Ticknor and Fields, 1854), 26.

10. No evidence of praise from these writers survives, but they were acquainted with Mathilde. The famous Jewish German poet Heinrich Heine (1797–1856) contributed to the *Neue Kölnische Zeitung*, which the Annekes edited in 1848 and 1849. Ferdinand Freiligrath (1810–1876) was another poet who championed German unification, publishing a newspaper with Karl Marx in Cologne in 1848. Friedrich von Sallet (1812–1843) was known for writing poems critical of religion. Manfred Gebhardt, *Mathilde Franziska Anneke: Madame, Soldat und Suffragette: Biografie* (Berlin: Neues Leben, 1988), 26, 74; *Encyclopædia Britannica*, 11:94–95; Daniel Jacoby, "Sallet, Friedrich von," *Allgemeine Deutsche Biographie* (Leipzig: Duncker & Humblot, 1891), 33:717–27.

11. Episcopalian priest James Cook Richmond was about to become rector of St. Paul's Church in Milwaukee. Frank A. Flower, *History of Milwaukee, Wisconsin* (Chicago: Western Historical Company, 188), 865.

12. Possibly Henry W. Spalding, who was ordained as an Episcopalian priest in Milwaukee in 1860. *Milwaukee Daily Sentinel*, January 1, 1860.

13. These clues are not sufficient to identify Faxon.

14. Affectionately.

Mary Booth to her mother Adeline Corss
Milwaukee, March 4, 1859
(English original)

My dear Mother:

I am <u>awful</u> sick, much sicker <u>I feel</u> than when I was the worst.

Monday I went to Waukesha[15] to attend the wedding of Prof. Daniels[16] & Miss Gove, which was Tuesday. I took cold, & have an <u>infernal</u> neuralgia[17] in my face & teeth. One of my front teeth is so sore it cant be touched, the filling came out of it before we came in this house, & I could not have courage to have it in. My face is swolen horridly. My nose being stretched from ear to ear. I have to lie on the lounge all the time, & can only sit up a short time. The Dr. says it is far better to be in my face than on my lungs again, in which case it would have been very bad. But I cough enough, any way, & wish I did more, rather than be <u>cussed</u> with such devilish torment. It makes me mad—the first time I have been for a very long time, & I guess blaspheming a little will do me good.

Sherman is in Madison.[18] I expect him home to night. Madam Anneke staid with me last night & night before. I was dreadful sick, & she sent her husband for chloroform in the evening for me, & I put it on my tooth & face, & it helped it. She would not let me smell of it. . . .

Madam Anneke's mother wears a cross of large diamonds <u>set in iron</u>, and also a ring, because her husband had iron mines. She always dresses in black velvet & is a most elegant woman although she cannot speak one word of English. Madam Anneke is herself grandmother of two children—her daughter's, who is only twenty years old.[19] She wishes I could have been with her in battle!!

I guess I would'nt stand and be shot at. It would take Jan[e] for that,

---

15. A town twenty miles west of Milwaukee.

16. College professor and one-time state geologist Edward Daniels lived in Ripon, Wisconsin. He had been arrested with Sherman after the Glover affair and continued to support him. Flower, *History of Milwaukee*, 250.

17. A widely used term for stabbing "nerve" pain. "Neuralgia," *OED Online*, Oxford University Press, accessed July 30, 2020, http://www.oed.com/view/Entry/126356.

18. Wisconsin's capital lies eighty miles west of Milwaukee.

19. Johanna ("Fanny") von Tabouillot had married Paul Störger and taken his surname. The couple did not live together consistently because Störger had business in Cuba and Fanny raised their children in Newark until moving to Milwaukee in 1866. There is only evidence that one of Fanny's children was born before 1859, but perhaps another died.

with her "Mazeppa"[20] notions. She had two horses a day. She has written a book about the Battle, & also her autobiography,[21] which I hope to be able to read sometime—& has published in all, fifty books.—She writes poetry & will translate mine as a soon as she understands English more. She is very large, & the most beautiful, delicate, child-like face you ever saw. She hates American womens rights females.[22] It was her love of her country & her husband, especially him, that led her to battle. She, & Carl Shurtz[23] were her husband's Agatants.[24] They were exiled from the country after the Revolution. Mr. Richmond was in Germany at the time, & says she <u>was</u> [&] <u>is</u> the glory of Germany. She has been painted as Madonna in two <u>churches</u> as a compliment to her fame as a poetess.[25] Mr. Richmond says she is in all respects a most wonderful woman. She came in while Mr. Davis[26] was here, & he did not give me another look. His wife said to me—"Jackson has found a wonder now." Lillian[27] came to us when we were in bed in the morning & said, "<u>The little bird dreamed of you both last night</u>, in the dark he dreamed of the Light." Madam Anneke kissed her half to death, & said

---

Mathilde to Franziska Hammacher, October 24, 1860, in *"Ich gestehe, die Herrschaft der fluchwürdigen 'Demokratie' dieses Landes macht mich betrübt,"* 41.

20. George Gordon Byron's narrative poem "Mazeppa" (1819) details the ordeal of a soldier lashed to a wild horse. George Byron, *The Complete Poetical Works*, ed. Jerome J. McGann (Oxford: Clarendon Press, 1986), 4:172–200.

21. Mathilde Franziska Anneke, *Memoiren einer Frau aus dem badisch-pfälzischen Feldzuge* (Newark, N.J.: Buchdruckerei von F. Anneke, 1853).

22. Mathilde's approach to women's rights differed from that of Anglo-American leaders such as Elizabeth Cady Stanton and Susan B. Anthony. American feminism during this period was associated with temperance, Protestant moralizing, and, sometimes, hostility to immigrants, none of which Mathilde endorsed. Yet her work with other feminists shows that she respected them as partners in a common struggle.

23. The most successful of the Forty-Eighters, Carl Schurz (1829–1906), would become a Union general in the Civil War, a U.S. senator from Missouri, and secretary of the interior. In 1849, he had been Fritz Anneke's subordinate in the revolutionary forces in Baden, and when Mary wrote, he was working as a lawyer in Milwaukee and trying to win the Republican Party's nomination for governor of Wisconsin. Schurz was a political ally of Sherman Booth, although the seduction charges ended their relationship. Hans L. Trefousse, *Carl Schurz: A Biography*, 2nd ed. (New York: Fordham University Press, 1998).

24. An adjutant is a senior military aide to a commanding officer.

25. If true, the paintings must date from Mathilde's brief time as a religious writer in the late 1830s and early 1840s, before she became hostile to traditional religion. Karin Hockamp, *"Von vielem Geist und großer Herzensgüte": Mathilde Franziska Anneke, 1817–1884* (Bochum: Brockmeyer, 2012), 16–18.

26. We could not identify Jackson Davis.

27. Mary's four-year-old daughter, whom she often called Lili.

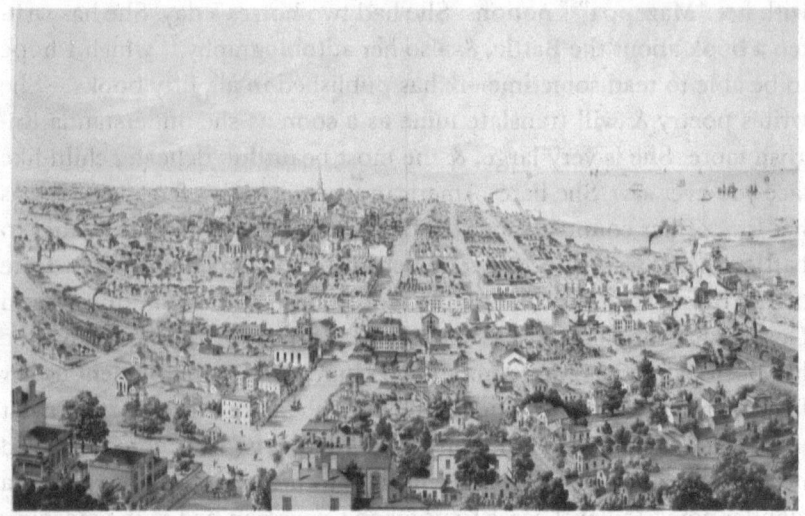

Lithograph of Milwaukee in the 1850s. George J. Robertson and D. W. Moody, "Milwaukee, Wisconsin," lithograph, 1854.
Courtesy of Library of Congress.

"never a child uttered an expression more poetical." Ella dances most beautiful, & is pleasant & good natured. They have gone to see <u>Fanny Crouch</u>.[28] Ella[29] teaches Madam Anneke's boy the Bible, & he her, German. I will write to Jane about it.

 Mary

I have strung out a long letter at last <u>by spells</u>.

Fritz Anneke to Mathilde Anneke
Detroit, May 30, 1859

My beloved Mathilde Franziska Maria!

 I had almost finished writing my letter to you when it happened: Someone knocked on the door to my room at the Hotel Mauch—that same room we stayed in last year—and as I get up I accidentally drag

---

28. The English-born undertaker Jonathan Crouch and his wife Rachael had a three-year-old daughter named Fanny. U.S. Census, Population Schedules (1860), 4th Ward, Milwaukee, Wisc., p. 4, dwelling 38, family 32.

29. Mary's other daughter, Mary Ella Booth, 9.

the tablecloth with me, and with it my letter paper, the letter to you, and the ink jar. Sadly, a large ink stain on the carpet and a completely ruined letter were the results. Now I quickly need to write the letter all over again in a rush.

Not until the moment we had to say goodbye did we realize—you as much as I—just how much we love each other. And had we known how much pain it would cause to go our separate ways, I may not have left and you may not have let me leave. I also think that—to put both our minds at ease—you may have decided to rest close to my heart that night. That is the very reason I came to your bed.—The moment we had to say goodbye, Mathilde, I will never forget!

Karl,[30] Emil,[31] and Booth accompanied me to the ship. You will know by now that I negotiated with Booth then.[32] He owes you $5. You will have received my farewell greetings by now. I was granted a free journey to Detroit. The lake was very rough and so we had to stay in the parlor and close to the oven. I spent my time on the ship thinking of you and the children and studying French vocabulary. In the course of the afternoon, I went on deck for a moment, leaving my dictionary in the parlor. Upon my return, I found that my letter had disappeared without a trace. All my investigations were fruitless. The passengers and waiters hadn't seen it. On landing in Grand Haven,[33] however, the letter was suddenly in its place again. It seemed that the thief had felt ashamed of himself. I could tell you several stories about the group of travelers, the journey, the strangely formed coastline of Grand Haven, and about the place itself. But I don't have the time right now. Maybe I'll write about it, and you'll be able to read the printed version. On landing in Grand Haven, I discovered a fellow countryman among the passengers. He hailed from Olpe[34] and had already lived close to Lake Superior for 14 years. He knew Rainard Weiskirch[35] very well and

---

30. Fritz's brother, Carl Anneke. The Annekes used the spellings Carl and Karl interchangeably.

31. Likely Emil Weiskirch, the husband of Mathilde's sister Johanna.

32. The negotiations probably involved Fritz's work as a correspondent. Booth had just sold the *Milwaukee Free Democrat*, one of the newspapers for which Fritz wrote. Jerome A. Watrous, *Memoirs of Milwaukee County* (Madison, Wisc.: Western Historical Association, 1909), 1:445–47.

33. A Michigan town almost due east of Milwaukee across Lake Michigan.

34. A town in Prussian Westphalia about forty-five miles west of Cologne.

35. Probably a relation by marriage to Mathilde's sister Johanna Weiskirch.

had been to Iserlohn,[36] Dortmund etc. He was a very knowledgeable and well-informed man. We traveled together for the rest of the journey and arrived at the Hotel Mauch together yesterday morning at 6 a.m.

Detroit is blooming like a garden in the spring right now. It truly is a beautiful place. At least several of its streets deserve that distinction, like Jefferson Avenue and Fort St. There are marvelous trees on those streets, as well as nice houses and gorgeous gardens surrounding each of them. . . .

You will probably not receive another letter from me before I arrive in New York. And now a thousand greetings and kisses to you from your Fritz and think of him with love.

Greetings to Grandma,[37] Karl, Mr. Booth, etc.

Mathilde Franziska Anneke to Fritz Anneke
Milwaukee, June 1859

Dear good Fritz!

Well, with Maria's[38] letter, you will have received the first message from us by now. Our little children ask about you often, and I try to comfort them with the prospect of reuniting with you soon. This morning I woke up early with them, dressed them nicely, and had breakfast with them alone. We talked about you. I will spend my time wisely now, because I've agreed to translate a novella for Leslie.[39] I wrote the

---

36. A town in Prussian Westphalia not far from Dortmund.
37. Mathilde's mother, Elisabeth Giesler.
38. Mary's.
39. Mathilde had written regularly for the German-language edition of Frank Leslie's famous *Illustrated Newspaper* since 1858. The popular weekly employed a more successful feminist writer, Louisa May Alcott, and was circulating an estimated twenty-five thousand copies of the German version alone by 1870. After Mathilde declined an invitation to work for free, Leslie visited her personally in Newark and agreed to pay her for her work. Maria Wagner, *Mathilde Franziska Anneke in Selbstzeugnissen und Dokumenten* (Frankfurt am Main: Fischer, 1980), 90; Karl J. R. Arndt and May E. Olsen, *German-American Newspapers and Periodicals, 1732–1955: History and Bibliography* (Heidelberg: Quelle & Meyer, 1961; reprint, New York: Johnson Reprint Corporation, 1965), 360.

As later letters explain, Mathilde translated a serialized novel from one of Frank Leslie's periodicals into German. The original author did not, in fact, finish the story, so Mathilde completed it herself. She published it as *Das Geisterhaus in New-York* (The haunted house in New York) under her own name without identifying the original author or acknowledg-

first column[40] yesterday afternoon. I do not have any more difficulty writing now than I had 20 years ago, and so why shouldn't I undertake it? He promised to pay 1 dollar per column and promised to send the $16 he owes me in 8 days. Tell me your opinion when you collect what he still owes us. Tell me if I can risk this, that is if he would indeed pay me. He wants 3 columns per week.

A shameful newspaper article written to humiliate you has been published in today's edition of the *Seebote*.[41] You need to read it. I sent the *Banner*[42] a simple counterstatement today. I am enclosing both documents.

I hope and wish, dear Fritz, that you are healthy. I am healthy again now—more or less.

Our situation here remains unchanged. Maria is rather healthy and affectionate towards me and the children. I do not want to tell any more about myself.—

Farewell, dear Fritz. Perhaps you won't leave American soil too soon and will receive another letter from us. If this is in fact my last farewell, then please know that I am sending you this with tears in my eyes. Farewell and never forget the mother of your six children.

Mathilde Franziska Anneke to Fritz Anneke
Milwaukee, [June or July] 1859

Dear good Fritz!

When Maria and I walked over to the post office yesterday, arm in arm, I was so happy to receive your nice long letter from Detroit. Your little letters for the children and Maria also brought us much joy. While walking over to Grandmother's house, we kept reading your letters.

---

ing that the text was mostly a translation. *Das Geisterhaus in New-York* (Jena and Leipzig: Hermann Costenoble, 1864).

40. Throughout, column ("Spalte") refers to a column of type rather than the whole piece of writing.

41. The *Seebote* started as a Catholic-friendly alternative to Milwaukee's secular German-language press in 1851. By 1859, it was essentially a Democratic newspaper. Alison Clark Efford, "The Appeal of Racial Neutrality in the Civil War–Era North: German Americans and the Democratic New Departure," *Journal of the Civil War Era* 5 (2015): 68–96.

42. Milwaukee's largest German-language newspaper in 1859, the *Wisconsin Banner und Volksfreund* supported Democratic candidates. Alison Clark Efford, *German Immigrants, Race, and Citizenship in the Civil War Era* (New York: Cambridge University Press, 2013), 72.

Maria was not satisfied with my poor translation of your letter. It would be better if you would respond to her funny little letters in English, her "sweet mother tongue." You can probably tell from the letters she wrote you how she has tried to comfort me. And that did not fail to have the desired effect on me because her immortal sense of humor often made me smile through my tears and even laugh out loud. I hope, dear Fritz, that you will have gotten over some of the most terrible pain of separation from the children and me. I for one try to deal with the direness of our separation as much as possible by carefully looking after those two gems of ours, whom I am now caring for alone. The love of my friend Maria and hard work also help me deal with this pain. But even after overcoming this pain, there is still so much melancholy in our current times. It causes a feeling of numbness in me against everything except for my children and Maria. If only I can preserve my health until I can one day bring the children back to you again, I shall be happy. It was not just at the moment we had to say goodbye, dear Fritz, that I realized once again how much I loved you. I've been aware more than anything of my love for you in its varying degrees from the moment it awakened until now. I knew before you left that a separation would cause endless grief for all of us. But I also knew that the misfortune of spending my life with you as your wife but not loved by you would feel even more endless. Dear Fritz, we should never have married. We should have stayed friends, and we may have both led happier lives. And indeed, we love each other more like friends now. We love each other since we are most intimately related through the children we have together. But we do not love each other like lovers who both feel that their desire for each other fills their existence and can only be satisfied by the touch of pure lips when they kiss. My endless love for you was not able to convince you of this truth and—all alone—it had to bleed to death. Through our dear good little children, we could have found a lost Eden of pure love again—and we still can, my dear Fritz. And once you are possibly with us again, let the living word[43] help us find out how and what we feel. I would like to chat with you much longer, but I am very exhausted after working on the boring translation.

---

43. "Das lebendige Wort" is a biblical allusion. It is not clear whether Mathilde was being ironic or simply using a common turn of phrase.

And Fessel[44] has strictly forbidden me to experience any kind of stress. I did not feel very well one night, and Maria and Booth took particularly good care of me. I'm now doing well again.

Emil wrote to Carl on Monday saying he had heard that I was ill and asking if we needed anything. I was touched by Emil's brotherly love. He hadn't received your letter yet. My correction in the *Banner* has set the entire press here in motion. Even the *Seebote* has rectified things now, so I hear.

I now have a pleasant little writing place in my bedroom. Maria used her well-known decorating talent to make it a lovely place for me here. I now have clean air, sunshine, and a nice view while writing. We are very much looking forward to letters from you. Me especially. Grandmother sends her regards and so do the others. I will celebrate Carl A[nneke]'s birthday with him tomorrow and bring him two nice glasses. I did take notice of your other comments. I will risk writing you again. And that's why I won't say farewell just yet.

Hold dear, your loving Mathilde.

Franziska Maria says[45] *"comm hier Americaner Maria, und schreibe zu dein Leben." Du bist ein bösewicht das was du bist.*[46] *Franziska Maria has conceived a "wonderful" affection for you since you went away. She persists in saying you are not cross.*

We sit now at a "wonderful" table in our bedroom & "Maria"[47] *writes & I plague her & kiss her half to death. We are not troubled by any masculine visitors except the Dr. & he comes every day. I think his health improves, as you know it is for his own good that he comes.*

Ich mein lieb zu meiner Liebe, and write soon

Dein Americaner schelm[48]

Maria

---

44. Mecklenburg-born Christian Fessel (1801–1881) was a physician who had been involved in liberal dissent in Europe from the 1820s to 1848. Louis Frederick Frank, *The Medical History of Milwaukee, 1824–1914* (Milwaukee: Germania Publishing Company, 1915), 18–22.

45. Mary inserted her own comment in mixed English and German into Mathilde's letter, calling her "Franziska Maria."

46. "Franziska Maria says 'come here American Maria and write about your life.' You are a villain, that's what you are."

47. Here Mary is referring to Mathilde.

48. "I will be nice to my love, and write soon, your playful American."

Mathilde Franziska Anneke to Fritz Anneke
Milwaukee, July 1859

My dear good Fritz!

Sunday morning

So now we probably do not stand on the same land. We're no longer together on American soil! I hope to receive your last farewell letter today or tomorrow. Yesterday, sometime in the afternoon when I picked up your letter, Maria and Grandmother and I went for a walk to the lake. And my thoughts were traveling with you "across the blue sea." If it safely carries you across, then I will bless it. "On Wings of Song"[49] is the melody I hear in my mind while the weather outside is quite stormy—I think I'm alone in the "land of the wind" and you have already arrived in more beautiful regions. I wonder whether you've received most of our letters before your departure! Excluding the letter that arrived yesterday, you still owe us half a dozen replies. There's the lovely first letter that Maria wrote about how much I cried after your departure and how she tried to comfort me. And how Booth himself came on a carriage and pair and invited us—me, the children, Grandmother, and Maria—for a nice ride into the country. We drove for about 8 miles and visited farmers in a wonderful-smelling forest and a beautiful flower garden. They invited us for supper, and we ate plenty of maple sugar and drank maple syrup. We also had fruits and bread—everything was prepared in the traditional farmer's way. It was already past 9 o'clock when we returned. Maria wrote to you the day after, and the day after that she wrote to you again.

Tuesday. I can't get any sleep, and I don't know whether it's because I'm anxious about you or what it is. I got up at half past four this morning and began working on my translation. Maria was sound asleep and so were all of our little children. Percy's school festival was held yesterday at Melms.[50] Maria and her Lili took the boat down there, and my little Hertha and I followed in an omnibus. It was a pity that it

---

49. Heinrich Heine's poem "Auf Flügeln des Gesanges" (1823) became popular after Felix Mendelssohn set it to music in 1834. In English translation, it is known as "On Wings of Song." Heinrich Heine, *Buch der Lieder* (Hamburg: Hoffmann und Campe, 1827), 117–18; Larry Todd, *Mendelssohn: A Life in Music* (Oxford: Oxford University Press, 2003), 309, 330; Hal Draper, trans. and ed., *The Complete Poems of Heinrich Heine: A Modern English Version* (Boston: Suhrkamp/Insel, 1982), 54.

50. The Melms Brewery operated a beer garden in Milwaukee's Menomonee Valley.

was such a cold day, but Percy enjoyed himself and his friend Mazzini[51] was there too. My little Hertha never stopped holding my hand. She has great difficulty walking, and I think an operation is imminent now. A dark cloud looms over our communication. I see you haven't received the letters we had written to you. On the second day after our sad farewell I had such an intense bout of cramps, and I was suddenly so deeply worried about our little children that I did not know what to do. I thought I would have permanent attacks now and that there was no hope of recovery. Additionally, I was overcome by the oppressive feeling that the Booths would constantly be burdened with taking care of me, etc. But now my worries have turned into the firm hope that I will get well again. As early as this week I will begin a health cure of sorts, meaning I will start drinking (an imitation of) Carlsbad mineral water.[52] I started with a pre-cure, a different effervescent mixture without iron tincture, and it truly benefits me and helps me with my anxiety. As to my corpulence: I am very noticeably losing weight and Maria is already worried that I could lose my embonpoint[53]—one of my characteristic features that she likes so much. I was very worried about Maria for several days, and I stayed up with her for an entire night because she was feeling such pain and disappointment. I helped her down the other side of that cliff, perhaps a bit roughly, but powerfully, because in the end her heart and being could have been shattered to pieces. I assume that her disloyal friend,[54] in his vanity, did not mention or show you the letter that I had already written. But this man just does not answer letters and does not return things that we've specifically asked for. It seems like we will have to take more extreme measures here. Maria's health is much, much better. The calm that has returned after this resignation has helped her in her recovery. She looks very nice again, oh so pretty! She now wants a divorce more than ever before. She wants it because of her children, and she wants it for herself—

Thomas W. Merrill, "Melms v. Pabst Brewing Co: The Doctrine of Waste in American Property Law," *Marquette Lawyer* (Summer 2011), 8–22.

51. Percy possibly had a friend nicknamed after the Italian revolutionary Giuseppe Mazzini. Census takers found no Mazzinis in Milwaukee in 1860.

52. The water from the Karlsbad Springs in Baden was widely believed to have therapeutic properties. Perhaps Mathilde had salts that allowed her to imitate its properties in Milwaukee.

53. French for corpulence.

54. This seems to be a reference to J. A. Biedermann, a music teacher and tenor with whom Mary had a romantically charged friendship. He comes up in later letters.

and she is right. What will become of the trial, I cannot say.⁵⁵ Booth is behaving terribly.

On another day. This night—I always spend part of the night at the side of our dear little Hertha—she cuddled me, firmly held on to me, and almost shouted for joy: "My dear Papa." She soon became aware that it was me and not you, pressed me to her heart as if to say that well, everything was fine then too.

And now today she tells Lilie that her Papa had spent the night sleeping next to her and then left again this morning. Naturally, I will not wake her from this wonderful dream. Whenever Lili jumps into her father's arms, Hertha follows her, equally rejoicing in the prospect of seeing her father. And when she then sees Lili's father and not her own, she quietly comes back into my arms. There's so much desolation in her eyes! But what can be done? Percy speaks of you often, and he has now started drawing maps and has started drawing your route. He regularly attends school, but I don't think he learns much. The institute⁵⁶ seems to me to be of little value. It was at the school festival that I came to this realization. Your second to last letter—and tomorrow I will pick up your farewell note—downright saddened me. I see how few resources you have left. Was it truly not possible to claim the money that Lexow⁵⁷ or Leslie owes us? After all, heaven knows whether I will receive payment from Leslie. I will not send him another part of my translation before both Hölzlhuber⁵⁸ and I have received our payment. I also haven't

---

55. Beginning on July 25, 1859, Sherman Booth faced a two-week trial for "seducing" Caroline N. Cook, a fourteen-year-old neighbor who was staying overnight at his house to care for the children. Cook would testify that after she refused to go to bed with him, Booth came wordlessly into the bedroom she was sharing with her sister, took off his clothes, lay on top of her, and penetrated her. After performing the act twice, he carried her into another room and repeated it once more. *The Trial of Sherman M. Booth for Seduction* (Milwaukee, Wisc.: Wm. E. Tunis & Co., 1859), 7–8.

56. Forty-Eighter Peter Engelmann was the principal of the well-regarded German-English Academy, a private school established in 1851, which Percy attended. Kathleen Neils Conzen, *Immigrant Milwaukee: Accommodation and Community in a Frontier City* (Cambridge, Mass.: Harvard University Press, 1976), 181–82.

57. Born in Schleswig-Holstein, Forty-Eighter Rudolph Lexow had settled in New York, where he edited the *Criminal-Zeitung und Belletrisches Journal*, an enormously popular political and literary weekly that changed name over the decades. *New York Times*, July 17, 1909; Arndt and Olsen, *German-American Newspapers*, 345–46.

58. Austrian painter Franz Hölzlhuber (1826–1898) traveled in the United States in the late 1850s, residing for a time in Milwaukee. "Franz Hölzlhuber's Watercolors," Wisconsin Historical Society, accessed July 30, 2020, https://www.wisconsinhistory.org/Records/Article/CS359.

received anything from Madison and other places yet. I've outfitted our children with new clothing. Maria is currently sewing two dresses for Hertha. Maria is always her loving self. Several nights ago, she revealed something interesting to me. Something that she has never told anyone ever before, neither Booth nor B[iedermann].[59] And only at my request would she allow me to tell you that she is the descendant of an Indian. This revelation was so amusing to me; the manner in which she disclosed this, her pride, and then also her self-denial. It cost us half a night of sleep. I think her great-grandmother was a daughter of the forest, one of the last Mohicans.[60] Her great grandfather, a Corsican, married the daughter of a tribal chief. I told her that you had said before that Indian blood was running through her veins. She's happy that you did not say that to her, because she would have hated you for it. She says her ancestry has caused her much sorrow her entire life and that her evil mother always blamed all evil in her on her Indian heritage.

Why did you call me "you sweet thing"?[61] *You* know I am not. *Was I ever "sweet" to you? Tell me that Mr. Fritz! Mary. Is that a greeting over the See?*[62] *What you think? Yes, it is. Never mind! That is* sweet *consolation!!*

You see that she's lost nothing of her humor, not even after I just received a letter from Biedermann.

Franziska Maria is "wonderful" kind and lovely to you now you are away, "never mind" so long as you are not here—ist sie *sehr sehr böse!*[63] *She can write the* truth *about herself which it would be impolite in me to do.*

You see, dear Fritz, ever since the playful Indianae[64]—I won't call her by any other name now—took up my pen, all decency has vanished from my letter. As I wrote before, B[iedermann] has sent a letter and in it he declares in his terribly confusing writing style that he would never stop loving her, but that he is aware that he cannot reunite with her and so on. It did have a considerable impact on Maria because she told me

---

59. See n. 54 (chapter 1).
60. Soon after James Fenimore Cooper's *Last of the Mohicans* was published in 1826, abridged and edited translations began to appear in German Europe. Cooper was one of the best-known foreign authors among Germans at the time. Preston A. Barba, "Cooper in Germany," *Indiana University Studies* 21 (1914): 51–104.
61. Mary inserted a comment.
62. Mary seems to be parodying Mathilde's response to receiving a letter from "over the sea."
63. "She is very, very angry!"
64. Latin for a female Indian.

he could not stop loving her the same way she couldn't stop loving him and so on. I wonder how this whole romance novel is going to end. Grandmother is her old self. Johanna and Emil are happy together, and that's all. Carl Anneke complains a lot, and just like Krues expressed it at the festival,[65] he looks like he takes his medicine.[66]

I can't think of anything else—*oh, Mr. Fritz*[67]—*your picture and mine hang opposite each other at <u>Grosmother's</u>—They look <u>wonderful</u>—and smile very sweetly on each other, as we <u>never</u> did. Franziska & I are going with the Editorial convention to Grand Rapids*[68] *to night. We shall return Saturday morning. We saw Dr. Kane's Panorama*[69] *last night. I have a picture of Grandmother which looks like the Devil.*

Well, I will send this letter to Beust.[70] Please send my kind regards to him and all of his loved ones. You also have to send my regards to Ottilie Kapp, maiden name Rappard, who now lives in Zürich.[71] I will keep sending all subsequent letters to Beust. We are looking forward to your first letter after you've hopefully safely reached European shores. You will find helpful friends in London—I have no doubt. Kinkel[72] and Freiligrath are there, and they are certainly not weary. For your sake, I will hope for the best.

I was invited to the excursion of the editors' conference held here beginning yesterday. It has been decided to travel to Grand Haven and Grand Rapids together. We will talk about you often, and I will be thinking of you as you've recently passed both of these places. Your let-

---

65. This reference is unclear.
66. Carl Anneke worked as a pharmacist.
67. Mary interrupts.
68. A town in Michigan.
69. Panoramic paintings of Elisha Kent Kane's Arctic expeditions were on display in Milwaukee in June 1859. *Milwaukee Daily Sentinel*, June 8, 1859.
70. Friedrich ("Fritz") von Beust was, like Fritz, a former Prussian officer who resigned to participate in the revolutionary movement in Cologne. A supporter of Marx and Engels's communist party, Beust published a newspaper with the Annekes until authorities suppressed it in 1848. In 1859, he was running a private school in Zürich. Ludwig Julius Fränkel, "Beust, Friedrich (von)," in *Allgemeine Deutsche Biographie* (Munich: Historischen Kommission bei der Bayerischen Akademie der Wissenschaften, 1903), 47:754–58.
71. When Mathilde moved to Zürich, she would again enjoy the company of her old friend, author and educator Ottilie Kapp. *Titan: A Monthly Magazine* 25 (1857): 561–78. Kapp's daughter Cäcilie would return to the United States with Mathilde in 1865.
72. Johann Gottfried Kinkel (1815–1882) was a poet, university professor, and Forty-Eighter who fled to England after Carl Schurz helped him escape from a Prussian prison in 1850. Otto Maußer, "Kinkel, Gottfried," in *Allgemeine Deutsche Biographie* (1910), 55:515–28.

ters, all of them with no exception, and your curl of hair have their special little place in our home. I often go there with Hertha and Percy and tell them about you. The children will not forget you. Farewell, dear Fritz.—Stay healthy!

Think of us and send my love to Father[73]—and to my homeland that I will probably never see again. We keep your little pictures with your letters. One beautiful morning—before we'd found this safe asylum for them—I caught Hertha who had put them in her little drawer to slide them back and forth. When I caught her doing that, she suddenly had a sad expression on her little face and said she wanted to drive Papa around. The *N.Y. Demokrat* has dedicated an obituary to you.[74] The *Banner* is still in press today and has not been published yet.

Farewell, farewell, farewell.
Your loving Tilla.

Mathilde Franziska Anneke to Fritz Anneke
Milwaukee, [June or July 1859]

Beloved Fritz!

How long it's been since we've last heard from you! All last week I went for the mail in vain, hoping that the letter you promised to send from Southhampton[75] would be there. But I always came back home empty-handed and with a heavy heart. Hopefully, you will have received our letter upon your arrival in Zürich. Nothing or nothing much has happened in our lives since then. I am preoccupied with my little children, my Maria, and my work. Nothing's changed regarding Booth. His trial may be adjourned for 2 weeks. Grandmother was ill but is now healthy again. Little Hertha is a dear little heart. She is beginning to express less desire to see you, but that doesn't mean she's forgotten about you. Her little feet aren't getting any better unfortunately, and an operation has become necessary. As soon as my resources allow it,

---

73. Fritz's father Christian Anneke.
74. The *New-Yorker Demokrat* was the weekly edition of the *New Yorker Herold*. Arndt and Olsen, *German-American Newspapers*, 349, 410. The "obituary" Mathilde had in mind was probably a piece of commentary on Fritz leaving the United States for political oblivion.
75. Southampton was southern England's main emigrant port in the mid-nineteenth century. Mathilde misspelled it throughout.

we will no longer wait on that. I had two new pairs of shoes made for her already, but neither is good enough for her to wear. I carry her in my arms much of the time. Percy is a little more industrious since I've taken him out of the Engelmann school and now that he attends Zündt's school.[76] The new school is certainly a little more expensive, but I am much calmer now that I know he has better supervision.

I suppose Franzisk[a] Maria wishes very sweet to you. I suppose, also, you don't know that "Mr. Augustus"[77] *and Dr. Munk*[78] *are in love with her! Maria—*

While I was putting the children to bed, Maria's playful nature got the better of her again and she played this prank on me. I now continue in all seriousness. Percy is busy until 6 o'clock in the evening. He speaks about you with a longing smile on his face; and he hopes that you will return to us soon. My dear Maria and I never leave each other for a moment. We love each other, and we share both joy and sorrow like sisters. In the mornings I now drink my imitation Carlsbad mineral water, take a short walk, and begin my work after breakfast. I'm translating the novel for Leslie, and I receive 3 dollars for 3 columns every week. As to the old debt: I have not yet received a cent from him and not from Lexow either, whom I'd pressed for 1½ dollars per column. Neither did Cramer[79] remunerate me for the translation, nor have I been able to collect money elsewhere. I had plenty of expenses, however. My cure always costs money—But why tell you about these petty matters? I have not had one of my bad seizures again—the one I had after your departure when I had to alarm the entire house. *Franziska Maria has done for tonight.*

Yours as ever M. B.

---

76. Ernst Anton Zündt (1819–1897) was a Swabian-born writer who would later become known for his lyric poetry, but he held various positions, including stage manager, newspaper editor, and private teacher. "Zündt, Ernst Anton," *National Cyclopaedia of American Biography* (New York: James T. White & Company, 1909), 11:371.

77. Possibly Baden-born Augustus Greulich, a local politician. U.S. Census, Population Schedules (1860), 2nd Ward, Milwaukee, Wisc., p. 31, dwelling 266, family 282; Flower, *History of Milwaukee*, 264.

78. Probably the widowed physician Emanuel Munk (1806–1899), an enthusiastic Republican from Prussia's Polish province of Posen. Frank, *Medical History of Milwaukee*, 27–28.

79. New York–born William E. Cramer edited the *Evening Wisconsin*. Donald E. Oehlerts, *Guide to Wisconsin Newspapers, 1833–1957* (Madison, Wisc.: State Historical Society of Wisconsin, 1858), 171.

Fritz Anneke to Mathilde Franziska Anneke
Zürich, July 1, 1859

My beloved Mathilde!

What memories I've relived since yesterday! I'm at the guesthouse "tiefen Brunnen." I'm staying in the same room we stayed in 10 years ago. And I think only and only of that time. My eyes always darken here, and now my paper is getting wet, my hands are shaking, and I cannot make any progress writing.

I was just at the garden by the lake, and I plucked a little purple rose from which I'm sending petals enclosed, as well as a leaf from the grapevine stocks where little Fritz learned how to walk and where he always picked grapes! The beautiful garden and house look just like back in those days. And the farmyard also looks the same. This is where little Fritz and I were looking for fruit and where he uttered his first word: "tree."

Herr Coßmann[80] and his wife recognized me immediately. Life has treated them well. They have eight children now. . . . And farmhand Ernst is also still alive, but his wife is dead, and his Babettchen is married, and he himself has taken to drink. He's apathetic and does not travel through Switzerland anymore. He was also unable to remember us. But when I showed him his own handwriting in a letter I had in my wallet, he recognized it.

Upon arrival in Strasbourg[81] yesterday afternoon I could neither find Father nor a letter from him. And then I went to the Montagne Verte[82] immediately. The innkeeper on the other bank of the River Ill recognized me at once. I saw our old house there as well, just from the outside, and the places on the Ill where we went swimming, boating, and fishing. And the meadow where little Karoline ran toward us saying: "the little animal is here!" Little Karoline is also dead and so is her mother, Frau Münch.[83] They died in Africa. And our good old friend

---

80. Mathilde later refers to the fact that the Koßmanns had run the inn. Perhaps she is referring to the same family.

81. Located on the west bank of the Rhine in the historically contested area of Alsace, Strasbourg was a French city in 1859, as it is today. Between 1871 and 1918, it was part of the German Empire.

82. Fritz describes part of Strasbourg bordering the Ill River.

83. We found no further information on these two people.

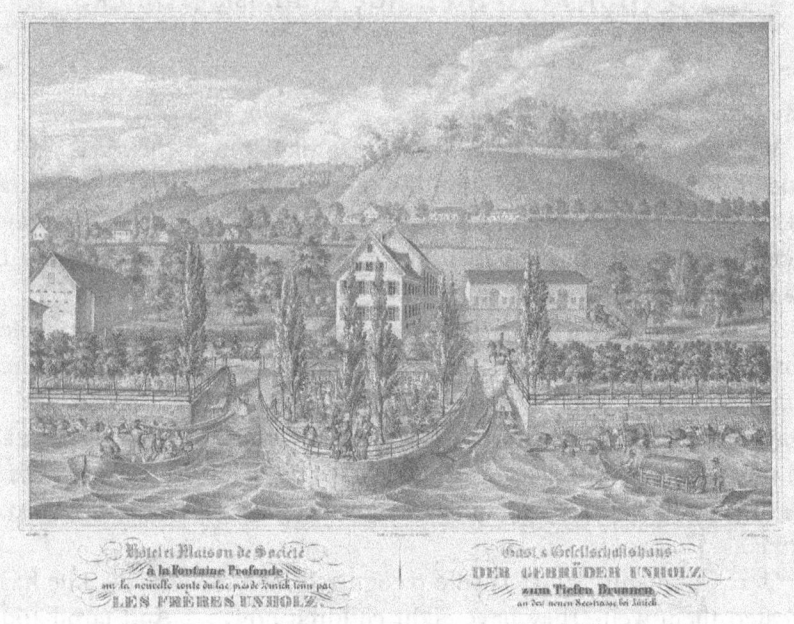

Postcard ca. 1864 of the hotel "zum Tiefen Brunnen"
in Zürich, where Fritz stayed in 1859.
Courtesy of Zentralbibliothek Zürich,
Graphische Sammlung und Fotoarchiv, Zürich, Switzerland.

Dr. Lobstein who had invited us to a farewell "democratic breakfast"?[84] Death carried him off mercilessly also.

I soon turned my back on Strasbourg. When I returned from the Montagne Verte and came back to the inn "Rebstock," I received a letter from Father telling me that he could not come to Strasbourg on account of passport problems and because he was overwhelmed with work with no one to fill in for him. He would come visit me in Zürich if at all possible, and if not, he would send me a letter to Zürich at any rate. I now expect him today or tomorrow. If he does not come, I will travel to Italy the moment I have the resources. I had $41 in Milwaukee and a total of $61 with Emil's contribution. And now my little savings

---

84. This is likely a reference to a breakfast organized by members of the "Demokratischer Verein," where Mathilde and Fritz first met. Hockamp, *Von vielem Geist und großer Hersensgüte*, 19.

have melted down to 65 francs or $13. I cannot get far with that kind of money. Including the advance payment to Schwedler[85] for the journey, $35, I have spent $83 since I left Milwaukee. I have economized a great deal, but the long stays in different places, several purchases, and some random expenses, e.g. $2 for passport matters, expensive prices here and there, and all of that quickly melted away my savings.

My dear Mathilde, I need to refer you to my newspaper correspondence to read about most of my travel experiences. I must economize with my time as much as with my money. I do not devote any time to mere amusement. I only focus on necessary travel and the collection of writing material. I have material again now for a hundred correspondences, but most of it would be relevant for literary papers only. With this letter I will mail my first correspondence to the *Free Democrat*—the one I began in Strasbourg but was unable to complete there. You will like it, and the readers of that paper too, as long as they are not offended a little in their American arrogance. I will enclose a little note to you just like I did before when sending correspondences to the *Sentinel*, [*Illinois Staatszeitung*], *N.Y. Demokrat*, and *Westliche Blätter*.[86] I will now first write to the *Atlas*[87] and then the papers in Detroit, etc. I had my laundry cleaned for an extremely low price in Strasbourg. It took four hours, and I received it looking better than ever before. I left the place yesterday morning at 7 and arrived here around 6 in the evening. I saw Father Rhine only for a moment in Basel[88] when we drove in an omnibus from one train station to the next. And then at the last stop in France I had to show my passport. No one asked to see it in Swit-

---

85. Friedrich Schwedler edited various permutations of the *New Yorker Herold* (including the *New-Yorker Staats-Demokrat* and the *New-Yorker Demokrat*). Arndt and Olsen, *German-American Newspapers*, 369–70, 410.

86. Where Mathilde abbreviates a German-language newspaper title, we provide a fuller version in square brackets. Run by Forty-Eighters, the *Illinois Staatszeitung* was Chicago's largest German newspaper and an important antislavery, Republican organ. The *Westliche Blätter* was the Sunday edition of the *Anzeiger des Westens*, a St. Louis newspaper that also supported the Republican Party and opposed slavery under the leadership of Heinrich Börnstein during the late 1850s and early 1860s. Arndt and Olsen, *German-American Newspapers*, 73–74, 274.

87. Forty-Eighter Bernhard Domschke published the German American *Atlas* in Milwaukee from 1856 to 1861. For a time, Carl Schurz contributed articles to the Republican newspaper. Arndt and Olsen, *German-American Newspapers*, 671–71; Trefousse, *Carl Schurz*, 72–73.

88. Swiss city on the Rhine at the borders with France and Baden.

zerland. As I left Basel and continued my journey, I also saw Dornachbruck[89] from a distance where we climbed to the peak of that beautiful mountain and when we reached the top you put your arms around me. We then passed through Liestal, Aarau, and Baden.[90] It's been a delightful journey.

I was standing here in the garden at the lakeshore for one hour looking at the blue-green water and the glassy surface. I was looking at the nice little steamers, the clumsy boats, all the beautiful houses and villages on both sides of the lake, and the mountain chains to the right and to the left.

The top of the old Uetliberg,[91] which we climbed together during a romantic nighttime excursion, was covered in a mist of clouds. The other surrounding mountains could only be seen when a ray of light somehow found its way through this wall of fog and clouds.

Oh, that dull and dreary country, "where, in freedom's mighty stable stalled alike is every clown."[92] How is it even possible to stay there for such a long period of time when all of the world's treasures can be found on this side of the ocean? If I shall return, then only to come for you. My numerous arrangements to write newspaper correspondences will be an optimal chance for me to provide for us working from here permanently. I will be able to keep many of them for good, and then I can build on them, and little by little I will be able to make new arrangements in Germany and maybe England. Maybe I will even try to seek correspondence arrangements in Germany. I will write you more about this another time.

After a long search, I found Beust last night. He does not live in the former inn by the lake anymore. He now lives a little further up and closer to the city. Beust, Anna,[93] and their two handsome boys are faring well. He has 5 boarders and a school with about 50 pupils. They

---

89. A former town on the Birs River now mostly incorporated into the municipality of Dornach. "Dornarchbrugg," *ortsnamen.ch: Das Portal der schweizerischen Ortsnamenforschung*, accessed July 30, 2020, https://search.ortsnamen.ch/record/109001534.
90. Smaller towns on the way southeast from Basel to Zürich.
91. A small peak overlooking Zürich.
92. Heinrich Heine used these words in reference to the United States in the 1851 poem "Jetzt wohin?" (Where to now?). The translation here follows Margaret Armour, trans., *The Poetical Works of Heinrich Heine* (London: William Heinemann, 1917), 230.
93. Anna Beust (née Lipka) was a cousin of Marx's collaborator Friedrich Engels. Markus Bürgi, "Friedrich Engels' Aufenthalt in der Schweiz 1893," *Marx-Engels Jahrbuch* (2004): 187.

were very disappointed that I did not board with them from the start, and they wanted to keep me there without further ado. But I did return to my guesthouse "tiefen Brunnen" late at night in pitch-black darkness, walking on mountain and forest paths. Everyone was sound asleep when I arrived. In general, people here carefully put out all lamps and go to bed at 9 o'clock.

I was interrupted by Anna Beust at this point. She came in a carriage to take me away from my guesthouse and welcome me to her home, where I'm now sitting in my room after lunch, writing this letter to you. I have received Father's letters now: one for me, one for Fritz Beust, and one for Anna Beust. I am very upset about his letters. As I expected, Father will not come because urgent work keeps him there. He doesn't send me any money either, but rather complains about difficult times, losses etc. His health is very weak. He speaks ill of me in most terrible ways in his letters to Fritz Beust and to his wife. He writes that I have been playing nothing but silly games since 1845 and that I just betrayed him again by adventurously and blindly rushing into a war trying to write correspondences. In his letters, he asks them to keep me from going. I assume that this is also the reason why he refuses to give me money. Anna Beust, who looks as youthful as ever and is just as cheerful and buoyant as in the olden days, was outraged by Father's letters. Then and there, she wrote him a response, six pages long, and she read him the riot act. I am now stranded here, because I can't travel to Italy with my 65 francs. I would get to the border at best, and then I would need to rely on begging and robbing.

But what hurts my feelings is that this thwarts my plan, which was so well thought out and had worked so well until now. It is mortifying that I am now experiencing this uncomfortable humiliation with the papers I've contacted. The only thing I can do now is to write as many articles from here as possible and ask the well-to-do newspaper editors for advances. It will certainly take four weeks until I can collect some money, probably 5 or 6. In case you have requested and received money from Börnstein[94] after reading my earlier letter from Southampton, and if you are in pocket, I ask you to send me something. But

---

94. Born in Hamburg, Heinrich Börnstein (1805–1892) was a teacher, journalist, writer, and theater entrepreneur who collaborated with Marx in Paris in the 1850s. After moving to St. Louis, he published the *Anzeiger des Westens*. Heinrich Boernstein, *Memoirs of a Nobody: The Missouri Years of an Austrian Radical, 1849–1866*, trans. and ed. Steven Rowan (St. Louis, Mo.: Missouri Historical Society Press, 1997).

please send it to F. Beust because in the end there could be a happy coincidence, and I could acquire resources and then would have left already before the arrival of your reply. American bills of exchange, however, probably have to be taken care of here so they can be turned into money or Italian currency. I will earn a handsome income from my Milwaukee correspondences. The traditional Eidgenöss'sches Freischießen[95] will be held here again and starts the day after tomorrow on July 3. It will provide me with plenty of writing material.—Tomorrow, it will be three weeks since I left American soil. And this means I should have received letters from you a long time ago. I expected a letter from you to arrive with the Hamburg steamer that landed in Southampton two days after the steamer that I took. And in fact, long since then another steamer has arrived in Liverpool. Did the damn, negligent American mail play another trick on us?—I must close now, my dear Mathilde, because I have to write to Maria and the children and then need to work on my correspondences right away.

Farewell, my dear, dear Mathilde. You won't receive another longer, direct letter for some time now, but the little notes, similar to the first four, will just keep coming to you very often. Kiss the dear children from me and send my best to Grandmother, Karl, Emil, Henriette,[96] Johanna, Booth, and everyone asking about me. Anna Beust, as well as Bertha Lipka[97] and their mother, who live close by, send their special greetings to Karl. Beust and his wife also send you their warm regards. Bertha Lipka looks very old and very lean. As I had expected, Fritz Beust is very well-informed about the war and he has splendid maps, statistical notes etc. The Swiss press, as small as it is, does provide good material about the war, and so reporting about it from here is going rather well. And not to forget, I recommend that you use quite thin paper for your letters, because the French mail <u>only</u> delivers ¼ ounce for standard postage.

Yours, Fritz.

---

95. A famous competitive sharpshooting festival.

96. Fritz's brother Carl Anneke's wife.

97. Bertha Lipka was Anna Beust's younger sister, another first cousin of Friedrich Engels.

Mary Booth to her mother Adeline Corss
Milwaukee, July 3, 1859
(English original)

My dear mother:

We received your letter yesterday. I will send Jane the music by Lorenzo.[98] My Stars! You ask "where is the money coming from to go to Italy"—that's the question! I should like first to see even one dollar. Sherman pays every cent he gets for debts & lawyers. He has now engaged a man, (with whom he has been closeted all day) to hunt up evidence for him—against the girl, (& me, too, I suppose). Madam Anneke came up stairs & found him in our bed room,[99] talking with the girl who was making the bed. & The bed in a radiant condition. We both being (_nix_[100])—Sherman had sent him up—but I tell you he had to catch it most awfully, as he speaks German[.] Mad. A. fired off at him _tremendously_ in German. She asked him how he _dared_ to come in our sleeping room & marched him off quick. He is a fine looking man of good presence, about 55 years old. He is to go to the Cooks[101] & pretend to be an enemy of B. & find out all he can, and report to B.

An elegant Sundays work! and he is to work at such things all the time until the trial, which is to commence one week from to-morrow. The day is now set. S. pays this man $25 & must raise this week one thousand dollars for his lawyers—where he is to get it I cannot say, nor imagine. Mr. Arnold[102] told S. to employ this man. What do you think—he was on the jury that convicted him in the Slave Case. A. said

---

98. Reporter Lorenzo L. Crounse was a very close friend of the Corss family. Only nineteen in 1859, he had worked with Sherman Booth at the *Free Democrat* before joining with a partner to buy out the paper in March 1859 when Booth was arrested for "seduction." Watrous, *Memoirs of Milwaukee County*, 1:445, 1:465.

99. One author claims that Mathilde found Sherman in the bedroom, but the reference is clearly to the lawyer, and Caroline N. Cook was no longer babysitting for the Booths by July. Diane S. Butler, "The Public Life and Private Affairs of Sherman M. Booth," *Wisconsin Magazine of History* 82, no. 3 (spring 1999): 187.

100. Mary probably means "strike that."

101. The family of Caroline N. Cook, Sherman Booth's victim.

102. Jonathan E. Arnold was one of Milwaukee's most successful criminal attorneys in the mid-nineteenth century. As the letters show, Sherman Booth would fire him before the trial. Watrous, *Memoirs of Milwaukee County*, 1:663–64.

that when there was not Evidence enough, this man would see that there _was_ in some way or other.

Mrs. Merrill[103] looks like a gohst "being" so "_sick_" for fear of having to testify. She is really sick on account of it. I have only seen her three times—and then not long. Madam Anneke dont think it is good for me to talk about it with her, or any one more than is need. Mary[104] thinks you ought to be here by all means, but I do not feel that I shall be brought up, although she does. She says I am deceived in thinking all will be right in regard to me—but I do not feel afraid. Madam Anneke will go to the trial all the time with an old German editor, & if I am spoken off wrong she will attend to it, & she can influence S. to quit it, or she will make a fuss that he wont like. She has talked to him, & now he is better than a few days ago.

When he is not, then I am sick—I am now about as well as when you were here.

If it should be necessary for you to come, which I cannot think it will, I will telegraph to you.

Mathilde Franziska Anneke to Fritz Anneke
Milwaukee, July 15–18, 1859

Beloved Fritz! Percy came home from the post office yesterday afternoon with the very first little letter assuring me that you are on firm ground again. Schwedler sent it to me with a few friendly lines and noted that at your special request he will send me the weekly *N.[Y.] Demokrat* starting with the first one that includes your correspondence. The 6 rose petals you sent and the news that you were busy drinking wine made all of us very happy, including Maria and myself. We received another message from you yesterday evening when I got your letter from Southhampton only 2 hours later—the one you wrote on the ship. Grandmother just came in while I was reading your letter,

---

103. A few women with the last name Merrill lived in Milwaukee.

104. Possibly Mary Briggs, an otherwise unidentified friend mentioned in later letters. Mary to Adeline Corss, August 8, 1859, Box 2, Folder 5, p. 124, Sherman M. Booth Family Papers, Wisconsin Historical Society, Milwaukee Area Research Center, University of Wisconsin–Milwaukee Libraries Special Collections and Archives. Also available online Sherman M. Booth Papers, "The State of Wisconsin Collection," accessed August 30, 2020, http://digital.library.wisc.edu/1711.dl/WI.SBCb2f5. (Hereafter "Booth Family Papers.")

and then we were both just so glad that you had happily made it to the other side of the Atlantic. It was a family celebration. I did send Booth to the *Sentinel* offices right away to see whether they had received your correspondence and enclosed little note to me. The answer was no. He was waiting impatiently for it and said if there was anything he could help me with—if I wanted to travel and so on—I only needed to ask him. The [*Illinois Staatszeitung*] sent me your enclosed little note with the 6 rose petals today.

The first of your correspondences that I thus read was the one printed in the [*Illinois Staatszeitung*]. It is about ¾ of a column long, and I like it very much. I cut out every one of your articles, and Maria has taken on the task of "getting" them into a large binder. St. Ruppius[105] may have taken the correspondence that was sent to the *Westliche Blätter* with him to St. Louis. Or he may not have received it yet. That is to say that Rup[pius] stealthily left for St. Louis yesterday morning. And as Zündt tells me, he will continue the paper there under the direction of Börnstein (?) (and this could be true). Z[ündt] is supposed to provide articles for him from here. And Ruppius did not pay the poor Märklin[106] for his work on the last two issues of the paper. Quite generally speaking, it is a curious case with the *papers* these days. I was in need of money and requested the 3 dollars that the *Atlas* owes me. The new manager, Herr Otterburg[107] (because Cramer was dismissed from this position), has responded to me that instead of payment I had received

---

105. Mathilde frequently used the German abbreviation "Hl" ("St.") to mock men who were apparently convinced of their own righteousness.

Saxon-born Forty-Eighter Otto Ruppius had edited Milwaukee's *Gradaus*, but he had just moved to St. Louis to continue his writing and editing career there. U.S. Census, Population Schedules (1860), 4th Ward, St. Louis, Missouri, p. 215, dwelling 1102, family 1489; Arndt and Olsen, *German-American Newspapers*, 683, 694.

106. Edmund Märklin (1816–1892) worked as a pharmacist but published poetry throughout his life and became well-known among German Americans. Märklin had been compelled to flee Europe after writing revolutionary songs and poems and fighting with the nationalist forces in Baden in 1849. He married Caroline Giesler, the widow of one of Mathilde's brothers. *Jahrbücher der Deutsch-Amerikanischen Turnerei* 3 (1894): 174–76; U.S. Census, Population Schedules (1860), 7th Ward, Milwaukee, Wisc., p. 138, dwelling 943, family 889.

107. Marcus Otterburg was the Jewish Bavarian manager of the *Milwaukee Atlas*. Editor Bernhard Domschke boarded with the Otterburg family, and that relationship would help Otterburg secure a consulship in Mexico after Lincoln was elected president. U.S. Census, Population Schedules (1860), 7th Ward, Milwaukee, Wisc., p. 79, dwelling 541, family 488; *New York Times*, June 30, 1867.

the *Atlas* free of charge for quite some time now. And about the *Banner*: The *Gradaus*[108] is now published under the name *Volksblatt*. Herzberg is the owner.—But I shall now get back to writing about our family celebration. My little money dilemma did not last long because Lexow, whom I had asked for 1½ [dollars] per column, has sent me $25 for "Frauenbilder," my piece on the perceptions of women. He has also sent 2½ dollars for four correspondences—in all, $35. I then bought a pair of new boots for Percy and a little doll for Hertha and told them that Papa had sent it. I paid my mailman and bought a summer hat—a pretty bold purchase as the hat is made of straw and has a wide brim. I also bought two bottles of wine [illegible] and we drank lemonade in your honor.

You are right to assume that little Percy still likes to sleep in. Hertha is the first one awake. Sunday mornings are the exception. He is never still in bed then when I get up. On Sundays, he is eager to do gymnastics and usually has already put on his Turner[109] outfit. I had it made for him, and he receives it every Sunday evening with the other clean laundry. On Sundays, he runs to Turner Hall with a piece of bread in his hand. He stays there until 10 or 11 o'clock. He enjoys going to Zuendt's private school, and I sleep much better now that he is there. Little Hertha wants to go to school also and says: "Well, when I go to school, I too can make a little letter for my Papa."

July 16.

My poor Maria is in bed. She is suffering from a swollen face. She had previously been pretty healthy for some time, although she did have to deal with many heartaches. Your stories about Biedermann did not please her in the least. She says you're jealous and that's why you are seeing her lost friend through black-colored glasses. The former may be true, but her conclusion is not. Booth's case will come before

---

108. Ernst Anton Zündt and Otto Ruppius began publishing the *Gradaus* newspaper in Milwaukee in the late 1850s. Its successor, the *Volksblatt*, apparently lasted less than a year. Arndt and Olsen, *German-American Newspapers*, 694.

109. Founded in Berlin in 1811, the Turnverein was a nationalistic gymnastics society with roots in the resistance to the Napoleonic occupation of German lands. Many Turners had been heavily involved in the Revolutions of 1848 in Europe, and in the United States, Turners tended to support antislavery and working-class politics, while continuing to promote German culture, sociability, and physical training. Efford, *German Immigrants, Race, and Citizenship*, 25–27, 41–43.

the *Court* in 8 days. In that regard, things have changed as he has now taken the case from his former lawyer Arnold and has handed the case over to Bottler,[110] who is Mary's lawyer. In what way this is supposed to improve the situation for Maria I dare not say yet. Bottler, though, has few values, like most men. He is just a man of a more elegant reputation than others. And he has always shown his sympathy for B[ooth], more so than he has shown interest in the actual work Maria hired him to do. Be that as it may! Deep in her heart Maria has no other wish but to free herself from this lewd *husband in law*, and indeed, she is right. Even if he denies her and the children any *support*—she is still right. I would not want all the world to see him as my lawfully wedded husband either. We are aware of his good qualities—you and I both. But the evil instincts that lead him to seduce innocent girls—you may not have heard about his lewd desires as much as I am hearing about them right now. He is evil in the true sense of the word. He keeps his distance from me—he is afraid of me. He has not further provoked me, but I have still assumed a somewhat firmer attitude since you left. He has not been allowed to enter my room, which is always locked, and so on.

The reason why he refused to employ Arnold again is probably lack of money. He was supposed to pay him 1,000 doll now, and then again after the trial and his release. Things are looking grim when it comes to his money. He only helps his family with some expenses and does not pay for others at all. And this worries me. I happily share all I have with Maria, and so does she. How much will poor Maria have left after the trial has ended? I don't know, and she does not know either. And yet—this much is true—I will remain her true friend. I will never leave her. She will never leave me.

Your correspondence for the *Sentinel* has just arrived. He[111] sends me the little letter. Your article will be published on Monday (today is Saturday). The *Free Democrat* is waiting expectantly. I think he will be the first one to pay. I haven't heard from your favorite, the [*Westliche Blät-*

---

110. A lawyer by the name of William F. Butler practiced in Milwaukee in 1860. Mathilde misspelled the name. U.S. Census, Population Schedules (1860), 1st Ward, Milwaukee, Wisc., p. 239, dwelling 1724, family 1695.

111. Mathilde probably means Rufus King, the editor of the *Sentinel*. She often identified editors with their newspapers in this way. Charles King, "Rufus King: Soldier, Editor, and Statesman," *Wisconsin Magazine of History* 4, no. 4 (1921): 371–81.

ter]. The [*Criminal-Zeitung*],[112] with its fabricated articles supposedly reporting directly from the war zone, is an institution. And this is why people believe these articles are real. I am looking forward to your correspondence in the *Staats-Demokrat*.[113] The *Atlas*'s Herr de Longe[114] tells me they have long been waiting for your correspondence and is asking whether you will write to them. Today, I found my last correspondence in the [*Criminal-Zeitung*], the one about the editors' conference excursion to Grand Rapids, my most favorite little city. This tour brought us much joy. The hosts of the *Railroad Comp[any]* made sure we had all modern conveniences. Maria was rather cheerful, the weather was beautiful that day, and so was the blue lake. We were gone for two nights and one day. Hölzlhuber's sketch and my reading exercise for Frank Leslie are both ready. He has asked for it, but he will not receive it until he's paid what he still owes us. Booth wrote to him about it on our behalf. Upon your arrival in Zürich, you will hopefully have received my letter, the first one I directed there. You will have met with Father in Strasbourg. I look forward to hearing about it. Carl Anneke arrived in Grand Rapids yesterday, and he is daydreaming about moving there. He will meet with Emil there.

Monday morning.

I just read your English correspondence "*from our European Correspondent*" with great ease. Nothing—not a word—is unclear to me. The English is much easier to understand than my story about Eliot Granger.[115]

During breakfast, Booth tells me: "the correspondence is rather good." They only had to fix your "Germanic English" at the *Sentinel*. Maria thinks the correspondence is too dry and your proletarian pride too obvious. There was no need to let the *fashionable* people know that you were traveling in second class. She would have liked the correspondence to be somewhat more ornamental for the *ladies*. By the

---

112. Rudolph Lexow's *Criminal-Zeitung und Belletrisches Journal*. See n. 57 (chapter 1).

113. This may have been a slip on Mathilde's part. The *Staats-Demokrat* seems to have been the former name of Schwedler's *New Yorker Demokrat*. Arndt and Olsen, *German-American Newspapers*, 410.

114. We were unable to find further information.

115. Mathilde's footnote: "This story will appear in the next issues of the *Stripes and Star* and as soon as it appears, I will translate it."

The *Stars and Stripes* was a short-lived Frank Leslie magazine of which no issues appear to have survived. (See *Frank Leslie's Illustrated Newspaper*, January 1, 1859, 72.) Eliot Granger was the main character in *Das Geisterhaus in New-York*. See n. 39 (chapter 1).

way, she says, "your English is quite nice." About local news, dear Fritz: The beautiful Youngs-Hall[116] lies in ruins. Gothic Hall has also disappeared, and our friend Negmann[117] is without bread again. The European war brings their elite—their high society—to us once again. The Wendt family[118] will return in September and Finkler[119] and his wife and all the rest of them as well. I am now reading that the [*Westliche*] *Blätter* has indeed merged with the *Anzeiger des Westens*[120] with Ruppius as co-editor of the *Anzeiger*. Well, that should be enough mergers for now, don't you think?

I also just read your third correspondence in the *New Yorker Democrat*, "From Our Own Correspondent," and that's my favorite one. My dear lovely chatterbox is playing around me all morning and rattling on in English. I wish you could hear it. You have probably never heard such cute English! Even Maria notes how nice Hertha's English is. She is such a lovely smart little girl! Once you're in a place and position to receive a letter from me then and there, I will send you another nice little letter from the children. I did receive the evergreen branchlet from the graves of our dead children.

Don't forget our rose petals, and keep sending us *some little* curls. Percy is busy looking for bugs, and he already has a little collection on his wooden board. And now that I need to mail this letter, I've misplaced Percy's letter to you and just cannot find it. But you shall soon have one from him. I will send another letter soon after this one.

Next week will probably bring us many events, and then I will write again immediately. Naturally, I haven't received any remuneration so far. I plan on including a list in every letter, telling you which payments I have received.

---

116. Young's Block housed many businesses, including the wine and cigar store Gothic Hall. *Milwaukee Daily Sentinel*, May 25, 1859.

117. We have been unable to identify Negmann.

118. Possibly feminist Mathilde Wendt and her distiller husband Charles, German immigrants who lived in Milwaukee in 1860. Michaela Bank, *Women of Two Countries: German-American Women, Women's Rights, and Nativism, 1848–1890* (New York: Berghahn Books, 2012), 33–34; U.S. Census, Population Schedules (1860), 1st Ward, Milwaukee, Wisc., p. 295, dwelling 2052, family 2117.

119. Nassau-born Forty-Eighter Wilhelm Finkler (1821–1879) was a politically active liquor dealer who would return to Germany after distinguished service in the Union Army. U.S. Census, Population Schedules (1860), 7th Ward, Milwaukee, Wisc., p. 97, dwelling 675, family 574; *Milwaukee Daily Sentinel*, July 13, 1874; *Milwaukee Herold*, April 2, 1922.

120. See n. 147 (chapter 1).

Now have you gotten signs of life from some of our friends? How glad Father must have been to see you.

How did you fare with your money? Will you soon be able to have bills of exchange sent to you (from each one individually)? How did you find the Beusts? Tell me about our old friends in your next letter and whether you've heard from Franziska.[121]

I've just received a letter from Dr. Brandis,[122] and he writes that Leslie cannot have the last installment of the English novel. That means that I now have to end my work on the translation—unless I feel inclined to write the final part of the novel myself. If only the story wasn't put together in this terrible American manner, then it would be my pleasure to do this. But with all the *rowdy pack* that has already appeared and that I need to keep in the story, I think it will be difficult for me to finish writing the novel. I am at chapter 10 with the translation and would need to write twenty more chapters to bring about a reasonable ending. As courageous as ever, and in heartfelt love, yours, Mathilde.

Mary Booth to her mother Adeline Corss
Milwaukee, July 17, 1859
(English original)

My dear Mother:

I received your letter day before yesterday, but being sick all day yesterday with neuralgia in my face I could not answer it until now. My

---

121. Mathilde had known Franziska ("Zischen") Rollmann Hammacher since childhood, and the two were very close. Most sources, including a 1940 biography to which Mathilde's daughter Hertha Anneke Sanne contributed, report that the two women were cousins, but we find no evidence of a blood relationship. Mathilde called Franziska's mother "Tante" (aunt) and her children called Franziska "Tante," but Mathilde and Franziska corresponded as though their families had no contact except through them. Henriette M. Heinzen and Hertha Anneke Sanne, "Biographical Notes in Commemoration of Fritz Anneke and Mathilde Franziska Anneke" (1940), 9, unpublished manuscript, Box 8, Folders 1–2, Anneke Papers. Mathilde to Franziska Hammacher, February 4–6, 1861 and [October] 1862, in *"Ich gestehe, die Herrschaft der fluchwürdigen 'Demokratie' dieses Landes macht mich betrübt,"* 54, 140.

122. Herman M. Brandis had trained as a physician but worked as a pharmacist and then editor for the German imprint of *Frank Leslie's Illustrated Newspaper*. The Hanover-born Brandis lived in Hoboken, New Jersey in 1859. Carl Wilhelm Schlegel, *Schlegel's German-American Families in the United States* (New York: American Historical Society, 1918), 3:289–90.

face is swolen & looks <u>awful</u>, but not worse than it feels. S.'s trial has not come off yet, & there is no certainty whatever when it will. So you need not worry yourself any more about it. When it comes let it come & never mind it.

S——n[123] has discharged Mr. Arnold and taken Mr. Butler in his place. I am very glad, as Mr. Butler has his interest at heart, and Mr. A. had not. It is the best thing that could have been done. People are beginning to have very much sympathy for him, owing to the belief that he is a poor injured individual & that he was <u>drive[n]</u> to it. He says Hortensius Paine[124] said yesterday that he ought not to have lived with me another day, after I informed of him, & if he had not[,] no jury in the world would have convicted him, <u>knowing the circumstances</u>. He is now in friendship with Dr. Baker,[125] who, if it were nescessary, would have enough of manufactured evidence for him. Mr. Butler has no doubt that he cannot be convicted. He believes he will come out right. He grows more & more sure of his case every day. I mean S——n—he thinks that he is a horribly injured man, & says the world will soon know it. He says all the time that <u>I</u> have brought it all upon him &c. & just so sure as I am a little more sick then he begins again.

It is certain that we should starve were it not for Madam Anneke. She buys medicin for me, & has now got for me nine bottles of wine. Sherman has never a <u>bit</u> of money—not <u>a little</u>. There is no Church in St. Paul's. Mr. Richmond has gone. Spalding preaches in Mr. Thomson's Church.[126] Sherman has employed a man who was on the "Jury of Decons"[127] which convicted him before to hunt up testimony of the girl's bad character for him, & he now says his strong hope for him is that <u>my appearance</u> at the last, to hear the closing plea, will turn the jury. Mr. Butler says so too. He said to me "you <u>thought</u> he was guilty, & that you did right, but <u>now you have changed your mind</u>, you believe now he was not, & I shall say. She comes here as his friend, his wife, &c.—& for

---

123. Sherman Booth.
124. Lawyer Hortensius Paine, brother of Judge Byron Paine, had defended Sherman Booth in his 1854 trial for his involvement in the Glover affair. Watrous, *Memoirs of Milwaukee County*, 1:544.
125. Erasmus D. Baker practiced medicine in Milwaukee. U.S. Census, Population Schedules (1860), 4th Ward, Milwaukee, Wisc., p. 87, dwelling 664, family 662.
126. Henry M. Thompson was rector of the Episcopalian Free Church of the Atonement. *Milwaukee Daily Sentinel*, January 15, 1859.
127. The reference suggests that a committee of church leaders censured Sherman Booth for his actions.

her sake & her children's you must not convict him" &c. What do you think of that? Lorenzo says I <u>never</u> must do it, nobody would respect me. & Madam Anneke says I <u>shall</u> not. She will go herself, & see what is said & done. She is not afraid of any body, & she is too firm in character to be hurt by anything. Lorenzo says I ought to go East when he goes, that nothing else would do but that is utterly impossible. He is afraid I shall <u>have</u> to go to court, if I am sick or not. I see Mrs. Merrill very seldom. I am not strong enough to go out much, & I don't like to go there at that house where there are so many low men boarders. Mrs. Cook[128] raves now against Mary[129] & I. She says are as bad as S——n &c.—She is a "poor <u>creatur</u>" & has to take much morphine to keep her alive. A Baptist minister who is editor at Grand Rapids came over here to attend the trial & staid three days. He will come again, & as he is a good, fine man I am glad of it, as he diverts S——n's mind.

Sherman says he shall not live with me <u>ever</u> another day if he is convicted!—<u>That tickles me!</u> How could he when he was in States Prison? If he <u>is</u> convicted he will move for a new trial. We have all the time new girls,[130] but it can't be helped. I talked with this one before she came & told her all how I expected her to act &c.—

Tell Ella I have two nightgowns of both kinds for her, only one is made yet. I will send them by Lorenzo. I have urged S. to send money for Ella.

Fritz Anneke to Mathilde Franziska
Samedan, Switzerland, July 19, 1859

Beloved Mathilde!

Beust and I have been here in this snowy region[131] since the 16th, staying with Emmermann,[132] who has been working here as a forester since he traveled the region years ago. The peace in Italy badly hurt my correspondence arrangements. Even if I had rushed there as soon as

---

128. Probably Adeline Cook, the mother of the girl Sherman Booth assaulted.
129. Possibly Mary Briggs. See n. 104 (chapter 1).
130. Presumably household servants.
131. Samedan is a small town in eastern Switzerland near the border with what was then the Italian kingdom of Lombardy-Venetia. It is situated in the alpine Engadine Valley region, which includes the resort town of St. Moritz.
132. We found no further information.

possible, I would not have reached Italy in time for the Battle of Solferino on June 24.[133] We just landed in Southampton that day. And then while I was in Zürich, there came this unfortunate ceasefire and a few days later this even more unfortunate peace. I would need to go to Italy to have at least some kind of justification to work on my correspondences from Europe. It will take a while until things are in order and "regulated" again in Italy. And until then, there will be many difficulties and battles. And to witness these firsthand would be my main task there. Whether the revolution will raise its head in Italy now will largely depend on whether the French troops stay. If they do stay and if they function as execution troops[134] to suppress the general discontent of Italians with the disgraceful peace, which can be seen most distinctly in the resignation of the Cavour Ministry; and if the execution troops are used to reinstall the princes of Tuscany, Modena, and Parma, as well as to recapture the Papal States for the Pope—well, then there is not much that the Italians can do about it in the interim, unless the French soldiers consider themselves above such fetch-and-carry tasks. According to an authenticated message that's arrived from Milan, many French officers have broken their swords to pieces and have removed their epaulettes and medals out of anger over this inglorious peace. As may be imagined, Garibaldi[135] and particularly Mazzini are not idle now. But what they are actually doing now and what their plans are?—It's impossible to learn anything about them here. The only things I hear are the most uncertain of rumors. Authenticated messages do not arrive here until late.

I departed together with Beust on the 14th. We took the steamer to Rapperswyl at the end of Lake Zürich. Then we took the railroad to

---

133. Troops from France and the northern Italian kingdom of Sardinia defeated Austrian forces at Solferino, Lombardy on June 24. In the subsequent armistice and peace agreement, Austria ceded Lombardy to Sardinia and accepted the creation of an Italian confederation under the "honorary presidency of the pope." This settlement fell far short of the goals of Sardinian Prime Minister Camillo Benso, Count of Cavour, who had sought France's help in completely eliminating Austrian control of Italian lands in order to effect Italian unification. Arnold Blumberg, *A Carefully Planned Accident: The Italian War of 1859* (Selinsgrove, Penn.: Susquehanna University Press, 1990), 135, 140.

134. Fritz's unusual term, "Exekutionstruppe," played on the fact that in both languages execution means killing and carrying out.

135. Italian military leader Giuseppe Garibaldi was an international icon famed for his work to unify Italy under a republican government, including in 1848. Alfonso Scirocco, *Garibaldi: Citizen of the World* (Princeton, N.J.: Princeton University Press, 2007).

Chur,[136] and from there we walked to Churwalden on the same night. It was a pleasant journey: First the beautiful Lake Zürich with its lovely shores, the ruins of the castle of the Count of Rapperswyl, which was destroyed by the Swiss many years ago. The ruins are located on a high peninsula in Lake Zürich. We had plenty of time to explore it. Then the wild mountains on both sides of the railroad tracks, the small Lake Walen with its rugged cliffs 4–5000 feet on high, Father Rhine in his youth, and the little city of Chur, located in a basin and completely embedded in giant hills. . . .

Mary Booth to her mother Adeline Corss
Milwaukee, August 4, 1859
(English original)

My dear Mother:
The trial has now been going on for 8 days.

Mr. Carson,[137] & Carpenter have made their pleas. Mr. Palmer is now giving his. Ryan will close to-morrow.

S. has not a bit of Fear. They have succeeding in crossing the girl's testimony, & she, poor thing, dare not tell all—& although S. expects an acquittal, I expect the jury to disagree. I dare not send you the papers with testimony for fear Jane should get hold of them. It will come out in a book. Then I will send it.

Tell Ella that Lillian has a new plaything—a <u>little mouse</u>. It runs all over her hands & arms, & much to my horror, she kisses it, & crys when it runs away. She is a very good & mild child now. I am not very well <u>myself</u>, & dont know <u>nothing</u> what to do. The Dr. comes to see me every other day.

Give my love to Ella & all. Yours aff Mary.

---

136. About fifty-five miles farther southeast.

137. Edward G. Ryan and District Attorney Dighton Corson prosecuted Sherman Booth's case, while Henry L. Palmer and Matthew H. Carpenter defended him. *The Trial of Sherman M. Booth for Seduction*, 4.

Mathilde Franziska Anneke to Fritz Anneke
Milwaukee, August 2–17, 1859

My dear Fritz!

It was just recently on July 22 that I celebrated the day of birth of our unforgettable child, our Fritz. I celebrated the day we reunited with him in Strasbourg.[138] My dear Maria and I had driven out to her gravesite[139] alone. And there in the shade of the large vine-clad oak, I had a good cry and told her what a difficult day it had been for me. Returning from the hills, I steered the horse in the direction of the post office and received your dear letter from Zürich—the first one from that El Dorado of wistful memories. I shed tears, bitter tears, all evening reading your letter. I felt so overpowered by memories of little Fritz when I got to the part about the dark roses and little grapevine leaves. I saw our child again in his green dress and little blue velvet skirt—his little pale face. And I remembered how he gained weight drinking that good Swiss milk every day—oh God, how much has happened since then! We have buried our hopes. We have buried our children. All—all is lost. Nothing is left now of the things I had hoped for in those days. It was all a dream—a dream! And now I live in a very different world than back in those days: different children—different loved ones—different flowers—different lands—different air—different soil—different home.[140] I think I have lived out four different lives already!—Let me stop here and return to the meager little reality that we have left. If you ever had a successful plan, dear Fritz, it was this one! If only this premature peace does not abort it. Now that you are stranded, for the moment anyway, this peace came at a good time. At least we here felt that it made more sense for you to be in Zürich than in an abandoned war

---

138. Mathilde and Fritz reunited with their infant son in 1849 after fighting in Baden.

139. Mathilde seems to have used a visit to the grave of Mary's six-month-old baby, Alice (1852–1853), at Forest Home Cemetery to mourn her own lost children.

140. The original German reads "andere Lieben" (different loved ones) and "andere Luft" (different air). Maria Wagner incorrectly transcribed these words as "anders lieben" (love differently) and "andere Lust" (a different kind of desire). Wagner, *Mathilde Franziska Anneke*, 107. Several other works on Mathilde Anneke rely on Wagner's inaccurate transcriptions. See for example Gebhardt, *Mathilde Franziska Anneke*, 191; Joey Horsley and Luise F. Pusch, eds., *Frauengeschichten: Berühmte Frauen und ihre Freundinnen* (Göttingen: Wallstein Verlag, 2010), 7.

zone. The negotiations will, without a doubt, be interesting enough for some time, and everyone here is terribly anxious to hear more....

But my hair stood on end reading about the way Father greeted you in the homeland! It is a real miracle that such a welcome did not cause you to hate the entire Fatherland. These philistines—this philistinism! God knows that I would rather put up with the bears and wolves here in the jungle than to breathe the air of our homeland filled with artificiality and hidden brutality. No doubt Anna[141] has helped you take revenge for this. Such revenge is not worth anything to me. After all, we've had to swallow many such insults. I will never forget the time of your imprisonment because people blamed me for it. And then later a gift of money was supposed to help me get over this insult—I will never forget about this. And now you have to suffer another humiliation just like this. Poor Fritz—the love for your father and the longing to see him one more time drove you to abandon your second home and cross the ocean again.—Booth is standing at the gates. You won't believe this original yet despicable odd fellow! I believe he will be released. At any rate, as evil as he is, I don't want to see him in state prison.

Maria is doing better than I had anticipated. Her name has barely been mentioned in the trial so far. We've had three days of this trial already—and I think there will be three more and then it still won't be over.... Well, I certainly have what I need, but it's too bad that life is so expensive. B[ooth] himself is without money entirely. It's almost completely up to me to take care of this household. This has to change after the trial is over. How pleasant your stay in Zürich must be right now! How often I think about that beautiful country! Sometimes I feel as though I am homesick for the blue lake. And Herwegh[142] was at the marksmen's festival too! His poetry writing was awakened again by the Alpine glow. His poem is so nice! It was published in the papers here on July 6 and is attracting a wide audience. Send him my regards, will you!? Ask him if he'd like to send me poems. I would like to publish a German American almanac here and encourage German poets to participate! I would certainly find a publisher if poets like Herwegh would

---

141. Anna Beust. See n. 93 (chapter 1).

142. Georg Herwegh (1817–1875) was a German poet and translator who had established his radical credentials even before 1848. In the uprisings, he, like the Annekes, fought in Baden. From 1849 until 1866, he lived in exile in Zürich, where he was one of the Annekes' closest friends. *Encyclopædia Britannica*, 11th ed., 13:405.

join forces. Our oleander is in bloom, looking beautiful and reminding us of you. Maria claims it belongs to her—I claim it belongs to nobody. I take good care of all my flowers.

Today is the second of August already. The Booth trial is in full swing. No one doubts that he will be released. I will let you know the result. The *Banner* is very piqued that you're not sending correspondences, and the *Atlas* had also expected to have your first submission by now. This peace arrived at just the right moment for you. That is to say, I only hope that it will be a temporary one. The congress of envoys[143] will also be held in Zürich. Well, you should thank your lucky stars that you had to stay in Zürich. I wish you had written more about the marksmen's festival. It made headlines in all the papers. There must be other correspondents in Switzerland reporting for our local papers.

August 3. I just received your dear little letter through the *Michigan Journal*. So, you did go to Italy—too late to see the war, but not too late to see Italy. You did the right thing in any case. I would have embarked on such a trip with the good magnificent Beust as well. Is the little man still so buoyant? Why don't you send me pictures of the entire family when you get the chance? It's Percy's birthday soon, and I will give him nice presents on your behalf. Hertha asks me today: "Tell me, when are we going to see Papa in Italy? Are we going there by boat?" "Yes on a little ship floating on the water." She says "wata." If only you could hear her chattering.—

I think that it must have been a stormy time in Paris around the time of July 24.[144] I don't think there can be an effective peace settlement without a popular uprising. All this hesitation that can be felt in the air in the streets of Paris! I trust that the July sun will ignite what has to be ignited.—I think your correspondence could be interesting enough even without the slaughter in Italy after all. All the papers seem in need of European news. I met Gallo[145] yesterday, and he was wondering "why Anneke does not write to us." I told him your reasons. I

---

143. French, Sardinian, and Austrian representatives would meet to finalize the Treaty of Zürich (November 10, 1859), which formally ended the conflict in the northern Italian lands. Blumberg, *A Carefully Planned Accident*, 143–63.

144. The willingness of Napoleon III of France to sign an armistice with Austria after the Battle of Solferino (June 24) angered Italian nationalists and other Europeans who hoped for a unified, democratic Italy. Blumberg, *A Carefully Planned Accident*, 141–42.

145. Gallo seems to be an editor, but we have not been able to identify him.

did tell him there was hope that you would write to them, however. The *Freie [Zeitung]*[146] has forwarded me your little letter. Have they even received your correspondence? I will ask. The second correspondence for the *Westliche Blätter* has arrived here, but it hasn't been published in the latest issue. In its stead, the quite nicely written excerpt about the sea travel taken from Bernays's[147] travel account has been printed. Ruppius does not write <u>anything</u> about a third correspondence. He seems to have taken a dim view of your first two correspondences. And indeed, I would have too when it comes to the first one. I had not expected you to write such dull things. I haven't read your second correspondence yet of course. You won't see any payment for it, I can tell you that much. And whether Börnstein is going to send you the bill of exchange as I requested—I will have to wait and see. The noble *Atlas* does not pay you the three dollars it owes you. I have already spent some of the 15 dollars. It would not have been necessary if Leslie had paid me five dollars last week as he should have. Dr. Brandis sends a registered letter and writes that he's sending five dollars enclosed—but there is <u>nothing</u> enclosed! If and where there is roguery involved here is anyone's guess. . . .

August 17. Dear Fritz, if my letter arrives later than expected, then you just need to forgive me this time. I do not know myself why I did not complete the letter sooner. I cannot and should not sit for a long time. I feel so miserable after working for an hour. My liver disease can probably never be properly cured. The Booth trial lasted 11 days. The proceedings were most ambiguous in nature. No decent German who intends to keep a good reputation was present at the trial. And this is how it ended: There will be a second trial. The jury could not come to an agreement, 7 were in favor and 5 were against him. The second trial is supposed to start in 6 weeks. Poor Maria, more and more she feels the urgency to get away from him. She detests him because of his passions as much as she tolerates him like a sister because of his

---

146. The Republican *New Jersey Freie Zeitung* was published in Newark. Arndt and Olsen, *German-American Newspapers*, 307.

147. Karl Ludwig Bernays (1815–1879) was a German-born journalist who worked with Heinrich Börnstein and Karl Marx in Paris and took part in the French Revolution of 1848. After leaving Europe, he settled in St. Louis, working on the *Anzeiger des Westerns*, serving at the secretary of Missouri's Republican Party, and holding various patronage positions. A. E. Zucker, ed. *The Forty-Eighters: Political Refugees of the German Revolution of 1848* (New York: Columbia University Press, 1950), 278.

good elements and qualities. In reality, he does not have much interest in providing for her. He only shows interest in her when he can make her a slave to his vanity.—I've been busy preparing for Percy's birthday these past several days. Your little picture has arrived, and he was happy about this personal note from you. Everything is ready now: an entirely new outfit, black pants, new boots (it only took him 4 weeks to ruin brand new boots), a new coat, 4 new shirts, a *portemonnaie*,[148] a little notebook, marbles, pencils, and writing books. Maria has invited company over for him tomorrow—our entire family, Booth's family, Ida, Alma, Franklin, and two members of the Zündt family.[149] She will bake a cake and make fruit lemonade. Booth has bought 1/9 ts.[150] of *kandy* for this purpose and so on. I'm worried about our little fellow. He doesn't listen, he is disorganized—he dreams all day. . . .

Farewell and do not forget us, your loving Mathilde.—

---

148. French for wallet.
149. Alma and Ida Weiskirch were the young daughters of Mathilde's sister Johanna. Franklin Giesler was the seven-year-old son of Caroline Märklin, the widow of Mathilde's brother. See n. 106 (chapter 1).
150. Mathilde is possibly using an abbreviation for teaspoons in a hyperbolic reference to Booth's stinginess.

CHAPTER 2

Europe Bound

September 1859–August 1860

ALTHOUGH PROSECUTORS DECLINED TO RETRY SHERMAN BOOTH for "seduction," Mary, Mathilde, and Fritz's lives would not settle into an easy routine. For several months in late 1859 and early 1860, Booth lived in his Milwaukee home with Mary, Mathilde, and the children, Percy, Hertha, and Lillian. While the other members of his household still found joy in each other's company, the rift between the two Booths made for plenty of tension.

Financial concerns exacerbated the personal strains in both the Booth and Anneke families. Almost every letter that Mathilde wrote to Fritz in Europe included long lists of editors who had failed to pay them for their work. Mathilde had so little money that she could not always scrounge up enough for postage. Even when she could afford stamps, international mail service was unreliable. Fritz and Mathilde routinely wrote to each other several times a week, but many of the letters arrived months late, or not at all. Under these conditions, their correspondence became repetitive and sometimes reproachful.

The personal dramas continued to unfold against a backdrop of legal and political intrigue. Sherman Booth was arrested again on March 1, 1860, this time for his part in encouraging Wisconsinites to participate in the Glover jailbreak back in 1854. In earlier trials, the state supreme court had twice cleared Booth, supporting the idea that Joshua Glover's incarceration had been illegal in the first place because the Fugitive Slave Act of 1850 was unconstitutional. For years, the Wisconsin judges had managed to delay federal review of the case, but in 1859, the U.S. Supreme Court had overturned the state decisions, setting the stage for Booth to be arrested once more.[1] While Booth was imprisoned during 1860, Mary, Mathilde, and other supporters schemed con-

---

1. H. Robert Baker, *The Rescue of Joshua Glover: A Fugitive Slave, the Constitution, and the Coming of the Civil War* (Athens, Ohio: Ohio University Press, 2006), 94, 130, 169.

stantly to break him out. Despite making ingenious efforts on Booth's behalf, Mathilde and Mary were also preparing to leave him as soon as they could. They would sail out of New York in August 1860.

Fritz Anneke to Mathilde Franziska Anneke
Zürich, September 10, 1859

Dear Mathilde!

I need to write you a longer letter now despite not hearing from you. It's been 71 days today since I wrote you from here about not having seen Father, not going to see Father, and telling you that he would not or could not give me money. It's been 33 days since I received your letter dated July 20. You had promised to send another letter after that one soon, but it's been 33 days now—almost five weeks! Have you forgotten all about me in the meantime or did your letter get lost? I have no other explanation for your silence. By now you will have received my letter from Milan dated August 20, the reply to your letter dated July 20, which I did not receive until August 18, and you will have gotten all of my little notes enclosed in my newspaper submissions before you receive this one.

It is indeed burdensome to be completely cut off from all communication. And then the financial difficulties put a heavy burden on me, a burden that gets even heavier when I don't hear from you. . . . I do not know which of my correspondences will be published and which ones will gain favor. I know just as little about your financial means and my prospects of keeping myself alive here. There can be no talk of me returning to America now. There will be war[2] again between now and next year, and it would be foolish to waste time and money on the voyage back. And other than that, I truly don't see how I could gain possession of the necessary monetary resources. In my letter from Milan I had proposed to you to come back across the Atlantic this year if at all possible. Whether this is feasible and a good idea—that's best for you to judge from there. . . .

---

2. On the Italian peninsula.

I did stamp my letter from Milan. I cannot afford stamps for this one, and so I will leave it up to fate whether you'll be able to afford the postal charges for it or whether you won't because Maria has again spent the money on *candy*.

You would feel at home here in Zürich, where there are at least 30 to 40 magazines and thousands of books and brochures from "your field." To be sure, women here never go to the museum, but you would break with this undesirable tradition.

But it is truly just too painful not to hear from you, my dear children, and Indianae[3] at all anymore!

I'm enclosing several flowers. I plucked the small wild ones on the Via mala, and the domestic ones are from the Campo dolcino in Italy, not far from the Splügen Pass.[4] Zürich is bursting with flowers, especially the path from my guesthouse "tiefen Brunnen" to the city. There is an abundance of dahlias, roses, asters, bindweeds, oleander, geraniums, fuchsias, and so on. And the blossom trees that you call "peonies"—there are plenty of them here and in all colors.

I don't know what else to write you at this moment except that I am almost dying with the desire to finally hear from you again. I will see that this letter gets to the post office now.

Do not completely forget
your Fritz.

Mathilde Franziska Anneke to Fritz Anneke
Milwaukee, September 23, 1859

Dear good Fritz!

Your courteous letter dated August 19, the first one I've received from Milan, came my way on Sept. 9. Today is September 19 already, and I only have myself to blame for not responding sooner. But if you could see me in all my *troubles*, you would have a little patience with me. . . .

Our little children are faring well. Percy is enormously difficult to raise. He goes through a tremendous number of clothes and shoes. He

---

3. Mary. See n. 64 (chapter 1).
4. The Via mala is a famously treacherous route through a gorge near Thusis, Switzerland, while the municipality of Campodolcino is situated north of Milan near Italy's (then Lombardy-Venetia's) border with Switzerland. Splügen Pass lies on that alpine border.

ruined the latter, a pair of shoes that cost 10 shillings,[5] within 3 weeks. I can raise my little Hertha for less than no money. She shall now have good winter clothing because it is already quite wintry here. Maria sews everything for us. She has just completed a nice little winter hat for Hertha and little nightgowns and other little dresses. Hertha is playing nicely with Lilian now. Maria is sterner with her than she usually is, and that is an advantage in Hertha's case.—My way of living is very monotonous. I sit at my desk all day, or I patch something. Every now and then we go to Grandmother's in the evenings. I never go anywhere without Maria. We never leave each other, not even for an hour. She sits next to me while we're working, and we are happy to have found each other never to leave each other. I get to know her good and lovely soul better each day, and I love her little weaknesses in life as much as her good qualities. I know she loves me too, and I feel fortunate to be loved and understood again.

Your lovely plan to come here this winter, dear Fritz, is falling through. Where shall we get anything here for our oilcloth or for our furniture? Money can almost be relegated to the realms of fantasy here. It is a sad state here, and I do not know how it will end. Stirn[6] pays me nothing. Does he not sell anything as he claims? Maybe. I have doctors' bills amounting to 11 doll for Fessel and 7 for Müller.[7] Now that she has the little machine for her foot, little Hertha's operation has become almost unnecessary to me. Her feet are getting noticeably better. She steps evenly on the front part of her foot and races against anyone. She herself says, "My little foot is now good enough and does not have to be cut." The child does not forget her Papa. But Percy too has a big smile on his face when he speaks about you. The love the children have for each other is touching. Little Hertha dominates Percy. They are happy in this house and they make use of the play area and

---

5. In the nineteenth-century United States, "shilling" was an informal term for an eighth of a dollar. Walter D. Kamphoefner, Wolfgang Helbich, and Ulrike Sommer, eds., *News from the Land of Freedom*, trans. Susan Carter Vogel (Ithaca, N.Y.: Cornell University Press, 1991), 608.

6. Possibly Henry Stirn, a Hesse-born maker of picture frame molding and civically active local businessman. U.S. Census, Population Schedules (1860), Milwaukee, Wisc., p. 37, dwelling 315, family 339; *Milwaukee Daily Sentinel*, February 26, 1859, August 28, 1860, and September 26, 1862.

7. Carl Müller was a Saxon-born physician who would serve in the Civil War. Louis Frederick Frank, *The Medical History of Milwaukee, 1834–1914* (Milwaukee: Germania Publishing Co., 1915), 31.

the large rooms. And the Booths are just so considerate and indulgent. One would almost think that these are their own children. He is as polite and good with them as Maria is truly loving. When I am not feeling well, I have good care that I cannot get anywhere else. My health is not yet stable. My liver and gallstones or whatever it is are rumbling constantly. I've been sitting too much for a while, and so next week I think I will take up several of the *ensemble companies* on their generous offers. I've accepted St. Movius's[8] invitation to a cruise on one of the newly built *steamers* named "Detroit" and "Milwaukie." I have *tickets* for Maria and me. On the next nice fall morning, we will embark on a journey to Grand Haven. Right now, it's cold, and we have unpleasant weather. Tonight, we will go to the opera. There are only very few *tickets* available, but I've received two from the club. Now that I bring them in regular correspondences, it seems as though I was able to win their favor. Märklin and Linchen[9] come to visit us occasionally in the evenings, and Carl and Henriette also enjoy staying in our welcoming *parlor*. I'd invited only smaller groups of people, including St. Klien[10] because he is a good piano player. I did this to entertain Maria and so that she would have some distraction. Merklin sends you his love and so does Grandmother. Emil has a great deal of bad luck in his *business*. Johanna now has a nice little daughter, her third. Carl and Henriette have moved their pharmacy to Dr. Munk's place. This is supposed to be a better location, and the rent is only half of what they had paid at the old location at the marketplace. Herr Balatka[11] is theater director for the next winter season. Sobolewsky,[12] a Hungarian composer who has

---

8. Julius Movius was the German-born general agent for both the Great Western Railroad and the Detroit and Milwaukee Railroad. Under his direction, the latter invested in ships that crossed Lake Michigan from Milwaukee to Grand Haven, Michigan. David R. P. Guay, *Great Western Railway of Canada: Southern Ontario's Pioneer Railway* (Toronto: Dundurn, 2015), 198.

9. Caroline ("Linchen") Märklin, the widow of one of Mathilde's brothers. See n. 106 (chapter 1).

10. Mathilde probably meant to write "Klein," but none of the Milwaukee men with this common surname stands out as a likely guest.

11. Austrian Forty-Eighter Hans Balatka (1827–1899) helped found Milwaukee's Musikverein and directed it during the 1850s. Kathleen Neils Conzen, *Immigrant Milwaukee: Accommodation and Community in a Frontier City* (Cambridge, Mass.: Harvard University Press, 1976), 175.

12. Johann Friedrich Eduard Sobolewski was in fact a Polish violinist, composer, and conductor who had studied in Berlin and lived in Milwaukee briefly before moving on to

settled here in Milwaukee, has written a beautiful opera about Indians: "The Flower of the Forest." In 14 days, the local musical society will perform it for the first time.[13] These things always provide interesting material for my *papers*. Maria has written you all about the political *affairs*. As had to be expected, Carl Schurz's American party has deserted.[14] I think the young man is lucky that he is not the party's Excellency now. He is already vain enough as to be almost unfit. I had a real scare witnessing this show that the party has put on. This behavior of the party *bosses*! This heroic *Atlas* and all the other trumpeters like the *Illinois* [*Staatszeitung*]. I tell you I have never seen anything more pitiful.

I've had a continuous headache for three days now. I can't make any progress writing. And I'd like to know what was wrong with you, dear Fritz. Because of the dishonest R[uppius], I was deprived of nearly all of your messages. I want to know whether I can still come into possession of the letters and correspondences. I mail out correspondences frequently, almost every 4–5 days.

Maria: *You stupid thing, you, if you wish to know the <u>length</u> of your correspondence in the Sentinel, I will tell you: I have just measured it, & it is six yards and quarter long.—*

She does not tolerate the fact that I go through the trouble of measuring every single correspondence that we have in our house. The *Sentinel* usually published them in 1½ columns. The same is true for the *Illinois Staatszeitung* with the exception of your first correspondences, which are a bit shorter. The *Atlas* usually reserved two columns and a bit more for your articles. . . .

Stay healthy and be fresh and cheerful.[15] Little Hertha sends you kisses and so does little Percy.

St. Louis. Nicolas Slonimsky and Laura Kuhn, eds., *Baker's Biographical Dictionary of Musicians* (New York: Schirmer, 2001), 5:3391.

13. The Musikverein, founded by German immigrants, was an important force on Milwaukee's cultural scene. Conzen, *Immigrant Milwaukee*, 175.

14. German Americans tried to convince the Wisconsin Republican Party to nominate Schurz for governor. When they were unsuccessful, Schurz declined to take a position lower down the ticket. German Americans attributed the failure to nativism, which perhaps explains Mathilde's reference to the "American" party. The anti-immigrant Know Nothing Party, which briefly flourished in the mid-1850s, was officially called the American Party. Hans L. Trefousse, *Carl Schurz: A Biography*, 2nd ed. (New York: Fordham University Press, 1998), 76–77.

15. This phrase echoes the Turnverein motto "Frisch, Fromm, Fröhlich, Frei" (Fresh, Pi-

I'm also sending my greetings and my kisses.
Your loving
Mathilde Franziska

Mary Booth to her daughter Ella Booth
Milwaukee, October 2, 1859
(English original)

My dear Ella:

Last week the State Fair was here. I presume I should not have gone but Mr. Dexter[16] came with a new carraige, & tickets for us so we went, Mrs. Anneke, Lillian, Herta and I. As he came Herta & Lillian & I were just going out of the door to the consecration of Mr. Richmond's new church[17]—but as he was as good as to come for us we thought we would go. When we came home we found your grandfather & grandmother Booth[18] here. They went home yesterday & I think they had a very good visit. Mr. & Mrs. Daniels were here too during the Fair. She went off & left, by mistake, the most beautiful boquet of flowers you ever saw. I have been to Mr. Richmond's church to day with Lillian & Herta. It is very near Mrs. Weiskirch's, and he having a horse by his door, I asked him to bring us home, which he did.

Herta can walk much better than she could since she had the new machine for her foot. She is crazy to go to "Uncle Richmond's" church. Lillian thinks there is no person in the world like him. That is why I shall go there, because I can have no peace with her if I do not. He is going soon to Europe & I shall go to the old church while he is gone,

---

ous, Cheerful, Free). Georg Hirth and F. Rudolf Gasch, eds., *Das gesamte Turnwesen: Ein Lesebuch für deutsche Turner*, 2nd ed., vol. 3 (Leipzig: Verlag von Rud. Lion, 1893).

16. Possibly David H. Dexter, a farmer who lived west of Milwaukee. U.S. Census, Population Schedules (1860), Township of Wauwatosa, Wisconsin, p. 118, dwelling 874, family 844.

17. Mary had a close relationship with Rev. James Richmond and had previously told her sister that he had been "driven out" of his parish after a conflict with influential parishioners. He took up the position of rector at St. Paul's Episcopal Church. Mary to Jane Corss, February 15, 1859, Box 2, Folder 5, Booth Family Papers.

18. Sherman Booth's father Selah and stepmother Harriett lived in Waupun, Wisconsin. U.S. Census, Population Schedules (1860), North Ward, Village Waupun, Fond du Lac County Wisconsin, p. 7, dwelling 47, family 50.

& when he comes again I can rent my old pew. There are no pews to be rented in his church.

We have a little fire in the grate in the palor when it is cold evenings & Mrs. Anneke plays chess with the "felly."[19] The "Chap" was at the fair almost all the time—

Last Monday we went to Grand Haven on the boat & back again. We did not even see the place. The "felly" lost his cane in the lake there, but expects to get it again. Mrs. Anneke was not well, still the trip did her good. A bird flew before the boat & around on it all the way home—

I have not seen Emily[20] since she came home.

A new German literary club has been formed of which Mrs. Anneke was chosen President and myself Vice President, which was done, I suppose as a compliment to her, because they knew it would please her. Mr. Richmond & I will be the only English members. He said he wished to come & they would all like to have him as he speaks German beautifully. It is something as a lyceum—& has both gentlemen & ladies.

There has been a beautiful opera composed by an old man in the city called the "Flower of the forest" the incidents of which are taken from the American Revolution, & there are Indians in it, & the "flower of the forest" herself came to me to ask what she should wear, & I took her to see Mary Cook's[21] beautiful "Hiawatha"[22] costume—she will make one very much like it, & trim it with feathers instead of beads—

This is the first opera ever composed in America.[23] The man has written many in Europe,—& this will go there & be very popular. He teaches the musical society it himself & leads it, instead of Mr. Balatka. When it is performed, after the first act he will be presented with a laurel crown from the American public. Two little girls, Lillian May

---

19. Selah Booth was nicknamed "Felly," and the family called his wife "Chap."
20. It is not clear to whom Mary refers.
21. A lot of women named Mary Cook lived in Milwaukee. Is seems unlikely that this one was a relative of Sherman Booth's victim Caroline N. Cook.
22. In 1855, Henry Wadsworth Longfellow wrote an epic poem based on a fictionalized version of Hiawatha, the pre-European leader who helped form the Iroquois Confederacy. Although Hiawatha was male, Mary seems to be referring to a woman. William Nelson Fenton, *The Great Law and the Longhouse: A Political History of the Iroquois Confederacy* (Norman: University of Oklahoma Press, 1998), 59–65.
23. In fact, William Henry Fry's *Leonora* (1845) is credited with being the first publicly performed grand opera composed by an American. Elize K. Kirk, "United States," in *The New Grove Dictionary of Opera*, ed. Stanley Sadie (London: Macmillan Press, 1992), 4:869.

& Alma Weiskirch,[24] will bring it lying on a white satin pillow, & Mr. Richmond, or somebody will take it from them & with a few remarks in English & German place it on his head. Then the little Mary Cook (who used to live in Cyrus' house) will come in her beautiful Indian costume with her lap full of flowers and drop them at his feet. The Goddess of Liberty will stand in the back ground.

I think Lillian will be glad when she is older to know that she has done it. She & Alma will have on their white dress[es] with flowers around their necks—& perhaps wreaths on their heads.

Alma & Ida fought so to go in "Uncle Richmond's" church that their grandmother had to take them.

I was sorry not to have any thing to send Gram[25] on her birth day for a present. Mrs. Pope[26] lives in a new house of your grandfather's in Waupun in the same yard. Give my love to Gram & Jane, & write as often as you can. I cannot say if we shall go to see the Great Eastern[27] or not. Your aff. Mother—

My dear Daughter[28]—I have just read your mother's letter. I think of you every day & love you very much. When do you want to come home? It is beautiful weather. I hope you are well[.]

Good Bye, Your aff. Father

Mathilde Franziska Anneke to Fritz Anneke
Milwaukee, October 1859

Dear Fritz! It is Sunday morning and Maria and her little daughter are in church. I've just played with my little children for a while, and now I want to seize the moment and write to you. You are not expect-

---

24. Mary's daughter and Mathilde's niece. See n. 149 (chapter 1).

25. Mary's mother, Adeline Corss.

26. At the time of the 1860 census, a seventy-four-year-old New Hampshire–born woman named E. O. Pope lived in Ripon, not far from Waupun. U.S. Census, Population Schedules (1860), 2nd Ward, Ripon, Wisconsin, p. 115, dwelling 881, family 871.

27. When it was launched in 1858, the English ship the *Great Eastern* was the largest ever built. It visited New York in June and July 1860 to great fanfare, but Mary Booth probably did not arrive in the city soon enough to take Ella. *New York Times*, July 19, 1860.

28. Sherman Booth added a few lines along the edge of the first page.

ing a letter from me, and whether you are happy to get it—I do not know. I do not understand your feelings. I do not understand you! The distance between us is endless. Let me respond to your two little notes. I've received one through the *Sentinel* or rather with the correspondence for the *Sentinel*, and the polite *Illinois Staatszeitung* has sent me the other one. In the first one you are outraged that my letter is dated July 20 to August 20. In what way do you have the right to fault me for writing you a few words about our lives almost every day but not sending these words to you as instantly as both you and I would have hoped? Well, that is for you to decide after I've informed you about the simple fact that I did not have a cent to pay for stamps—for more than eight days. And after I told you that the only reason your children and I were not at risk of starvation was because I had credit enough for bread and food here in our blessed West. And I would have used this loan money to buy stamps, but I already needed to buy shoes and other immediately necessary things on credit. The five dollars that I'd borrowed for this purpose from Emil, who by the way had a rather difficult summer, might not have exhausted my credit with him. But you know too well from experience how difficult it is to borrow when we're in dire need of it. Your utter despair at being without money for fourteen days—and then the dismal jeremiads you decide to send me across the ocean about the random delay that is your own and only your own fault. How can you write such things to me, to me, the person you had left behind here in a much, much more difficult and anxious situation? I've been ill, almost deathly ill. And these cruelties are proof of everything I would have realized a long time ago had I not been too blind to see it. I am not complaining—not even when in reality I do not have the money that I should have on paper. I despise complaining whenever I am still able to help myself. When I keep my sorrow and hardship a secret, however, you seem to come to the conclusion that life is a bed of roses for me and even that I am feasting like the Sybarites at your expense![29] I thank you, dear Fritz, for whom I once suffered. I thank you for the punishment that your painful rage has put on my already martyred heart. . . .

---

29. Residents of the ancient Greek city of Sybaris on the Italian Peninsula had a reputation for indulging themselves. "Sybarite," in *OED Online*, Oxford University Press, accessed August 30, 2020, http://www.oed.com/view/Entry/196084.

As to your utter despair, it is proof of the faintheartedness of a human who calls himself a "man," such as I have never seen before in my entire life despite all my rich experiences and expertise in knowing people. Did you not have the confidence in yourself and the people around you to simply give your host a strong slap on the shoulder and say: "Look, old fellow, you know I am an honest man. I am waiting longer as expected to receive my payments. Will you give me something to eat and to drink? And maybe only until I come into possession of the most necessary resources? Will you do this for me, even if it may take 2 months until I receive money? See, I am not only honest, I am also rich because I have the brains to conquer the world on my own, and I can do it—I have confidence in myself." Putting these last few words into your mouth could almost sound cynical—but no: I had honestly hoped and thought that self-confidence had finally become one of your qualities. And that's because I remember the moment we had to say goodbye, when I literally asked you: "How are you going to surmount all those difficulties?" And then your response was—and I was happy to hear the strength in your voice: "If the difficulties seem insurmountable, then I will surmount them all the more."—You had surmounted all of these difficulties—I had given you exact reports about all of your successes.—And even when you did not receive your payment on the exact day and hour you'd expected to receive it—when not receiving the money so that <u>you, your children, and I</u> could live—your manhood still demands that you not despair—not "to vanish" as you say.—I would have heartfelt sympathy for you in this embarrassing situation of yours, but I've learned from experience that you take pleasure indulging in complaints about the unworthy state of society in order to appeal to the conscience of those who are to blame for this and say: ecce homo![30]

It was with great difficulty that I came in possession of the most necessary means to support daily life. I've gone to great lengths for us: I've written letters, and I've gone to the papers for you. I've worked to receive 40 dollars in payment myself, which luckily, I have received every week. I've been ill—and I even had to interrupt my health cure because I was so anxious and could not afford to spend money on medication.

---

30. According to the Latin translation of the Gospel of John, Pontius Pilate spoke these words ("Behold the man!") when presenting the scourged Jesus to a crowd shortly before his crucifixion. The Bible (Vulgate Version), John 19:5.

I did not tell you about any of this, and I would not have now if simply alluding to it had been enough. But it has become necessary to show you explicitly that there are stark contrasts between our approaches to life, despite the similarity of our respective circumstances.

I've gone to great pains to receive my payments and collect and benefit from yours. I cannot get anything from the *Atlas* unless I ask for it ten times. All I received for your letters was 2 dollars from their manager Otterburg. Just 2 dollars. The *Sentinel* keeps me busy. I was there 6 times already. Now Booth is trying to get our money from them. I received <u>12 dollars from the *Freie Zeitung*</u> after my last letter to you, which I sent on the 30th (enclosed with newspapers). I now regret having disappointed you since you thought I would <u>not</u> send you a letter. That's all. If I were not to live in this *comfortable* house but in a little hut with my two little children, whose well-being is my main interest in life, I would hardly need the money. But circumstances demand that the children and I cannot walk around in ragged beggars' clothing. That's simply the way it is. Herr Prieth[31] seems very happy about your correspondence, and I regret now having made a hasty judgment about him. The *Buffalo Teleg[raph]*[32] always sends me the issues with your articles. I received your last direct letter to me dated Sept. 10 on Sept. 28. I have to wait again until I have some money to buy stamps before I can mail this letter.

If you don't feel comfortable receiving letters or rather news from me, you just have to say the word. I would be happy to only report to you about the children and not bother you with matters about myself. I can stay silent about any and all issues concerning myself. I'm feeling healthy now, and I'll be able to handle it.

<u>On October 19th</u>

... I wish you the best of everything. I will not bother you with another letter, unless business or other urgent matters demand it. At the very least, I will not write to you before I receive your response to this letter.

Live happily! Your loving Mathilde.

---

31. Benedict Prieth published the *New Jersey Freie Zeitung*. Karl J. R. Arndt and May E. Olsen, *German-American Newspapers and Periodicals, 1732–1955: History and Bibliography* (Heidelberg: Quelle & Meyer, 1961; reprint, New York: Johnson Reprint Corporation, 1965), 307.

32. The *Buffalo Telegraph* was a German American newspaper that supported the Republican Party. Arndt and Olsen, *German-American Newspapers*, 328.

Mary Booth to her daughter Ella Booth
Milwaukee, December 30, 1859
(English original)

My dear Ella:

Yesterday, I sent you a blue net in a letter to Gram, which I forgot to say Madam Anneke bought for you, or rather, gave <u>me</u> money to buy it. I send you in this letter a net which I have made myself for you. [I]t is just finished. It is the first I ever did. All girls and ladies wear them here on the back part of thier heads. If Jane wants one I will make it for her & send in a letter.

Lillian is a good child now & when you come home she wont be ugly to you anymore. She is not naughty at all now. She wishes to see you very much. Mr. Richmond's Sunday school had a festival Tuesday. Lillian & Hertah went. Hertah will almost cry if told she is not a Christian child, & I dont allow Lillian to say so to her.

They had a very nice time & played beautifully, but Lillian would not eat. They played, going around in a ring, "choose the one that you love best" & some of the girls choose Mr. Richmond, & I guess they all wanted to.

You can tell Gram that if Mr. Carl Shurtz lectures in Hartford to send you to call on them as he has his wife[33] & little girl with him, & you are acquainted with her, & she would like to see you, so would her mother.

Hertah's grandmother gave me a pair of beautiful gauntlet gloves for a Christmas present. When you come home you will find a beautiful Sunday school to go to, & many very pretty & good children there who will be very happy to see you.

Lillian will learn you speak German,[34] as she speaks it as well as English. Every one is astonished to hear her speak it. Hertah's aunt sent her a beautiful doll, but Lillian likes her own rag baby the best.

---

33. Carl Schurz's wife Margarethe is remembered for briefly (1854–1856) operating the first German-style kindergarten in the United States. Ann Taylor Allen, "American and German Women in the Kindergarten Movement, 1850–1914," in *German Influences on Education in the United States to 1917*, ed. Henry Geitz, Jürgen Heideking, and Jurgen Herbst (Cambridge: Cambridge University Press, 1995), 85–103.

34. Perhaps Mary's awkward phrasing was supposed to imitate someone learning a new language.

Lillian and Hertah have red flannel sacques.[35] Lillian has not had even a little cold this winter, and I hope you have not.

This city has been so full of mad dogs this winter that every dog is now killed which is seen in the streets. They were never so many known before.

Lillian & I ride to Sunday school now every Sunday.

They was a wedding in church night before last—the first one.

Madam Anneke & I went, then we went to see Mr. Richmond. Franklin's father[36] made him an elegant christmas house & furniture table & all & put candles in it, all out of cigar boxes & put it in a green little yard with a fence around it & two christmas trees beside & a fountain. The most beautiful thing you ever saw. & out of the chimney there came smoke. He is going make a work box for me Mrs A. says, also from cigar boxes which are always made of mahogany.

Love to all. Your aff. Mother

Mathilde Franziska Anneke to Fritz Anneke
Milwaukee, January 16–25, 1860

Dear good Fritz! Well, you've truly made all of us so happy this time. That is to say, we've received your little box. We were sitting at the breakfast table about four mornings ago and received this by express mail. It was with due care that I pulled out the long German nails myself and then exposed the contents under the surprised gaze of Maria and the children. Little Hertha was shouting "well this is a very good Papa" time and again. First, we arranged the lovely garden figures. Percy arranged his battle lines. Maria adorned herself with the agraffe[37] and very much enjoyed looking at all the beautiful pictures and the wonderfully pretty Swiss houses in particular. The pictures, along with the little lead figures, are standing on the marble fireplace now. They are tastefully arranged in front of the *parlor* and in a way that the children can enjoy them without having the chance to ponder

---

35. A style of jacket, robe, or dress that flares out from the neck.
36. Mary presumably refers to Edmund Märklin, who had recently married Caroline Giesler (Mathilde's brother's widow) and become Franklin Giesler's stepfather. See n. 106 (chapter 1).
37. An ornamental clasp.

too much.... Naturally, the old Beranger[38] has given me the greatest pleasure. We've already delighted in reading about the old vagabonds. His farewell songs and all the others, with which I was still unfamiliar, brought some nourishment for my hungry soul. You won't believe just how much I lack intellectual nourishment here. Maria fills a great void in my emotional life. But you know all about the difficulties communicating in general with the Americans whom we have come to love. In some respects, there can be no thought of having a meaningful conversation from which we can gain results regarding our critical thinking and our knowledge. The differences between our attitudes and our languages still get in the way. Booth, with his *notions* and his hypocrisy about certain things, is often so repulsive to me that I break off all conversation with him. Maria's temper, her love, her inborn sense of beauty, her care for me—it is a compensation for many things. I love her more and more each day. I hardly have other company, and I rarely leave the house now since Maria has been suffering from the most severe pain in her face for the last three to four weeks. Grandmother is still our most frequent visitor. She thanks you for the beautiful present, of which she is so proud. She's been meaning to write to you God knows how many times, but you know how difficult that gets for her. She's reading your written and printed letters with utmost interest. She often claims that "Fritz is one of her favorite writers." I am often very worried about Mother. Johanna is often very unfriendly to her and so is Emil. She complains about it to me, but what can I do? If I were alone right now, then she would come live with me. But I don't want to invite her to live in the Booth house, even though Maria has offered it already. Having to part ways with Mother and also with my poor Fanny would make it much harder for me to return to the old Fatherland.—

Our little children are healthy. Percy is a good-looking, brave boy. He is now also very well-mannered, and you will be delighted with him. He has a passion for playing chess, and I constantly have to get the idea of joining the local chess club out of his head. He needs a better chess partner than Booth. You will have little Hertha's picture by now. I often think about how much you must enjoy it.

Anna Beust's advice to "make a package of my things and simply leave" does show me that people there are as ingenious as they have al-

---

38. Pierre-Jean de Béranger (1780–1857) was a French poet known for his satires of monarchy. *Encyclopædia Britannica*, 11th ed., 3:761–3.

ways been. Meanwhile, it has become cumbersome for me to even go from one house to the next. I cannot pack up and leave like in the old days when you only had to say the word and I would travel across countries and oceans. What couldn't I have done if you had wished it?—But traveling across the ocean alone with the children—what would they do if I fell ill again? And I am so prone to illness now that I am alone. Only leading a very regimented life helps prevent illnesses like I had this past spring. Little Hertha writes you a hundred little letters every day. This is her writing to you,[39] and it is supposed to say, "I am a good girl, and I do not drop my glass of milk at all." And now Lillian needs to write to Papa.[40] As you must know, Lillian just wrote that she thanks you for the nice things, and why don't you please send her a little horse.—I've read *Danton's Death*[41] again, dear Fritz. I gave *Orla*[42] to Johanna. I don't particularly like it anymore.—

I see you're exchanging letters with Father again. I have always delighted in his opinions, which he loves to impress upon the boring brother in Bonn.[43] Have you not been able to make the people understand that an American citizen can never and nowhere get "permanent employment"? Dear God, how these old and young backward-looking men madden me! And then the excerpt you take from his letter in his notoriously formal and bureaucratic writing style. One time he calls my poor Franziska[44] "the good one," and then again he speaks of her lightly calling her "oh so scruffy and sloppy." These are always the same stories about Hammacher. We should stop paying attention to it. Franziska only makes me bewail women in our society. She did not have the courage to show her good-for-nothing husband the door. This man has

---

39. Hertha inserted about a line and a half of scrawl imitating cursive writing.
40. Lili's scrawl.
41. Georg Büchner, *Dantons Tod* (Stuttgart: Phillip Reclam, 1835) is a famous German play about the French Revolution.
42. The dramatic verse *Orla*, written by a freethinker and socialist, was less well known than *Dantons Tod*. Albert Dulk, *Orla* (Zürich: Literarisches Comptoir Zürich und Winterthur, 1844).
43. Although not a relation, Friedrich Hammacher was a jurist and future statesman to whom Fritz had been very close in the 1840s. Although Hammacher married Mathilde's friend Franziska Rollmann, the relationship between Fritz and Hammacher broke down when Hammacher became less radical. Friedrich Anneke, *"Wäre ich auch zufällig ein Millionär geworden, meine Gesinnungen und Überzeugungen würden dadurch nicht gelitten haben—": Friedrich Annekes Briefe an Friedrich Hammacher, 1846–1859*, ed. Erhard Kiehnbaum (Wuppertal: Friedrich Engels-Haus, 1998).
44. Franziska Rollmann Hammacher. Ibid.

used the little intellectual superiority he has over her to rob her potentially forever of everything that was beautiful and lovely about her. He is using her, and she has become pathetic enough to let him use her. This is the fate of thousands of unhappy women. It is most painful for those who are consciously suffering! ...

January 25

... All this anxiety and apprehension—it's no way to live. And then, matching my still depressed mood, came the terrible accident that befell our poor, poor Grandmother! She went for a walk on Saturday afternoon and fell on Mason Street, not only breaking her thigh bone but also dislocating her pelvic bone. She was only accompanied by Ida and Alma and was lying on the street for ten minutes. Finally, an American family helped her. Four men put her on a sleigh and drove her home. They fetched two doctors: Hopfe[45] and Müller. When I was informed about this very late in the evening, these two doctors seemed inadequate, and I fetched Wollcott,[46] one of the most gifted surgeons. He then conducted the examinations and applied the bandages himself. The dislocation was reset under the most terrible pain. At best, the broken bones will heal. However, she will never walk again. This is a great, great misfortune for all of us! I just cannot yet get over this myself. I spent the night before last with Mother, and by the way, I'm sure that the *Journal of Com[merce]* could use you here, naturally only as a commercial, not political, employee.

I stayed with Mother, and these past days I took care of her as much as was in my power. The Booths continued their efforts to bring her here and give her the best room and the best care here with us. It would have been good for Mother, but she did not want to act against Johanna's wishes, especially not now. I am very worried—my worries are endless.—I could not stop crying for several days.—I think there was still so much I wanted to tell you about, but I can't remember now. You might like Booth's new plan. In any case, you would need to reorganize your activities if we wanted to count on living a decent life with our family in Europe. Mother's well-being of course is the most impor-

---

45. Emil Hopfe was another Saxon-born physician. U.S. Census, Population Schedules (1860), 7th Ward, Milwaukee, Wisc., p. 125, dwelling 855, family 793.

46. The eminent Erastus B. Wolcott, who would become surgeon general of the Wisconsin militia in the Civil War, is remembered for his pioneering work in renal surgery. (Mathilde misspelled his name.) Louis Frederick Frank, *The Medical History of Milwaukee, 1834–1914* (Milwaukee, Wisc.: Germania Publishing Co., 1915), 5–6.

tant thing for the moment. I cannot even think about leaving her in the next six months.—I have to see what I can do, how I can help. The *Telegraph* in Buffalo, those repeated villains, will hopefully not receive another line from you! I just got a mean letter from the very same paper yesterday, which included ten dollars. I will again write to Veasell[47] today so as to have one thing less to worry about.

The Turner board members have decided to give me an *appointment* as a speaker for the Wisconsin area.[48] Certainly, this is too much of an honor. But I will accept anyway because it comes with nice little journeys and some income. I am supposed to speak primarily about women's rights. This will help me escape this depressed mood for a while. I will take our little Turner Percy with me.

Our dear little children send their greetings and their kisses. I wish you could see them.

Farewell, farewell.

Your old Mathilde

Send my best to our friends in Zürich

Mary Booth to her mother Adeline Corss
Milwaukee, March 2, 1860
(English original)

My dear Mother:

Sherman was arrested yesterday at the Depot on his return from Madison, by the U.S. marshal on the old slave base. He is now confined in the Custom House, where the Post office is, it being the only Government building in the city. He has a fine room in the upper story, & I guess he won't care much. He stopped at the house in a carraige with the officer but I was not at home. Mrs. A. & I having gone to see Mary Briggs who was sick. Lillian saw him, & he left his papers & things here.

---

47. This individual, possibly connected with the *Buffalo Telegraph*, could not be identified.

48. Full membership in the Turnverein was restricted to men until 1904, and Turners were not necessarily supportive of women's rights, but they were impressed enough by Mathilde Anneke to employ her and make her an honorary member. Anke Ortlepp, "*Auf denn, Ihr Schwestern!*": *Deutschamerikanische Frauenvereine in Milwaukee, Wisconsin, 1844–1914* (Stuttgart: Franz Steiner, 2004), 107.

The officer said he could see his Counsel, so Gen. Paine[49] went, & they wouldn't let him speak except in presence of the officer which he would not do. S. wrote me a note, & said he wished all legal measures used to get him out, which is very foolish indeed, as his other trial[50] comes on in four weeks, & he better stay where he is to divert the public mind from that, & turn it in a channel where he can have sympathy, & good feeling towards. The State would demand him as its criminal, & the U. States as thiers. Then there would be an interesting fight between the two, which would be what he has always wanted.

He carried a pistol for weeks to shoot the officer who should arrest, until I scolded so much about it, & forbid it, that he has not done it of late. Mr. Sholes[51] said it would be right enough if any one had the courage to do it, which he never should have. But I think it would be awful, & very wicked. But S. talkes very big, but as you know he <u>cowardly</u> after all, although he's furious if any body says so. He would only have to stay the 30 days out,[52] which he was sentenced before, & until the $2000 fine was paid, which the <u>Freedom people</u> would do soon enough.

Mr. Sholes came here & offered very politely to do all in his power for the family, or otherwise, but Lorenzo has not come the house.

Fitch[53] has been heard to say that if the Free Dem. did not pay well he should never put a cent in it. It is filled with stupid foolishness, & the subscribers fall off continually. Lillian has made a pretty rag baby for Ella, all alone.

Mrs. King[54] was in last night, and is <u>going</u> to write you.

---

49. Lawyer James H. Paine was the father of Hortensius and Byron and had supported Sherman Booth since 1854. *Milwaukee Daily Sentinel*, February 22, 1879.

50. Probably a reference to plans for a new seduction trial, which never actually took place.

51. Charles C. Sholes was an antislavery politician and editor who had briefly co-owned the *Free Democrat* with Lorenzo Crounse in 1859. U.S. Census, Population Schedules (1860), 4th Ward, Kenosha, Wisconsin, p. 103, dwelling 812, family 735; *Milwaukee Daily Sentinel*, April 16, 1860; Frank A. Flower, *History of Milwaukee, Wisconsin* (Chicago: Western Historical Company, 188), 627.

52. Mary seems to mean that Sherman would have to wait out the 30 days in jail.

53. Thomas Fitch (1838–1923) worked at Booth's *Free Democrat* for a few years in the late 1850s before going on to a much more interesting career as an editor, Republican politician, and lawyer in western states. "Fitch, Thomas," Biographical Directory of the United States Congress, accessed July 30, 2020, http://bioguide.congress.gov/scripts/biodisplay.pl?index=F000159.

54. Likely Susan King, whose husband edited the *Milwaukee Sentinel*, which supported Booth. See n. 111 (chapter 1).

I have received very serious talks from the heads of my church in reference to my duty—the one on which you talked to Ryan,[55] in accordance to the opinion you then had, but of those things the less I say the better.

Love to all. [A]ff. yours Mary—

Mathilde Franziska Anneke to Fritz Anneke
Milwaukee, March 16–20, 1860

My dear Fritz!

...

Grandmother was very happy to receive the letter in which you express your love and sympathy. She is showing your letter to everyone who visits her. She's not wearing the bandage anymore, and she is now sitting in Booth's large red armchair. The doctors say that the fracture has healed well. She cannot move her leg, but it doesn't hurt now when other people touch it. I remain hopeful that she will be able to stand up once she is allowed to in 3 weeks. The leg is a little shorter now. She is happy that her situation has improved now. All of her friends have done their best to help make this easier for her.

Booth is still incarcerated. It's the same tyranny everywhere. These insufferable boors who are watching him don't let Maria and me visit him very often. You know, "tout comme chez nous"[56]—and oftentimes things here are worse. It's as if we are almost back to the glory of medieval times here too. It was laughable how much effort Uncle Sam put into this as we were waiting for the writ of habeas corpus.[57] All weapons from the U.S. *cutter* had been taken to the prison. There were horse pistols on each step of the large stairs. You will find more details about this in Booth's letter to you. I do not know how this is going to end. I cannot foresee if and how he is going to carry out his plan (the London plan). My life here, and in Milwaukie especially, is entirely repulsive to

---

55. We have not been able to identify Ryan. Mary perhaps refers to marital duty here, although it is not clear.

56. French for "everything is just like at home." Here Mathilde is apparently comparing Booth and Fritz's respective imprisonments.

57. Writs of habeas corpus, which ask a court to assess whether an individual's imprisonment is legal, originated in English common law.

me. If it weren't for Mother—Mother and Maria—I would have at least quickly relocated to the American East by now. In exile, it has always been my wish to see my homeland or Switzerland again. But I am not sure where my home is now. Is it where my children are buried? Or is it where I spent my happy youth picking flowers? And in the end, something as profane as money could decide which one I would choose to be my home. I do not have any and neither does Maria. Booth has long been meaning to sell land, but there is no money, and there are no buyers either. Plus, he would not have given anything to Maria anyway. The children and I share the fervent wish that I take them to Switzerland. But I do wish for them to return to America later in life. I will let fate decide about all this. I will not take the risk that my children and I may or may not happily reach the European shore. I will leave it up to you entirely to decide whether we should leave or stay. I cannot get you any work. I don't have any opportunity to try.

March 20. I had to stop writing due to indisposition. My pen fell from my hand—I was experiencing such pain—the old seizures in the liver were back. I have now started a new health cure that Frau Bruno[58] recommended to me. Frau Bruno has had gallstones for years, and now keeps them in a delicate little box. Will it help me? At least it seems like the seizures have become less painful.—I have a terrible headache today. Maria takes good care of me, always with the same love and attention. She's afraid that I might die on her because of the seizures. But once her fear is over, she is soon her old playful self again. You will find her unchanged. And she is healthy—

Your letter dated February 3 enclosed in the correspondence for the *Free Dem[okrat]* arrived here yesterday. It must have been lying in the ocean. You will have taken from my second to last letter that the "unsealed" letter has come into my hands and was firmly sealed. Hertha and Percy send their greetings and kisses. Hertha now often carries around her "dear Papa" for days—your picture in a little box. She keeps reminding us that we had promised her to go and see "Papa in Italy." Percy is a dear boy. He is not persistent in his studies, but he does show an interest in history, arithmetic, and a few other subjects. If he were attending a better school, then he would learn more. This world-

---

58. An Amelia Bruno, born in Baden and only 25 in 1860, lived in Milwaukee. U.S. Census, Population Schedules (1860), 1st Ward, Milwaukee, Wisc., p. 216, dwelling 1551, family 1516.

renowned academy with St. Engelmann at the helm is worth nothing. This is why Percy is taking a few lessons every day with me now during the school vacation. I am hardly writing anything as is, and so I can best use my time teaching the boy.—A change of scenery would be so good for him right now!

Beginning April 1, Carl Anneke will work for Finkler who has his business on Westwasserstraße[59] in a big brick building next to Stirn.[60] Merklin will manage his pharmacy. I want for Carl to be happy.

Schmittill[61] was here for 8 days. For the first time in 8 years he allowed himself this little rest. He is a good man, and he seems happy. Schmittill wants to take a stand for Carl with Father so that Father will give him money and he can pay his debts. Finkler has a nice warehouse again. Drug Meyer[62] was forced to relocate. I could fill many sheets of paper reporting local Milwaukee news. But I don't want to amuse you with that. I will only tell you this much: The city's bankruptcy is imminent. The *City Comptroller* and the *City Clerk* have both been arrested for stealing thousands of dollars.[63] There is some talk about bringing Booth to Mackinaw[64] tomorrow on the U.S. *Cutter* "Michigan." The local abolitionists, namely a few radical Americans, want to free him. It is strange that the habeas corpus writ doesn't get him freed. Not even the *County Court*. We are living in our large house with our dear little children, happily and quietly. Uncle Sam would not have to free him for us—but for his own sake and for the sake of our cause, I do wish that someone would show this bad bunch of slaveholders the door and that Booth would be set free in triumph.

Vogt's pamphlet about the "Brimstone Gang" has gotten much at-

---

59. Immigrants often Germanized the name of West Water Street.

60. See n. 6 (chapter 2).

61. Fritz's sister Ida married Sigmund Schmidtill from Bavaria in 1852. Alma Harris, "Die Nachkommen unserer Großeltern Carl u. Elisabeth Giesler im Jahre 1890," (n.d.), Box 70, Archiv der Mathilde Franziska Anneke, 1817–1884, Stadtarchiv Sprockhövel, Germany; U.S. Census, Population Schedules (1850), Milwaukee, Wisc., p. 539, dwelling 532, family 569.

62. Mathilde used the unusual German term "Gift Meyer" to refer to the drugstore of Hanover-born pharmacist Enno Meyer. U.S. Census, Population Schedules (1860), 2nd Ward, Milwaukee, Wisc., dwelling 146, family 151.

63. Acting City Clerk Robert B. Lynch would be found guilty of forgery and embezzlement, but he escaped to Canada while his case was under appeal. City Comptroller E. L. H. Gardiner managed to evade similar charges. Flower, *History of Milwaukee*, 275; *Milwaukee Daily Sentinel*, March 13, 1860.

64. A village in northern Michigan.

tention here in this country.⁶⁵ But Blind's piece in *Der Pionier*⁶⁶ does cast quite a shadow on the regent of the realm.⁶⁷ His description of the Marx clique was rather amusing to me. Certainly, it is all true.

*Franziska Maria has acted like the devil all day.*⁶⁸ *She deserts me continually and runs away from me in the street, & acts awful. My rose which you gave me on my last birth day, after having been dead all winter, is now putting forth beautiful leaves, I suppose from the inspiration of your spirit.*

By the way, I find Mr. Blind to be a despicable character. This European correspondent is such a braggart! I have nothing but praise for "Theodore Karcher,"⁶⁹ on the other hand. For a while people here thought he was a European correspondent too.—Dear Fritz, we will celebrate our birthdays in loving memory of you. I will buy some flowers for us from Wisconsin's dull, cold countryside, and I will pretend you've sent them to us from more beautiful domains. I've already bought a little parasol for Maria. She is making dozens of shirts for me that are different in style from the ones I usually wear. Maria is making all of these things for the children and me herself. She is already preparing our journey there.

Herr Schwedler has finally sent me 27 dollars. I spent all of it already on food and clothing and to pay our debts. Marxhausen⁷⁰ writes

---

65. In 1859, Forty-Eighter Karl Vogt, who was living in Switzerland, published a program for European politics that made him unpopular with many German leftists in exile. A feud ensued in which Vogt ridiculed Marx as the leader of the "Brimstone Gang." (The English name was a literal translation of the German term for an organization of unruly students.) Marx interrupted his work on political economy for a year to publish a rebuke. Marcello Musto, "Marx in the Years of Herr Vogt: Notes toward an Intellectual Biography," *Science & Society* 72, no. 4 (2008): 393–94.

66. Karl Blind (1826–1907) was another Forty-Eighter who had fought in Baden but now lived in London. Blind wrote extensively on German history and politics, including, here, for *Der Pionier*, a periodical published in Boston by Karl Heinzen (1809–1880), one of the most radical Forty-Eighters in the United States. Joseph McCabe, *A Biographical Dictionary of Modern Rationalists* (London: Watts & Co., 1920), 82; Mischa Honeck, *We Are the Revolutionists: German-Speaking Immigrants and American Abolitionists after 1848* (Athens, Ga.: University of Georgia Press, 2011), 137–71.

67. Vogt held this position in the 1848 rump parliament in Stuttgart, which was called after the Frankfurt parliament was dissolved. Heléna Tóth, *An Exiled Generation: German and Hungarian Refugees of Revolution, 1848–1871* (New York: Cambridge University Press, 2014), 173.

68. Mary inserted a short paragraph in English before Mathilde resumed writing.

69. Théodore Karcher (1821–1885) was a French writer, editor, and political figure. Jean-Pierre Kintz, *Nouveau dictionnaire de biographie alsacienne* (Strasbourg: Fédération des Sociétés d'Histoire et d'Archéologie d'Alsace, 1993), 20:1880.

70. August Marxhausen from Hesse published and edited German American news-

that I should wait for a few more days and then he will send money. St. Crounse only pays me occasionally ever since he got himself the young wife. The last seizures were followed by a terrible headache, which is tormenting me day and night. I can only complete this letter bit by bit. Mary and I just returned from visiting Booth in prison. His sentence is up. The slaveholders will probably not set him free, however. Maybe they will tie him up for a while aboard the U.S. ship and let him be the galley slave for a change. It is impossible to know what else they could have in mind for him. A few good old abolitionist harbors are preparing a liberation by force. But will they succeed? Will they have the courage to do it? Maybe they want to engage the peasantry in this cause.

We fetched your letter dated Feb. 21 from the post office. Dear Fritz, our little children and I thank you for the lovely little pictures. I also especially thank you for the beautiful books you have purchased for me. I was long hoping for some Ancient Greek literature. The encyclopedia of Classical archeology will be very helpful. It was my greatest wish to read more about Plutarch.[71] But you shouldn't suffer any deprivations to give me these treasures. I must have received the Napol. laconic letters[72] about three times. Dear Fritz, you see that we cannot discuss the London plan any further now. We have to await Booth's fate.

I will inform you immediately as soon as there are new developments that concern him or us. The letter to the [*Free Democrat*] we thought was lost has also—but I see I already told you that. Mother wanted to write you herself. Percy just went to see her, get little Hertha, and bring her your letters. It is a pleasure seeing our two little children together. Hertha truly dominates Percy. They are very fond of their Mama. Perci never leaves the house without hugging me first. He is sleeping upstairs in your old room alone now. This way I'd hear it if he were sleep-

---

papers in Detroit for over half a century. In 1859, he ran the *Michigan Journal* with his brother. *The City of Detroit, Michigan, 1701–1922* (Detroit: S. J. Clarke Publishing Company, 1922), 3:226.

71. The most famous works of the Greek thinker Plutarch (46–120 C.E.) are biographies.

72. This oblique reference is perhaps to the letters that Napoleon Bonaparte wrote to his wife Josephine, which were published many times in French, German, and English. The love letters are better known for being passionate rather than pithy, so perhaps Mathilde description of them as "laconic" is humorous. In German, as in English, "Napol. laconic" sounds like "Napoleonic." Henry Foljambe Hall, "Introduction," in *Napoleon's Letters to Josephine, 1796–1812* (London: J. M. Dent & Co., 1901), xv–xx.

walking. But he does not do that anyway. Grandmother has been in too much pain to write you during this stormy weather we've had for days now. She sends her love, and you will soon receive a letter from her! And you're writing that you intend to wait with your response anyway. Stay healthy. Maria sends her greetings and will write to you in the next letter. This letter will soon be followed by a letter from all of us.

Farewell, yours, Mathilde.

Mathilde Franziska Anneke to Fritz Anneke
Milwaukee, July 4, 1860

My dear Fritz! I will celebrate this Independence Day by writing to you. Our suitcases are packed, and Maria's passport has arrived. Mine cannot be issued before I bring in my naturalization papers. This can happen tomorrow. Senator Durkee[73] will take care of it in Washington: "the *money will come, because it must.*" I never realized before what blind faith you have in your lucky star.—We have decided to leave on the 20th of this month. But I cannot yet assure you that we will have the money to go on this adventure. I received your letter dated June 1 on the 26th and the one dated June 3 on the first of this month. I would have responded much sooner had I not spent one day after the other in eager anticipation. We were first waiting for Maria's passport and for money. Second, we were awaiting Booth's liberation. The latter had much to do with the first. Maria and I had been conspiring for 14 days. Daniels was at the forefront of this. He is the state geologist who fought in Kansas and who lives in Ripon (about 150 miles from here). We intended to stage our coup at 5 a.m. yesterday morning. It was easier to make the arrangements from here. On July second, we informed our allies who lived further away: Farmers—real old Republicans from the old New England states. They were all in incredible pain having to witness freedom denied to one of them on the day of their independence. On the same day, late in the evening, Percy and I drove for 13 miles with a swift horse in order to notify the men. Dan-

---

73. Republican Senator Charles Durkee personally assisted Mathilde and Mary in procuring passports and in a note to Mathilde described Mary as their "mutual friend." Charles Durkee to Mathilde, June 27, 1860, Box 2, Folder 6, Booth Family Papers.

iels arrived in the afternoon. All weapons and munitions were ready. We spent the night loading our weapons. Our allies arrived at 4 a.m. and at 5 a.m. Shortly after the post offices opened 8 more men arrived. These men brought pistols and ropes. They were strong, energetic people who were supposed to go upstairs to fight the guards while Daniels opened the door using the key I've already told you about and release the prisoner. Two of these eight men were missing. I had brought those men I vouched for, full of courage. Our reserve men were ready and another 25 at not too far a distance. Daniels's men, whom he had counted on, did not come. Only one, a student who had fought like a lion with Brown in Kansas,[74] arrived 5 hours later. He'd been ordered to come on the 4th and not the 3rd. Whether this was Daniels's fault I did not ask. Our house served as the headquarters for the inner circle. The time had come, and everything was ready except that not all of the men who had promised to participate in the first attack were there. The men then left the headquarters, and everyone assumed they would attack.—Shattered hopes! They came back with concerns, saying the attack should be postponed to ten or twelve o'clock. The less reliable reserve men had broken our secret much too soon. This procrastination turned out to be too long. I haven't found out yet whether this happened due to the cowardice of the leader or of several of our allies. B[ooth] was at his window signaling the men not to attack before half past twelve. Daniels had fallen ill. He was not just pretending. The heat is unbearable. Then his friend came, a real revolutionary who fights until he falls. Daniels should have let him lead the men. But he didn't. And then at twelve o'clock everything was ready once again. We had 50 reserve men now, and some of them had gathered at the post office. And then suddenly the guards regained their strength and—I claim it was cowardice—Daniels, who's first in line, starts backtracking from the armed guards while still on the first stair. It's the same old story. At that point, the guards are armed to the teeth again. Everyone's armed and the *post building* seems like a fortress. Naturally, we cannot take over the building. We can only get Booth out of there by blindsiding

---

74. Mathilde later identifies the student as (Oscar) La Grange (1837–1915), who fought in Kansas with John Brown and other antislavery militants in 1855, returned to Wisconsin to attend Ripon College, and became a brigadier general in the Civil War. *Dictionary of Wisconsin Biography* (Madison, Wisc.: The State Historical Society of Wisconsin, 1960), 220.

the guards. And this opportunity had been destroyed. Today, we put up handbills saying: "Free men! To the Custom House! at 2 o'clock to prove our Day of Independence a reality. Booth will address the people from his prison window!" His window is overlooking an alley. Daniels has traveled back home due to illness. La Grange—that is the Kansas *fighter*—will stay. He may leave for the night, but he will return!!—At two o'clock masses of people were there! Booth had written down his speech, and we had smuggled it out around noon. As Booth was approaching the window, so were his three guards! B[ooth] cannot speak to us. The guards close his windows and put the iron shields in front of them. La Grange jumps on the roof of an opposing shack and following a revolutionary introduction, he starts reading Booth's speech. That is what happened. A few brave ones in the crowd were willing to take revenge for this disregard of their freedom—but they would have been lost, had they actually tried to attack.—Dear Fritz, we had decided to do everything in our power to free Booth before our departure. I thought it could be done with ease. And indeed, if I had been allowed to lead the people—he would be free by now, upon my life! We are helpless at this moment.—Schurz has become a jaded politician. And you were absolutely right that he had received orders from his superiors. It is a fact that Seward gave the order "let state rights fall."[75] The red Paines as well as the wretched Domschke[76] all take the same line. The army of truly loyal abolitionists is small!

On the morning of July 3, I included Reis[77] in our conspiracy. He then came with several fellows, and he was very reliable and stood the test. St. Domschke has long stopped visiting him. I recruited Wilhelm Steinmeier[78] without his parents' knowledge. He was on the scene at

---

75. In early 1860, New York Senator William Seward had deliberately moderated his public pronouncements in hopes of winning the Republican presidential nomination. He had previously supported the position that northern states should not enforce the Fugitive Slave Act. Schurz had thrown his support behind the moderate Abraham Lincoln and distanced himself from Booth. Walter Stahr, *Seward: Lincoln's Indispensable Man* (New York: Simon & Schuster, 2012), 182–84, 132, 154; Trefousse, *Carl Schurz*, 83.

76. See n. 87 (chapter 1).

77. Possibly Constantine Reis, a Baden-born schoolteacher. U.S. Census, Population Schedules (1860), 2nd Ward, Milwaukee, Wisc., p. 81, dwelling 545, family 492.

78. The 1860 census enumerated William Steinmeyer as a nineteen-year-old gunsmith boarding with Carl and Henriette Anneke. U.S. Census, Population Schedules (1860), 2nd Ward, Milwaukee, Wisc., p. 38, dwelling 318, family 342.

4 a.m. We used him as our runner and delivery boy. And in case of an emergency, I would have given him the job of pistol loader. The boy did splendid work, and I have only good things to say about him, as you must know.

I must now get to responding to your last dear letter. The first one does not tell me much, and so I can disregard that one. Your travel plan is very detailed. We could begin our journey this moment if we had the money. It would still be terrible enough to leave Booth here in <u>prison</u>, but Booth himself and the people here have to take care of it. He truly does not do anything to help his family. I doubt he ever thinks about them and how they can get by. It is only when he wants to stir up sympathy that he mentions his starving family. Maria is truly a very, very unfortunate woman. We have 80 dollars in cash at the moment. . . . I can barely get rid of any of the furniture. Frau H[enriette] Anneke has been meaning to buy the cooking oven for 8 weeks now. I promised her the oven. And now she's given up on the idea. In the meantime, I could have sold the oven three times over. Maria had hoped to receive the *rent* a year in advance from her priest in the country.[79] However, he will only give her three months' worth. I cannot sell a single *lot* of land. The *building* hardly yields any money for Maria. She does not receive payment for old debts. The Republican members of Congress had promised to do so much and haven't done anything yet. Nevertheless, we still have hope. We are all well-equipped. Five of the most beautiful sturdy suitcases are packed. Mother has given me a beautiful black silk coat that cost 12 dollars. The children have all they need. Maria has worked incessantly. We are awaiting Doolitle[80] or Durkee in the next days. Then we can send another letter immediately telling you the exact time of our departure. The children cannot wait to leave now. Hertha just gave me another handful of rose petals that I am always supposed to send you. I think we should deny ourselves the pleasure of meeting you at the shore, even if all goes well. We intend to travel through France as quickly as possible to possibly meet you in St. Louis at the border between France and Switzerland. I am determined to get work,

---

79. The identity of Mary's tenant is not clear.
80. Republican James R. Doolittle was Wisconsin's other U.S. senator. (Mathilde misspelled the name.) James Grant Wilson and John Fiske, eds., *Appletons' Cyclopædia of American Biography* (New York: Appleton, 1891), 2:201–2.

whether it's for you or for me. I had also thought of Willich[81] before. I will write to him. I am doubtful regarding our household. If it shall be my duty to take care of it, then I will not have much time for my literary endeavors. If I have to think about feeding 6 hungry mouths two or three times a day, then there won't be much time left. We have become so frugal anyway—we are now as modest as republicans and as economical as Americans. You will barely be able to compete with us regarding these virtues. However, since *housekeeping* is cheaper and more comfortable in the long run, then we must surely choose it. I think you should wait to rent a place until we arrive, provided that it is possible to make all necessary arrangements within a few days. Well, all our hopes are on the 2 or 300 dollars that Maria <u>may</u> receive in the <u>next days</u>. We are also hoping to receive my payments from Detroit and New York. As soon as we are in possession of the most necessary funds we will depart. We are hoping to get a reduced rate for the journey aboard the ship. I don't think we'll get it for free. If there were a little more honesty in the Republican Party, then surely Maria would be able to depart in style. But every American has the same fatal *help yourself* attitude. Only Booth is an exception. He always wants others to help him. And he loves to complain and to use every opportunity to make *money*. Percy and Hertha are not writing to you anymore now that we will be with you again soon. It certainly is high time for them to see you again. Little Hertha only wants to be called Irla now. She's been telling me to write you for quite some time now. She is as close with Lilian now as if she were her little sister. Percy is a rather strong boy. I gave Hertha a new pair of shoes again yesterday. She needs a new pair every 5 weeks to be able to walk comfortably. I have to spend at least 4 dollars on shoes for the three children every 4 weeks. The little ones are playing in the yard all day long. Percy must walk a long way to school.

It won't be necessary to write to me here anymore. I hope we will be ready at the end of the month. I will write to you as soon as we have received some money. And I will write you from New York as well. Maria

---

81. Like Fritz, August Willich (1810–1878) had resigned from the Prussian army for political reasons, joined radicals such as Karl Marx and Friedrich Engels in Cologne in the 1840s, and fought for a German republic in Baden in 1849. In the United States, he edited the *Cincinnati Republikaner* and became a particularly vigorous opponent of slavery. He was beloved as a Union Army officer, rising to the rank of major general. Honeck, *We Are the Revolutionists*, 71–103.

will spend the time we have on the East Coast in Hartford with her Ella and her dear old folks. I will go to Newark for a day or two—to desolate Newark. I will take your advice and stay at the Shakespeare Hotel in New York. I will let you know all about our journey from there. I will let you know of our arrival in Southhampton or Le Havre.[82] I will also write to Theophil Beust[83] in the next few days regarding Uhl's daughter.[84] We were able to do quite a few things here for Fritz Beust's school as well. Why aren't you writing a long article about this in the English papers?[85] You tell me about a new restaurant at "Tiefen Brunnen." I did not know that the Roßmanns[86] were no longer the innkeepers there. I think we should choose our apartment close to the city, say by the lake? We will only bring beautiful things that can be transported easily. I will leave most of my books here. But I don't know myself yet where I will leave my things and what we will bring. You can expect another letter soon after this one. I will send it to the address of "Tiefen Brunnen," just like this one.

Farewell, dear Fritz. Our dear little children and I are hugging you. It is a cruel fate for all of us that our family has been torn apart. But we are hoping for a happy reunion soon. Stay healthy.

Your old <u>Mathilde</u> who loves you dearly.

You will be shocked at my corpulence. I gain weight every day despite the most frugal lifestyle. Poor Grandmother frequently takes the city train. She drags herself on her crutches for one block and then takes the train from the hill to Walker's Point and back for her own amusement. This is a very viable business in Milwaukie.

Your good friend Garenfeld in St. Louis has died from sunstroke.[87]

---

82. Le Havre, France was an important port for migrants.

83. Fritz Beust's brother Theophil immigrated to New Jersey in 1849, but he does not appear in the 1860 or 1870 censuses. In the 1880, his occupation was listed as "editor." "United States Passport Applications, 1795–1925," *FamilySearch*, accessed July 30, 2020, https://familysearch.org/ark:/61903/1:1:QKNT-6HX6; U.S. Census, Population Schedules (1880), Town of Union, New Jersey, p. 56, dwelling 98, family 399.

84. Likely the daughter of Anna Ottendorfer, whose deceased first husband had been Jacob Uhl. See n. 89 (chapter 2).

85. Mathilde means English-language newspapers in the United States.

86. Perhaps the same family Fritz referred to earlier as Coßmann. The handwriting is clear, but there could have been confusion over the name. See n. 80 (chapter 1).

87. Gustav Garenfeld had taught German in Milwaukee's Sixth Ward Public School before dying in a St. Louis saloon. *Milwaukee Daily Sentinel*, July 10, 1860.

Mathilde Franziska Anneke to Mary Booth
Newark, August 1, 1860
(English and German original)

Meine viel geliebte Maria![88]

I have retourned yesterday New York, tired to death, but happy in possession of your letter and very contended in arangements of our voyage. Your passport must be <u>undersigned day before sailing from french</u> consul! Baggage should be sent on board the day before sailing! I expect you also Friday, so early as possible. My friend Mrs Ottendorfer,[89] proprietor of *Staatszeitung*, shall received you with pleasure, when I am not myself on board. I have to tell you very much, when I have you again, my dear, dear Maria! I hope, you are contended with all my arangements which I have made. Many of my old friends in New York I have seen again. Struve[90] (our historian) General Blenker[91] & his wife, Lexow, proprietor of *Criminalzeitung*, all together have come to see me. Blenker has had yesterday his birthday—I call it that festival of his eternal youth—he had spoeken to his wife about those happy evening in Milwaukie and about my lovely dear friend. To morrow, I am going again to New York to receive my last money; our Gold is saved for Switzerland and more. In Paris you shall buy you an beautifull mantilla.[92] I was very oekonomical and I have collect my money very good. (Show

---

88. "My beloved Maria!"

89. Anna Uhl had operated the *New-Yorker Staats-Zeitung* with her first husband until his death in 1852. As publisher and editor, she worked alongside Forty-Eighter Oswald Ottendorfer, who took over as editor in chief in 1858 and assumed legal control of the business when the two married in 1859. With Anna Ottendorfer continuing in the role of business manager, the *Staats-Zeitung* became the country's largest German American newspaper and rivaled the *New York Times* and *New York Tribune* in circulation. James M. Bergquist, "Ottendorfer, Anna Behr Uhl," in *American National Biography* (New York: Oxford University Press, 1999), 16:841–42.

90. Gustav Struve (1805–1870) was a surgeon and journalist who had worked with Friedrich Hecker to establish a German republic by force in 1848 and 1849. A. E. Zucker, ed. *The Forty-Eighters: Political Refugees of the German Revolution of 1848* (New York: Columbia University Press, 1950), 346.

91. Louis Blenker was a Forty-Eighter who had fought in Baden in 1849. He settled in Rockford County, New York and would rise to the rank of brigadier general in the Union Army before dying of wounds suffered in falling from his horse in 1863. Zucker, *Forty-Eighters*, 280.

92. A traditional Spanish lace head covering.

nobody my scripture and burn it very quick, when you have half understand, what I had to say you.)

Last night I have received from Mr Booth a long long letter, which I wisch to answer when you have read it to. I am gladed, that you have answer him, as you say: You shall never an offence suffer.—

Wie viel habe ich an Dich gedacht: wie mit meiner ganzen Seele über dein finsteres Schicksal (dark faith) gedacht. Meine Maria! Mein Leben ist Dir gewidmet, ich trage mit Dir den Schmerz Deines Herzens. Sei stark und hoffe auf einen neuen Blumengarten. Die Blüten des verwelkten sind Gifthauch??. Sei nicht traurig, wenn Du auch Alles verloren hast, so hast Du die Liebe meines Herzens doch ewig, und sie muß dich trösten können, da sie <u>echt</u> ist.[93]

Give my thank and my Love to your sister Jane and to your family!

Forget not, that you must be Friday in New York, and Saturday morning 9 o clock with the children on board of steam boat <u>Bremen</u>, foot of Chamber Street, Pier 30. North River (now in port.)

Lebe wohl, mein Herzens kind! Küß mir Ella und Lilian und denke daß kein treues Herz auf der Welt für Dich schlägt, als das Herz Deiner[94]

Franziska Maria
Mathilde Franziska

Mary Booth to her daughter Ella Booth
New York, August 3, 1860
(English original)

My dear Ella:

We arrived in New York yesterday morning about four o clock. and at about five we took a carriage & went to the Hotel where all our things are—after awhile Lillian & I walked to the office of the "Staats Zeitung"

---

93. "How much I've thought about you and your dark fate with my entire soul. My Maria! I dedicate my life to you. I share your pain. Stay strong and keep hoping for a new flower garden. The dead flower garden is oppressive, isn't it?? Please don't be sad. Even if you've lost everything, you still have me. And my <u>true</u> love for you is eternal. It has to be a comfort to you."

Mathilde mistranslated *Schicksal* as "faith." It actually means fate.

94. "Farewell, my sweetheart! Kiss Ella and Lillian for me, and please know that no other heart beats for you like the heart of your Franziska Maria."

& left word for Madam Anneke that we had come—& in about two hours she came to us. We then went with her to Mrs. Offendof's—the proprietress of the "Staats Zeitung" to dinner—then to call on another German lady, where we had coffee. Then very far up town, where we were invited in a very lovely family, where we had wine. The gentleman then took us in a carriage over the central park, and we saw the swans. The park is wonderful. [I]t covers hundreds of acres. Then we took Fanny to the Newark Station, and came again to Mrs. Offendof's where we spent the night, Lillian having a beautiful bed by herself in a room next to ours. It is a superb house, & every thing surrounding it is lovely. The lady has now gone to her office, which is the most beautiful in all New York, and Madam Anneke will be gone all day on business, while I remain here. Fanny was in New York, yesterday, so that I saw her all day, & shall not go to Newark. She was so sick, however, that she could hardly walk. Lillian sits on a beautiful red velvet sofa, surrounded by cussions, & plays with a doll nearly as large as herself. She is very happy. I wish you could spend the day with her. We shall stay here all day & shall not go out, & also tonight. Madam Anneke, I shall not see again until to-morrow morning. She sends you a present of two dollars to buy something for your own expecial pleasure. She wished to send you five dollars, but I told her that she must not—that two would do very well. She was going to send you a box of things by express, but as she had not time to day to see to it[.] She sends the money instead. She sends you much love, & says we will send you some presents from Switzerland as soon as we can after we arrive. I forgot to ask her for our address there, but will get it to-morrow, & drop a line to Gram. Wm. H. Burleigh[95] is coming here to see me to day. I suppose that you know that your father is out of prison[96]—it is in the Tribune.[97]

---

95. William H. Burleigh, then harbormaster in New York City, had worked and campaigned with Sherman Booth in Connecticut in the 1840s. Owen W. Muelder, *Theodore Dwight Weld and the American Anti-Slavery Society* (Jefferson, N.C.: McFarland & Company, 2011), 73; *Semi-Centennial Historical and Biographical Record of the Class of 1841 in Yale University* (New Haven, Conn.: Tuttle, Morehouse & Taylor, 1892), 48.

96. Booth remained free from August 1 until October 8, when he was rearrested. President James Buchanan remitted his fines and ordered him released on March 2, 1861, just before Abraham Lincoln took office. Baker, *Rescue of Joshua Glover*, 168.

97. Mary almost certainly referred to Horace Greeley's large and influential *New-York Tribune*, an antislavery newspaper that published some of Karl Marx's writings. Adam-Max Tuchinsky, *Horace Greeley's New-York Tribune: Civil War–Era Socialism and the Crisis of Free Labor* (Ithaca, N.Y.: Cornell University Press, 2005).

He was taken out Wednesday by ten men, without any trouble, & taken off into the country. They did it at noon, in open day. They locked the keeper unto his room, which is opposite your fathers, & had no more trouble. You can thank Mr. Daniels for it. He was determined to have no blood shed, & did not. Lillian broke her doll's head yesterday, & Fanny bought her another. She is very much pleased with all the beautiful things she sees about.

Mrs. Anneke is sorry that you & Jane did not come with me. We are going through Germany & down the Rhine instead of through France, as it is so much more beautiful, & Mrs. Anneke has a passport from the U. States. She is delighted with the idea—so we shall go direct to Bremen. The lady at whose house I am has two sons at school in Zürich, Switzerland.

With much love Your Mother.

CHAPTER 3
Radical Refuge in the Alps

August 1860–March 1862

MARY AND MATHILDE, ALONG WITH PERCY, HERTHA, AND LILI, arrived in Europe in August 1860 to reunite with Fritz. We know relatively little about their experiences during the first year of their stay in Zürich because the three adults naturally did not exchange letters while they lived together under the same roof. In September 1861, however, Fritz returned to the United States to join the Union army, so Mathilde began writing to him regularly, sometimes several times a week. None of Fritz's letters have survived, and Mathilde complained that they did not always arrive.

On returning to the United States, Fritz busied himself trying to find a position that would allow him to command artillery forces in the field. On October 1, 1861, he was commissioned colonel of Wisconsin's First Artillery Regiment, but the following month he resigned in the first of a series of impetuous career moves.[1] For her part, Mathilde showed great interest in her husband's success. She and Mary discussed his service with a fascinating group of Zürich friends who shared their conviction that the Civil War was a manifestation of a global revolution and that it must end slavery. Their circle included many exiles from the German states: military writer Friedrich Rüstow, influential socialist Ferdinand Lassalle, poet Georg Herwegh, and writer Ludmilla Assing, whose sister Ottilie became known for her relationship to African American abolitionist Frederick Douglass. Much of the women's writing was also related to the war. They produced commentary for English- and German-language newspapers in Europe and the United States and fiction that addressed the inhumanity of slavery. They translated each other's writing, reworking it as they went.

Mathilde and Mary also sought to offer their children a middle-class childhood complete with rigorous academic education, music and

---

1. Wilhelm Schulte, *Fritz Anneke: Ein Leben für die Freiheit in Deutschland und in den USA* (Dortmund: Historischer Verein Dortmund, 1961), 67.

drawing lessons, and, in Mary's case, religious formation. They explored the lakes and mountains around Zürich and celebrated birthdays and holidays. Although they enjoyed raising their children in Switzerland, it was a demanding task because they were both so often in poor health and vainly awaiting payment from publishers and support from their husbands. The letters here give only a taste of the illness and penury that so often preoccupied them.

Mathilde Franziska Anneke to Fritz Anneke
Bremen, August 20, 1860
Percy's Birthday.

My dear Fritz!
    We received your last letter while traveling over the rolling ocean waves. The passengers had just boarded the little steamer at the beautiful island of Cowes[2] en route to Southhampton and Havre. We had already decided on traveling via Germany and could not follow your signal anymore. I asked a man from the Palatinate region, who'd been traveling with us, to tell the young Hepp[3] that I had gone to Bremen. I could only just shout to him from the ship. We arrived here last night after we had cast anchor in the Baltic Sea[4] in stormy weather and then had set sail in the Weser River.[5] It was raining constantly. Today is a day for resting and washing. The 15 days of ocean travel in a horribly stinking vessel have very much exhausted us. Little Hertha was suffering quite a bit. She has become so thin, and I have to watch her carefully now. We are having a very happy family day today. We are staying in a very modest little hotel named "Stadt Bremen," where we have a nice room and are ordering anything we'd like delivered to our room. It's raining outside—as always under North German skies. We are celebrating Percy's birthday, which <u>actually</u> is today. At noon, the table

---

    2. Cowes is in fact a seaport town on the England's Isle of Wight.
    3. Johann Adam Philipp Hepp (1797–1867) was a physician and exiled German Forty-Eighter who devoted his time in Zürich to the study of lichens. Ingvar Kärnefelt et al., "Lichenology in Germany: Past, Present, and Future," *Schlectendalia* 23 (2012): 12.
    4. Actually, the North Sea.
    5. The Weser River connects Bremerhaven to Bremen.

was set so nicely for our little dinner for five. We emptied a bottle of Rhenish wine from green barrels and that gave us plenty of opportunities to drink to you and all of us. Maria very much enjoyed German *Gemüthlichkeit*[6] on German soil. We gave Percy a little canon and the harmonica that he had wished for. After our celebratory meal I ordered a nice carriage for 12 groats[7] and took the little group to see the unique city and its lovely promenades. We were so happy to see the wonderful green spaces and the gorgeous flowers, and the children were continuously rejoicing. Oh, but how beautiful it is here—how differently beautiful than in America. We've just now returned from our carriage ride. We have shipped our 5 boxes, and I've enclosed the freight ticket here. I did not have to pay at all. They have now been directed to the freight forwarder Jersing & Son[8] in Basel, who will ship it to your address now. They should be arriving 6 days from today. This freight ticket is nothing other than the duplicate of the real freight ticket that has been enclosed with the freight and is an exact copy.

We'll be traveling to Dortmund now tomorrow via Minden and Hamm (passing Münster).[9] Whether the five of us will be welcome at Father's and Mother's,[10] I do not know. I have strong doubts, and I'm a little afraid to go there. I will likely walk the streets of Essen without being able to see my dear Franzisca.[11] I do not know which route we'll take from there. We hope to find letters from you waiting for us in Dortmund that tell us where to travel to next. If the trip to Switzerland is not too expensive, then we will bring a small amount of money with us. My hope is that Booth will also send us a little money soon.— As I return to the German homeland, I am thinking of no one as much as our little Fritz. Today, I have had his little image in front of me the entire day! I hope you received my lines sent from sea quickly. I sent a letter with the Southh[ampton] post office from our ship.

---

6. *Gemütlichkeit* (in current German spelling), generally considered untranslatable, encapsulates a sense of cozy good cheer.

7. Northern German version of a "Groschen," a small coin worth several Pfennig. Wolfgang Pfeifer et al., *Etymologisches Wörterbuch des Deutschen* (Munich: Deutscher Taschenbuch Verlag, 1997), 481.

8. Jersing und Sohn had a good reputation of long standing. Johannes Schweizer, *Reisebeschreibung nach Nordamerika und durch die bedeutendsten Theile desselben* (Ebuat, Switzerland: Abraham Keller, 1823), 46.

9. They were heading southwest from Bremen toward the Rhine.

10. Fritz's parents Christian and Charlotte Anneke.

11. Franziska Rollmann Hammacher. See n. 43 (chapter 2).

And so, I'm hoping for a happy reunion, dear Papa. We will have much to tell you. As soon as I can notify you of our arrival in Basel, I will.

The children send you their greetings. Your picture has certainly not vanished from their dear little hearts.

Farewell and stay healthy. We'll see you in a few days.

Your old Mathilde.

Mathilde Franziska Anneke to her mother Elisabeth Giesler
Zürich, January 1861

My dear, beloved Mother!

The first words of dearest love this year—I've received them from you. Your little letter and the polite lines written by Emil Weiskirch and Louise Giesler arrived yesterday morning. We were happy to receive the good news. We were already in a happy mood, but I can't even begin to tell you how happy it makes me to see your dear old handwriting again and to know that you're quite free of pain and cheerful. But you haven't told me whether you are able to walk and whether you've made progress with or without crutches, and no one else has thought of telling me either. We've started the new year with new work and new hope. As the bell struck 12, the resounding echo could be heard in the entire valley surrounding the lake. And being "in the homeland again for the first time" it felt festive. The bell chimes lasted an entire hour. I thought for a long time about you and all my loved ones and did not fall asleep until it was very late. Well, the year has passed without much sorrow for a change, because I have returned to a life that nourishes my mind and soul—and it seems impossible for me to live without that. When I return one day to the new fatherland, then I will have gathered the peace of mind not to despair again for the rest of my life. We are continuing our literary endeavors tirelessly and in unison. Engaging with special people, surrounded by this beautiful nature and having access to the rich sources of aesthetic knowledge makes one feel inspired and feel younger each day. Our apartment is truly a little magical castle. People who live in the most magnificent palaces in the city center envy us. From our windows, we communicate with the spirits of the Alps. In our imagination, we embark on an exciting journey with them, from one mountain top to the next. And with them we carouse at the crystalline castles made of eternal glacier ice. We do so in the morning, in the glowing sunset, as well as during the nocturnal moonlight. "It truly is a different world, so truly close to heaven."[12] Whenever I look out the window and see the valley and heights in new light and an ever-new glow, then I think about how much I bemoan that you have never seen this magical magnificence. Now the landscape is covered with a blanket of snow, and the mountain tops that appear as black shadows and silhouettes rising from the gulch look peculiar. The glow of the softest rose light glistened on the Albis mountain[13] which is rolling right past us at this moment. At the same time the entire lake assumed a rose red color. This veil of snow covered in the most tender scent of roses that is almost too much for the human senses to take in.— This competition of nature: air, earth, and water—and still this eternal unity and the victory of the purest beauty—as I was looking at this imagery in front of me, I was thinking about you and how you would have to—simply have to—enjoy this magical scenery with me—if only through my somewhat weak descriptions.

And then on Christmas Eve the lights of the homeland were shining again in the dark, hopeful green of the pine branches. Our little children were overjoyed. Fritz had surprising gifts for all of us. My old faithful friend, Professor Kapp,[14] then added even more presents for all three children. And one night we spent with the Herweghs[15] looking at their little tree. Theirs was more beautiful and precious than ours. We had dinner with them—it was the night before New Year's Eve. A friend, Rüstow,[16] came home from the Italian war and brought back

---

12. From Austrian composer Heinrich Proch's folksong "Von der Alpe tönt das Horn." Barbara Boisits, "Proch, Heinrich," in *Oesterreichisches Musiklexikon Online*, last modified May 6, 2001, https://www.musiklexikon.ac.at/ml/musik_P/Proch_Heinrich.xml; *Des lustigen Sängers Neuestes Liederbuch* (Brno: Verlag von Fr. Karasiat, 1866), 27.

13. A range south of the city proper, overlooking Lake Zürich.

14. Ottilie Kapp. See n. 71 (chapter 1).

15. Georg Herwegh's wife Emma (1817–1904) was well known in her own right for her democratic agitation, her espionage during the Revolutions of 1848, and her writing. Mathilde mentions the couple's children, Horace, Adda, and Marcel. Regula Ludi, "Herwegh [-Siegmund], Emma," in *Historischen Lexikon der Schweiz*, last modified February 26, 2008, http://www.hls-dhs-dss.ch/textes/d/D19132.php.

16. Friedrich Wilhelm Rüstow (1821–1878) was a former Prussian army officer who had been active in the Revolutions of 1848 and fought with Garibaldi to unify Italy before settling in Zürich to write on military affairs. Rudolf Juan, "Wilhelm Rüstow," in *Historisches*

many keepsakes from Garibaldi, e.g. a picture of him for Frau Herwegh. I hadn't seen such a good picture of him before. Even the picture Mr. Booth sent isn't half as nice. Rüstow also brought back memories, and everyone was interested in hearing those. There's a much sweeter atmosphere in the poet's family circle than I had imagined after hearing our friends' reports. Frau Emma[17] has a noble and beautiful mind that is probably rarely found. She loves her Georg with the diligence she thinks is necessary for caring for his poetic soul. He acknowledges this with great tenderness. Their oldest son, Horaz, a fresh young man of 16 years, is the genius son of genius parents: a true poet's child and as talented as one can be. Adda, their only daughter, is not pretty but very kind. Little Marcell will surely befriend our little children next spring. How do people like Maria's translations?[18] Maria surpasses me in diligence. We are both writing novels, and she is much further along than I am.[19] Hers will be very good. Mine won't be so bad either I think. Cotta will publish my first piece in the next few days, either in the *Morgenblatt* or in *Das Ausland*, I don't know which it will be.[20] I wrote about Garibaldi in Caprera in my last St. Louis correspondence.[21] You will likely not be able to read it. I cannot sit down and write for half an

---

Lexikon der Schweiz, last modified January 5, 2012, https://hls-dhs-dss.ch/de/articles/024226/2012-01-05/.

17. Emma Herwegh.

18. Mary's translations of poems by Georg Herwegh, Heinrich Heine, and others were published in American newspapers and would also appear alongside some of her own work in two very similar volumes: Mary H. C. Booth, *Wayside Blossoms among Flowers from German Gardens* (Heidelberg: Bangel & Schmitt, 1864); Mary Booth, *Wayside Blossoms* (Philadelphia: J. B. Lippincott, 1865).

19. On the writing of *Uhland in Texas*, the short novel Mary and Mathilde wrote together, see Mischa Honeck, *We Are the Revolutionists: German-Speaking Immigrants and American Abolitionists after 1848* (Athens, Ga.: University of Georgia Press, 2011), 127–33. For an edited version of the text, see Mathilde Franziska Anneke, *Die gebrochenen Ketten: Erzählungen, Reportagen und Reden, 1861–1873*, ed. Maria Wagner (Stuttgart: H. D. Heinze Akademischer Verlag, 1983).

20. Stuttgart's prestigious Cotta publishing house dates back to the seventeenth century and had published the work of Goethe and Schiller. Cotta's daily *Morgenblatt für gebildete Leser* included literary fiction and nonfiction "for educated readers," while the *Das Ausland* (Abroad) focused on the world beyond German Europe. Liselotte Lohrer, *Cotta: Geschichte eines Verlags, 1659–1959* (Stuttgart: n.p., 1959), 170–71.

21. Garibaldi made the Italian island of Caprera (off the coast of Sardinia) his home base from 1855 on. Alfronso Scirocco, *Garibaldi: Citizen of the World* (Princeton, N.J.: Princeton University Press, 2007), 201–2, 405–6.

hour. It is unbearable. Fritz though is writing more than ever. The *Gartenlaube* (you can get the paper there too and I highly recommend it) will publish his soldier stories which are written in a highly engaging manner.[22] We both have a firm agreement with the paper and receive 40 thalers per page. This engagement makes up for the disloyal American papers, which betray instead of pay. Only very few of them are behaving decently.

I assume there is great exultation over the Republican victory,[23] especially among the Germans, most of all "the lad Carl."[24] He easily gained laurels, but he does deserve some of the credit after all. Is Frau Schurz[25] still your friend? Then give her my best. I trust that I will once again meet her again on this earth.

I am extraordinarily happy that you are now living in a new, beautiful, and spacious house. I'd like to spend time with all of you again.— Winters here are very mild, although the good construction of houses certainly helps in keeping winters mild for people. All of our windows—and there are several dozen inside—are equipped with double-glazed windows. I can barely describe how comfortable that is. And all of those large porcelain stoves are helpful too. We mostly sit in the kitchen or in Fritz's room (that stove also warms our dining room and the children's room) and in the parlor (which is 24 feet long and 16 feet wide according to Percy's measures). The stove in the parlor also warms our bedroom. Our Minna is such a fine girl who can cook and roast anything and is a good worker all around.—

I fell ill yesterday and had to put aside my little letter. Once again, I was suffering from jaundice after weeks of much liver pain. Around noon, I made my way out of bed. It was Sunday, and I <u>was</u> put on the sofa wrapped in blankets. The weather was inclement. Then that evening Frau Herwegh along with Adda and Cäcilie Kapp[26] came to visit.

---

22. The *Gartenlaube* was a highly successful illustrated magazine published in Leipzig. Kirsten Belgum, *Popularizing the Nation: Audience, Representation, and the Production of Identity in* Die Gartenlaube, *1853–1900* (Lincoln: University of Nebraska Press, 1998).

23. The election of November 1860 sent Abraham Lincoln to the White House and Republican majorities to the House and Senate.

24. Carl Schurz.

25. On Margarethe Schurz, see n. 33 (chapter 2).

26. Cäcilie Kapp, daughter of Mathilde's old friend Ottilie, taught at her parents' school. She would develop a close relationship with Mathilde and return with her to Milwaukee in 1865 to run a girls' academy before becoming a professor of German at Vas-

They stayed here the entire evening drinking tea and did everything they could to cheer me up so that I feel much better today. Frau Emma,[27] whom I like more and more (the feeling is mutual), played on our piano. She played so magnificently that I am still enchanted by her sweet tunes. You won't believe what an artist she is. Her close contact with Liszt and Wagner[28] has educated her in this beautiful art, and her warm and noble soul is apparent in every note she plays. I will advise Emil to buy an instrument here and to take advantage of the opportunity he has with my staying here. And in general, I wish you could have some of the treasures we have here in daily abundance that cost nothing compared to the prices over there. The wine drinkers and [*illegible*] will envy us when they hear that we have the best Burgundy wine in our cellar. One bottle barely costs two francs. The red table wine, which we drink daily, would cost you 4 shillings at a wine store. We pay 15 cents for 2 bottles. How easy it would be to send a little barrel every six months, safely packed in a box. Freight and import for such things do not cost much, but it would be expensive and risky to send and import a musical instrument. That Louis[29] has asked you to take a look at my letter tells me that at least he and Maria do not deliberately want to forget about me. I had braced myself for this and had tried to accept this misfortune among many others. Please give my best to him and my sister Maria and tell them that I would be very happy to hear that they are faring well. I've recently received a letter from my Fanny. I'm always worried that she's ill. I cannot begin to tell you how much I worry about the child. I write to her every month.

Not a word from Pauline.[30] I wrote her again for New Year's, but she did not respond. I would have liked to send her little children a lit-

---

sar College. Maria Wagner, *Mathilde Franziska Anneke in Selbstzeugnissen und Dokumenten* (Frankfurt am Main: Fischer, 1980), 245.

27. Emma Herwegh.

28. Dresden Forty-Eighter and composer Richard Wagner (1813–1883) had also lived in Zürich in the 1850s, and Hungarian Franz Liszt (1811–1886) had visited him in 1856. Rainer Kleinertz, "Liszt, Wagner, and Unfolding Form: *Orpheus* and the Genesis of *Tristan and Isolde*," in *Franz Liszt and His World*, ed. Christopher H. Gibbs and Dana Gooley (Princeton, N.J.: Princeton University Press, 2006), 231.

29. Mathilde's sister Maria married Louis Scheffer. Alma Harris, "Die Nachkommen unserer Großeltern Carl u. Elisabeth Giesler im Jahre 1890," (n.d.), Box 70, Archiv der Mathilde Franziska Anneke, 1817–1884, Stadtarchiv Sprockhövel, Germany.

30. Pauline von Reitzenstein was another of Mathilde's sisters. Ibid.

tle box full of Swiss things, but now that she is not even answering, I won't.

You are not letting people read my letters, are you? Much of what I write concerns my inner life, and it's for your eyes only and those of our closest family members. You would do me a kindness if you could write to Fanny for me. You wouldn't believe how much I worry about her.

Fritz sends his greetings, dear Mother. He loves you very much, and I assume he will write to you soon. Since I had a serious talk with him, he has thankfully changed his attitude toward the family entirely. He is very nice and friendly to me, and as long as it stays that way, I ask nothing more. Our spiritual bond and our joint endeavors must keep our friendship alive because love was not meant to be. He realizes that and has been trying very hard over the past weeks.

Mary[31] is truly growing inner wealth and bold character. Her energy, her great talent and her breadth of mind will guarantee her a good reputation as an author in the future. She sends you greetings with all the old love she has for you. I constantly die laughing because of her humor. She does not have time to write to you now but will do so soon. Send our greetings to Richmond.[32] Send my greetings to my old friend Carl Geisberg[33] and your good dear friends. I will write you a long letter again soon if it brings you joy. My little children kiss your hand, dearest best Grandmother.

I press you close to my heart, and I hope to see you again.

Give my best to Zünd and Märklin, Linchen, and Franklin.[34] It's not right that these friends don't write me letters.

Farewell!

I am your faithful, loving old Tilla.

---

31. Interestingly, Mathilde began to refer to Mary Booth by the English version of her name in Switzerland.

32. James Cook Richmond. See n. 11 (chapter 1).

33. Prussian retailer Charles Geisberg claimed to carry the most extensive selection of stationery in Wisconsin. U.S. Census, Population Schedules (1860), 3rd Ward, Milwaukee, Wisc., p. 6, dwelling 48, family 46; *Milwaukee Daily Sentinel*, January 1, 1855.

34. On Ernst Anton Zündt, see n. 76 (chapter 1). On Edmund, Caroline ("Linchen"), and Franklin Märklin, see n. 149 (chapter 1).

Photograph of Zürich in the 1860s.
Courtesy of Baugeschichtliches Archiv, Zürich, Switzerland.

The Beust School (Erziehungsanstalt von F. Beust) in Zürich
as it looked at the time Percy Anneke attended.
Courtesy of Stadtarchiv Zürich, Zürich, Switzerland.

Mary Booth to her daughter Ella Booth
Zürich, August 25, 1861
(English original)

My dear Ella:

Here are two rose leaves that I gathered for you last Sunday from the grave of Lavater.[35] I suppose you will have received your box containing your birth day presents long before you get this letter. I hope so. I think that you will be glad to hear that you are going to have another box before long. Mr. Anneke is going to America in about three weeks, to the war, and he will take the box, & send it to you from New York by Express, the same as the other was to be sent—& probably has been before this time. It may be that this box will please you quite as much as the other, because it has pictures on it, but it has no key. It is made of light <u>pear wood</u> & the pictures look like fine engravings—it is linned with blue, & is very strong. I do not know yet what I shall have to put in it, but <u>something</u>.

We should all be glad to go to America too when Mr. A. goes, but we cannot. I wish to see you very much indeed, and so does Lillian, but we must wait until after the winter has gone. Lillian is learning very much, and I hope you will find her a much better girl than she used to be when you see her again.

I sent you a letter, in one to your father a few days ago written on pictured paper.

I hope to have a letter from you very soon saying that you are quite well & contented.

Lillian would have liked very much to have witnessed the baptism of your little friends.

She saw several babies baptized in the church the other day, & she asked when she came home if she could take her kitten to church, and have the priest give it a name as he did the babies by baptizing it. She said she knew God would be pleased to have it done & that he would not like it if it was not. Write soon. Lillian is anxious to have a letter from you. Love to all[.]

Your aff. <u>Mother</u>

---

35. Johann Kaspar Lavater (1741–1801) was a Swiss poet, theologian, and scientist. Gisela Luginbühl-Weber, "Lavater, Johann Kaspar," in *Historischen Lexikon der Schweiz*, last modified November 27, 2008, http://www.hls-dhs-dss.ch/textes/d/D10444.php.

Mathilde Franziska Anneke to Fritz Anneke
Zürich, September 7, 1861

My dear, dearest Fritz!

We hope our farewell greetings will reach you on the ocean waves. Our thoughts were with you each step of the way, and the children, Hertha especially, have asked almost every hour: "Where is my Papa now?" She still remembers the journey, and so the little one was able to follow you in her imagination. Now they are writing to you and painting pictures and pressing flowers.—Percy and I went home in sad silence on the morning of your farewell. We then sat on the bench down by the creek in the garden to rest and talked about you and our future life. After we arrived home, we both went to bed, and I got some rest until the proof-sheets arrived, which I then attended to with great care. I asked Percy to take them to the post office right away afterwards. The eleventh proof-sheet marked the ending of the second volume. . . .

I spent the day we had to say goodbye in silence and in tears. The domestic staff tried to cheer me up. Even Frau Zeller[36] gave me plums in an effort to comfort me. She brought them herself in a crystal bowl in the evening. Father Gritzner[37] and his sister donated an entire basket full of blue-black grapes. Frau Ott[38] asked about me several times a day. I spent time with Percy, and he will now tell you himself what the past few days have been like for him. . . .

Farewell then, dear Fritz. May the ocean waves swing you over to the

---

36. Susanna and "Ts." (presumably Thomas) Jacob Zeller were Mathilde and Mary's landlords. Gemeinde Hirlanden, Gemeindearchiv, Einwohnerkontrollliste, 1856–, pp. 90–91 and Hirslanden Bürgerbuch, 1828–1869, Stadtarchiv Zürich.

Because Zeller was such a common surname in the area, the Zellers sometimes used Susanna's maiden name as well, going by some variation of Zeller-Engelhardt. This practice confused one historian. *"Ich gestehe, die Herrschaft der fluchwürdigen 'Demokratie' dieses Landes macht mich betrübt . . .": Mathilde Franziska Annekes Briefe an Franziska und Friedrich Hammacher, 1860–1884*, ed. Erhard Kiehnbaum (Hamburg: Argument Verlag mit Ariadne, 2017), 12.

37. Maximilian Gritzner (1794–1872) was a Viennese Forty-Eighter who had served in the Frankfurt Parliament, lived for a time in the United States, and would soon open a sewing machine factory near Karlsruhe, Baden. Helge Dvorak, ed., *Biographisches Lexikon der Deutschen Burschenschaft*, vol. 1, part 2, (Heidelberg: Universitätsverlag C. Winter, 1998), 180–81.

38. Several families with the surname Ott lived in Zürich around this time. J. Caspar Pfister, *Verzeichniß der Bürger der Stadt Zürich im Jahr 1858* (Zürich: Friedrich Schlutheß, 1858), 188.

other shore with ease and may you happily join the fight for freedom on the other side. But may you stay in my and our children's lives and enjoy the future days in constant merriness and happiness of the heart.

Our dear little children send their greetings and their kisses. Mary politely sends her kisses in this letter.

Farewell, and I embrace you and am your

Mathilde who loves you dearly.

Mathilde Franziska Anneke to Fritz Anneke
Zürich, October 7, 1861

My dear Fritz!

Can you imagine our joy when the little Zürich paper reported on Sunday morning: The *Saxonia* safely reached New York harbor on Sept. 23 after 12 days and a happy journey![39] The many storms that were sweeping the coasts of Old England exactly the day after your departure truly frightened me. The destruction of the gigantic *Great Eastern* made me feel quite fearful that the *Saxonia* could face a similar fate.[40] A special correspondent for the *Augsburger*[41] was on board of the Great Eastern, because he wanted to arrive at the war site even faster than you. This correspondent, who seems to be a military man, described everything vividly in long articles in the *Allg[emeine]*. By the way, this correspondent then left the U.S. again with the next steamer. One can see how much the paper values news from the other side of the Atlantic!

We are now constantly awaiting direct messages from you. Would you answer our thousand questions? I wonder whether Blenker gave you the telegrams that were forwarded to you from Wisconsin as quickly as possible, and especially those from Washington! I wonder whether you've traveled to Washington or whether your path has taken you to the murderous West, which I hate so much and where you would have to first take the lives of your enemies and those who envy

---

39. The Hamburg America Line operated the steamship *Saxonia* on the Hamburg-Southampton-New York route. *New York Times*, September 7, 1863.

40. A detached rudder had made the *Great Eastern* uncontrollable, leading to destruction and injury on board. *New York Times*, October 2, 1861.

41. The *Augsburger Allgemeine Zeitung*, published by Cotta, was perhaps the leading German political newspaper of the time. Edward Henck, *Die Allgemeine Zeitung, 1798–1898: Beiträge zur Geschichte der deutschen Presse* (Munich: Verlag der Allgemeinen Zeitung, 1898).

you if you wanted to be fortunate and victorious in battle.—That's what is running through my head, dear Fritz.—And will the student Koch[42] find you? He left here on the 25th with a carriage full of letters to you from your little children and from us, etc. etc. Now we intend to wait in patience and trust that our love and our thoughts will protect you. Almost every paper that we get from over there talks about you and your imminent arrival.

We have been faring quite well. We are happy in the house and garden, where new sunshine is enlightening our lives. We are happy to be with our children and dedicate most of our time to them. We find much satisfaction in working and studying diligently. We never go out. We only go out when we have to and that is enough—or sometimes we take the children somewhere. On Saturday, for example, we spent the day from 2 to 7 at the Sonnenberg[43] where we greatly enjoyed the swings as well as grapes and milk and honey. That at least comes close to the much greater pleasure you brought us when we went on a longer journey to Schaffhausen[44] with the little ones. I was very cautious, dear Fritz, not to use any of the funds that you had sent us, knowing that Mr. Sherman would let us down in the most unscrupulous manner. He has not sent a single dollar since you've left. Of course, I used our resources to pay Frau Spörri[45] the 100 fr[46], and she soon reminded me of that. And I paid the 70 fr to Nußbaumer[47] and have been buying what we need for the winter—except for potatoes, fruits and other vegetables—and now our resources are quite reduced again already. Butchers and bakers are true bugbears. Meanwhile, when Beust gave me the bill of much more than 200 francs a few mornings ago,[48] and as my head was getting a little too hot over the lack of character of the American man Booth, I wrote a letter to this gentleman that will hopefully in any case do him good: *You will permit me to remind you in these short*

---

42. As later noted, this young man attended the Eidgenössische Polytechnische Schule, the federal university.

43. The Sonnenberg (Sun Mountain) is located in a bucolic area of Zürich not far from the family's home.

44. Schaffhausen lies 30 miles north of Zürich near the German border.

45. The Spörris listed in a local directory were mostly tailors or shoemakers. Pfister, *Verzeichniß der Bürger der Stadt Zürich*, 237.

46. Francs.

47. Possibly Gottfried Nußbaumer, listed as a "Cantonsprokurator" or financial administrator of the canton. Pfister, *Verzeichniß der Bürger der Stadt Zürich*, 186.

48. For Percy's schooling at the Erziehungsanstalt von F. Beust.

lines of your duties, which I think finaly is the highest time for you to fulfill.[49] *Marys wearness & sickness demand more than I can give her. She needs, what she has since three years* <u>not receive from you</u>, *warm cloths, that is e e e*[50] *not to speak of bonnet e e which can only be bought for cash money. Your child needs the same. So is it the highest time if you will retain the regards of Marys & my friends first that you pay the school money of your child. 2/ that that child shall be comfortable clothed. Do you suppose I should say you these things, if it was not the greatest need? I have far to much pride to do so, to remind you of your duties, which I have taken with pleasure and with good help of Fritz upon myself so long as you was in prison & in your other unfortunate time & since we have been in Europe. Did not Mary suffer under this neglect & had I enough to provide for her wants, I should not demand any thing of you. It was of the greatest need for Hertha to have had an operation performed upon her foot this winter.—It needs money—I cannot do my duty by my child in this and other manner, unless you do your duty by yours. I should have gone to Carlsbad e e I waited a long time before I would say these things to you, but I think it is not well for you to make any longer delay. Mary has her pride too. You treat her as if she had not any. When she would die you can have the consolation to hear my words again & hear what has brought her to her sickness. Yours truly.* I think I told him something about you in the postscript. Percy's vacation is beginning now. I will do a strict cure with him, and I hope it helps. I can never leave his sight. His grade report which he has brought home to me is so bad. . . . I wish to pay my debts to Beust so that he is in a better mood, and generally I'd like to get along better. There is no more important task for me now than to complete the education of our children, just as I am supposed to do. I had a warm overcoat made for Percy and a few winter clothes—and now must fix my shabby little Hertha. The shoemaker receives constant work from us, especially from Lily.—I was at the museum a few times also. And slowly I have been corresponding my way for *Allgemeine, Criminal,* and *Banner.*[51] I have been working along on my *Geisterhaus*[52] and have now arrived at the last chapter. . . .

Yours sincerely, Mathilde.

---

49. Mathilde copied her English-language letter.

50. Mathilde used symbols like small Es, equivalent to ellipses or "etc." to indicate omitted material.

51. *Augsburger Allgemeine Zeitung,* New York *Criminalzeitung,* and *Wisconsin Banner und Volksfreund.*

52. See n. 39 (chapter 1).

Mathilde Franziska Anneke to Fritz Anneke
Zürich, November 3, 1861

My dear Fritz!

It is Sunday morning. The sun is gilding our empty valley, and the autumn winds are blowing against the mountains. The Alps are right in front of us as if we could reach out and touch them. But the flowers are fading, and there is a big slate coal fire in the stove. The children are paying their friend Snell[53] a Sunday morning visit and will invite him for tea this evening.—And your old Mathilde is coming to visit her "dear Fritz," who is in the rosiest of moods as I wish and hope. I plant a big rough kiss on his cheek, press him firmly to my old heart. He whom I love from the depth of my heart. Where are you, where can I find you? Along the Potomac maybe—as was my wish from the beginning? I should not like to think that you are having many difficulties regarding your activities. But even if you do, then I am convinced that you will bravely overcome them and that you will fight for your position like a hero, even when you are facing those fools. The world belongs to the bold. But the brave possess it. You are not bold, but you are brave. It is now up to you and your spirit to go boldly after whatever you'd like to defend bravely. I will be happy if you have more opportunities to find a "good commander" in Blenker. He will then and always be your friend. I can't help but admit that your letter from Washington made me sink into depression a bit. And now on to [*illegible*] the letter you wrote by night from Milwaukie and close to Grandmother's bed. Your rheumatism and your *disappointments* are upsetting me a little. I am longing for this evening, because it might be possible to receive another message from you. Since your departure, I have not been receiving the *Criminal*[*zeitung*] anymore. What is the reason for that? I've certainly submitted nice and well-written articles to him. Just yesterday I wrote another one for him. And then I've been looking out for your article in the *Augsburger*,[54] which you promised would be there. Mean-

---

53. We have been unable to identify Snell, but he was possibly related to the left-wing politician, editor, and scholar Ludwig Snell (1785–1854). Katja Hürlimann, "Ludwig Snell," in *Historisches Lexikon der Schweiz*, last modified November 22, 2011, https://hls-dhs-dss.ch/de/articles/013521/2011 11 22.

54. Mathilde shortened the title of the *Augsburger Allgemeine Zeitung* in several different ways.

while, Herr Corvin Corvinsky[55] has arrived over there to serve up his half-baked stories to the *Augsburger*. I can't tell you how much I long to finally read something dignified written by you in that paper. Raster's[56] articles are good but rare. The *Allg[emeine]* is scrambling to get decent reports from the battlefield. And even if you just submit short articles as an overview it would be better than nothing. Corvin has published his memoirs here (in Amsterdam).[57] They're terrible twaddle, smart but vile, so I hear, and they aim to be seen as a historical source for 1848. No one is listening more attentively when a letter arrives from you than our dear little Hertha. The child truly holds you dear in her little heart. Percy has become quite well-behaved. Today, he is wearing a brand-new suit again made of winter cloth from which I had pants made and a camisole. Hertha is wearing a new woolen dress. As I started using the Bl[enker] money, and you wrote to me that I should, I quickly went to Linke[58] and bought all sorts of winter clothing *cash* for more than 100 francs. Two nice dresses, a new jacket for me, an undervest, socks, a few linen things, etc. etc. I was surprised at my own courage. Mary got nothing but a pair of warm shoes.

On October 24, then, your letter written on Sept. 26 in New York already arrived here. It was franked in New York on October 8th. . . .

I sent my last letter to the address of the *Banner & Volksfreund* in Milwaukee on October 21. I received your first letter on the 20th. My "brilliantly finished" *Geisterhaus* has been with the *Didaskalia*[59] editors for 10 days now, and if it is not too long for the paper, then I can hope that it will publish the first imprint. For the second one or a publication in two volumes, F. W. Grünow in Leipzig, a renowned publisher of nov-

---

55. Otto von Corvin, a Forty-Eighter who had fought in Baden, observed the Civil War as a correspondent for the *Augsburger Allgemeine Zeitung* and the *London Times*. Wilhelm Kaufmann, *Die deutschen im amerikanischen Bürgerkriege* (Munich: R. Oldenbourg, 1911), 489–90.

56. Forty-Eighter and journalist Hermann Raster would later become famous as editor of Chicago's *Illinois Staatszeitung*, but he was already an important Republican politician. A. E. Zucker, ed. *The Forty-Eighters: Political Refugees of the German Revolution of 1848* (New York: Columbia University Press, 1950), 329.

57. Otto von Corvin, *Erinnerungen eines Volkskämpfers*, 2 vols. (Amsterdam: Gebrüder Binger, 1861).

58. Forty-Eighter Thomas J. Linke owned a clothier in Zürich. *Amtsblatt des Kantons Zürich vom Jahre 1865* (Zürich: Orell, Füßli und Comp., 1865), 1:721; *Schweizerische Bauzeitung* 94, no. 20 (May 18, 1929): 253.

59. A literary supplement to the *Frankfurter Journal*. Honeck, *We Are the Revolutionists*, 206, n. 59.

els, is interested, if he likes the book. And I think he will. He is writing to me very politely. And then you might have the chance to praise my talent in speculation more than my talent for writing. And then if you don't give me too much grief and sorrow next winter, I will complete my *Sturmgeiger*,[60] which I will start working on again with much courage. . . .

November 7th.

To Kentucky then? With your regiment? Where is your regiment now? Ordered to Kentucky from Michigan's shores this fast via telegraph? Without weapons, without uniforms? How is that possible? Either a letter has been lost or you think I am capable of divination.

Well, I am happy that you are now finally doing what you have been longing for so fervently. Since you've been gone, I've only received messages from you intermittently. You once spoiled me by describing the smallest events in your letters. Now I don't know details about your journey, your arrival, your reunion with Fanny, and so on. And now that you are so much closer to the battlefield, there is no hope for me to hear much that is coherent from you. And it does not seem like you have been longing for letters from us at all so far, dear Fritz. Hasn't Herr Koch reached you yet with many letters for you? St. Koch, the student at the local polytechnic institute[61] who wanted to go with you but then followed you later.

I wonder whether this letter will reach you? We will take that risk. It's enough for today.

Percy and Hertha send their kisses. Lili and Hertha play together like twins. Percy and his friend Snell are inseparable. Mary and I find so much happiness thinking of our fatherland and worrying about its fighters. We are working without interruption.

Farewell, farewell. I press you to my heart.

   Your old Tilla.

---

60. Mary translated excerpts from "Sturmgeiger," which in 1863 appeared in *Daily Life*, a newspaper Sherman Booth published in Milwaukee. Honeck, *We Are the Revolutionists*, 206, n. 59.

61. Zürich's federally controlled Eidgenössische Polytechnische Schule had just been founded in 1855. It was already a reputable institution of higher learning, and today it is one of the world's leading universities, going by the name Eidgenössische Technische Hochschule (Swiss Federal Institute of Technology). *Die Eidgenössische Polytechnische Schule in Zürich* (Zürich: Zürcher and Furrer, 1889).

Colonel Rüstow still hopes to become commander-in-chief of the U.S. Army after all. This Bernays truly is a blabber.[62] He has solutions for the "the military man who will make history" as he calls him in the *Anz[eiger] des Westens*. But he has none for you, a citizen and pioneer in this war. I will be breathing down his neck again soon!

Mary Booth to her mother Adeline Corss
Zürich, November 8, 1861
(English original)

PRIVATE

My dear Mother:

Your letter has just this morning come.

I am sorry that Ella has not yet received the first box, as it was worth a dozen of the last, & had two dolls in it beside.

In regard to Sherman's sending money for Ella's clothes. I have written, & charged him to do so enough, but I hardly think he will regard any such requests concerning her so long as he is utterly regardless of Lillian & myself. & I have told him what Lillian must have—of myself I have nothing more to say to him—it does no good. In regard to selling your lots he wrote about it to me some time ago, & said—the same as you do. Save he said he had been offered three hundred dollars in money, & you say two. I am sorry you have to let them go—all I have is gone I suppose—(perhaps for the education of others of the Westcott tribe[63]—for all I know).

Sherman is not morally changed. [H]is life is what it always was—he insults women more than ever. This is true—far too true. What on Earth I shall ever do with, or about that man is more than I can say. I don't know but he has made me about as much trouble as I can bear. It is folly to dream that the leopard can change his skin, & if he could a man cannot. I am very sorry to be betrayed into this unhappy tone, as it may cause you uneasiness, & can probably do no good, but I must say that this land business of yours is rather too much. S. is not a good,

---

62. President Lincoln appointed Karl Bernays U.S. consul in Zürich in 1861. See n. 147 (chapter 1). Zucker, *Forty-Eighters*, 279.

63. We have not been able to identify this family.

or an <u>honest</u> businessman as I used to suppose—honest in an <u>orthodox</u> sense to be sure, but not through & through. [I]n little things he is mean, where he can be & folks not know it. He wrote me the most awful letters all the time that made me sick continually, until Madam Anneke wrote to him, & put a stop to it, now he usually writes a lot of love trash that means nothing—complains about his business, promises to send me money, & complains because he cant—accuses me of not <u>loving him</u> &c. What on Earth should I love him for?—because he has a little pride, or vanity about me?

Of course I have a sort of "<u>natural affection</u>" for him, but there wont be much of that even left pretty soon if he is'nt careful.

I do not wish to do anything that is not right, & have been as mild & forbearing as any one could be—& he thinks because I do not complain of any health, or wants that all can run along in the same way forever.

You had better burn this letter as soon as you read it, as it is not just the thing to be lying around.

If I were to go to America to day I should not go to S., of course not. I could not so throw away my character, or expose my children to his vulgar talk.

I know very well what poverty is, but its worst form is better than the influence we should be subject to in his presence. He is too false. I cannot spend my last hours in such an atmosphere. I let things run on, & take their course, & trust in Providence to take care of the rest. Anxiety would be useless, & too much feeling kills one, so I try to have neither.

Sherman sent the poem to Gerritt Smith.[64] I wrote to him in a letter (he reads it at all his lectures) and in the <u>same letter</u> he asked him to [for]give <u>me</u> the debt I <u>owed</u> him of a thousand dollars borrowed money, which he supposed was for me—to take the mortgaged acre for the <u>debt</u>, & <u>another acre</u>! Gerritt Smith wrote back that he did not like to do it, but he would <u>forgive me</u> $500 of the debt, & would only ask for the other five. If that were impossible he would take the land. So of course he has the land.

S. uses me, & my name in all possible ways.—makes away all land, & Every thing, & then thanks the Lord <u>we</u> have got it off our minds. That

---

64. A wealthy abolitionist from New York State, Gerrit Smith participated in partisan politics in the early 1850s, supported African American communities in the North, and helped to finance John Brown's raid on Harper's Ferry in 1859. John Stauffer, *The Black Hearts of Men: Radical Abolitionists and the Transformation of Race* (Cambridge, Mass: Harvard University Press, 2001).

man is a "blood-sucker," or a leech more properly speaking if there ever was one.

Mathilde Franziska Anneke to Fritz Anneke
Zürich, December 27, 1861

After Christmas.[65] ... Yesterday, on the second day of Christmas, Consul Bernays invited us for dinner. The ambassador[66] had been invited too, but he had written to us that he had to leave for Paris. We were happy about that invitation, because as we arrived we saw the Countess Hatzfeldt[67] without her *amant*[68] Rüstow but accompanied by the Herweghs and Lassalle[69] instead.

I had not met this lady and gentleman before, but that was just fine. Lassalle, who sat opposite me at the dinner, struck me as a highly educated, interesting, and good-natured man. The Countess on the other hand—I thought she was neither beautiful, nor witty, nor liberal as our friend Bernays said. I thought she had the scent of a corpse, like a made-up female wreck. I can only wish all men the best of luck with her. Lasalle approached me with such kindness—and the Countess did

---

65. Mathilde did not start with a salutation.
66. Mathilde was friends with George G. Fogg, a Republican politician and editor who served as minister resident to Switzerland from 1861 to 1865. "Fogg, George Gilmann," in *Biographical Directory of the United States Congress*, accessed July 30, 2020, http://bioguide.congress.gov/scripts/biodisplay.pl?index=F000234.
67. Sophie Josepha Ernestine, the Countess of Hatzfeldt, was the companion of Ferdinand Lassalle, who was twenty years her junior. They met in 1846 when Hatzfeldt was seeking assistance in an eight-year legal struggle with a highly abusive husband. She repaid Lassalle with lifelong financial and moral support, although their romantic interest in each other waned. Hans Wolfram von Hentig, "Hatzfeldt, Sophie Josepha Ernestine Gräfin von," in *Neue Deutsche Biographie* (Berlin: Duncker und Humblot, 1969), 8:67; David Footman, *Ferdinand Lassalle: Romantic Revolutionary* (New York: Greenwood Press, 1947), x–xi, 51–61.
68. Lover in French.
69. Ferdinand Lassalle (1825–1864) had participated in the Revolutions of 1848 and moved in similar circles to the Annekes, corresponding with Heinrich Heine, Marx, and Engels. He is best known for arguing that the interests of the masses could be well served by a political party operating within a system in which all men could vote, an opinion that made him an adversary of Marx and an unlikely ally of Prussian statesman Otto von Bismarck. The party that Lassalle formed helped to establish the Socialist Democratic Party of Germany (SPD) after his death. Iring Fetscher, "Lassalle, Ferdinand," in *Neue Deutsche Biographie* (1982), 13:661–69.

as well. He let her introduce him to me and asked with much interest about his former prison companion.[70] As we said goodbye he asked me kindly to send you his greetings and to refresh your positive memories of him. The relationship of the two odd persons, Lassalle and the Countess, made the following impression on me. Las[salle] was a young lad when she seduced him. His glowing spirit and his distinctive strength have been both enjoyable and helpful to her. In any case, he has been her genius. He has always kept her on the surface when she was about to sink, and he has always been at her side in faithful friendship, as long as necessary. Of course, he does not love her anymore—they do not live together like husband and wife anymore, as Emma says. He is on a high intellectual pedestal and is treating her a little *en bagatelle*. She whitewashes[71] many things—namely "liberal"—and if she speaks too much nonsense then Lasalle gets angry. First, he tries to hide his anger, but then he can't stand it anymore and starts lecturing wildly. And then it gets interesting with this fellow when he radically tears apart everything that is contradiction and nonsense. Occasionally he develops a philosophy of law and a legal philosophy with such dialectic and incisiveness of the mind that it is a pleasure to listen to him. For people like us, who seldom have the chance to hear something like that, it's a true pleasure. I forgot about roast goose and rabbit pâté and listened to the man. I thought about Mother a lot, the good old woman who was enchanted with his speeches for the defense back then.[72]

The Herweghs still have not accepted the professorship in Naples. . . .

It is late. Percy was sitting next to me for a long time and reading *Robinson*[73] with great pleasure. All have gone to sleep. Farewell, dear Fritz. Stay healthy. Write as often as you can. It is our only joy.—And where to send letters now?—To ? in Indianapolis.

 Farewell, farewell

 Your loving Mathilde

---

70. Fritz and Lassalle were apparently jailed in the same Prussian prison in Westphalia late in 1848. Footman, *Ferdinand Lassalle*, 65; Schulte, *Fritz Anneke*, 32.

71. The meaning here is unclear in the original. Perhaps Hatzfeldt dismissed ideas by calling them "liberal."

72. Elisabeth Giesler apparently knew Lassalle.

73. *Robinson Crusoe*, the eighteenth-century English novel about a castaway's adventures. Daniel Defoe, *Robinson Crusoe*, ed. Thomas Keymer (Oxford: Oxford University Press, 2007).

Mathilde Franziska Anneke to her mother Elisabeth Giesler
Zürich, January 1862

My best and most beloved Mother!

I have been meaning to write you every day since New Year's Day. But the daily chores, the daily worries, raising the children—in short, because of all my duties—I barely found an hour to chat with you, dear Mother. And yet I feel most comfortable at your side, and I think that there is no one in the world I can talk to from the soul the way I can with you.

How did all of you start the new year? Surely not as light-heartedly as in the past. Yes, these are serious times. The world's fate will be decided in the near and dark future, and our own fate depends on it—more or less. How will the battles of the Union develop? Who would be able to say? Will the battles be bloody for our family as well? I think Julius[74] made the right decision when he joined the cavalry. I hope he will return healthy and be a good father for his family. Louise[75] loves him greatly, and he feels the same for his entire family. Booth's letters tell me that Louis[76] also wants to swing the sword for the God of Battle.—Maybe it's best that all men resort to that <u>last argument</u> in these times. Send my greetings to the warriors. I'd rather stand with them in battle than be made petty by a life of worries about the fate of humanity and the quotidian concerns.

On Christmas, dear Mother, we lit candles on a dark pine for our little children. Our gifts were modest, and only through Franziska's[77] continuous love did they receive more presents on the Second Day of Christmas.[78] The first and only little box that we received in the mail in good old German tradition had such interesting contents that it made us so joyful and happy. We spent New Year's Eve with the Herweghs, who were hosting a big party. We met your old "distant lover" Lassalle

---

74. Julius Giesler, one of Mathilde's brothers. Harris, "Die Nachkommen unserer Großeltern Carl u. Elisabeth Giesler im Jahre 1890."
75. Julius Giesler's wife, Mathilde's sister-in-law. Ibid.
76. Presumably Mathilde's brother-in-law, Louis Scheffer.
77. Franziska Rollmann Hammacher.
78. Germans traditionally extend the festivities to December 26.

(who will send you a picture of himself via Fritz) and the still oddly beautiful Countess von Hatzfeldt. The previous day, she had invited Mary and me to a grand dinner, which she had arranged in a truly royal manner at her hotel, Bauer am See.

I must admit that the days of this European luxury have been an interesting change compared to the days in America, where there was no luxury and where we had to do without any of this. I had to think of you often and had planned to send you descriptions and observations of this life here. But then I decided to quickly attend to my silent muse again to finally finish a longer work. And then I delved into my novel *Sturmgeiger und Kajütenprinz* again. I think it will be quite "nice." Maria is delighted, and Emma Herwegh would like to know how it is going to end. Now and then I let someone read out parts of the novel to her. On New Year's Day then, dear Mother, I put the words "For my beloved Mother!" on the first page of the growing manuscript. Since then I have been able to work even better than before. Your "*spirit*" is helping me overcome all difficulties. You have always given me courage, and you still do from far, far away from me. On New Year's Day, as all others would give their best wishes to you, I did it in this way. I hope it put a smile on your face.—My *Geisterhaus* has now been in Leipzig for more than 2 months. Only the gods know when it will finally be printed.

Recently, I've been receiving lovely little letters from Pauline and her little children now and then. Then we received a little box with socks knitted by little Louise[79] for our little ones and little aprons, etc. etc. I will send the little box back to her filled with Swiss things, and I hope she will be delighted. The children are exchanging cards and pictures. They were both[80] cheering at receiving the pieces of gold that I had sent them. I think Pauline is doing well. I hear her children are lovely, and it's a fact that the little scoundrel[81] is writing me nice letters. Much—much later! Please tell him to write often.

I haven't had a letter from Fritz in 10 days, but before that I often received two in a week. It was a bit of a compensation for the days of worry which were doubly difficult when the children were asking: Why

---

79. Louise von Reitzenstein, daughter of Mathilde's sister Pauline and her husband Albin von Reitzenstein. Harris, "Die Nachkommen unserer Großeltern Carl u. Elisabeth Giesler im Jahre 1890."
80. Mathilde's niece and nephew Louise and Albin von Reitzenstein.
81. Albin von Reitzenstein, Jr.

is Papa not writing to us? Is he in battle already? and so on. I'm afraid that in the evenings in Indiana as well as in Wisconsin he will have to deal with *Knownothingism*[82] and other difficulties. But I hope he will overcome them. Why don't you write to him as often as you can, dear Mother? We celebrated his birthday "in the circle of happy revelers."[83] The revelers were Mary and I, Percy, Hertha, and Lili. We sat around our little *bowl* and were eating cake. Then late in the day came the Countess H. who "is crazy about us." She drank a glass to Columbia and Fritz, and then she left again. She is a highly witty woman, indeed. God knows she is free and independent but also decent and noble. I prefer her over a thousand gossiping nuns who are vile at heart. She arranged a noble dinner in our honor. There was an interesting group of people surrounding her, and I had the pleasure of dancing a waltz with Herwegh and sitting next to him at dinner. The same way the larger contrasts have changed in my life, so have the smaller ones. Just three days prior I was suffering terribly from cramps. I'd love to go to Tarasp[84] or Carlsbad as soon as possible if I could leave the children alone with Mary. But there are so many obstacles. Her own illness and keeping the household together, which is my duty of course.

You would have so much joy seeing my Percy and also the small and lovely little Hertha, dear Mother. I will describe them to you so you can get an idea. I am quite proud of my beautiful boy who is so nice and well-behaved now. He is studying diligently and is so polite that I can take him anywhere and be proud of my son. How much easier it is raising children here! All three of them are taking painting lessons now and will be able to show you their success soon. All three of them have incredible talents, which I can foster now that God and the war have provided me with a lot of money(!!).

And just now I received a letter from the hearty Märklin. It did make me quite happy. The right view of the things over there gives me a

---

82. The American (or "Know Nothing") Party was a significant anti-immigrant political movement that flourished briefly in the mid-1850s. German Americans continued to use the term to refer to nativism in subsequent decades. Tyler Anbinder, *Nativism and Slavery: The Northern Know Nothings and the Politics of the 1850's* (New York: Oxford University Press, 1992).

83. From the German folksong, "Im Kreise froher, munterer Zecherer." C. Täglichsbeck and J. Müleisen, eds., *Göpel's deutsches Lieder und Commers-Buch*, 2nd ed. (Stuttgart: Verlag von Karl Göpel, 1858), 321.

84. A small village in the alpine Engadine Valley region of Switzerland.

much clearer picture, which has blurred before my eyes after reading the many contradicting reports in the papers here. I will respond to him soon. Please give my best to him and Linchen for now.

No word from Fritz yet. Surely, he is already in battle in Kentucky or still at the rear after all.—According to today's news, things are being taken care of more energetically now. But still no sign of a radical cure. How and when will it end!—

I don't write for *Banner* anymore. Märklin tells me that he quite enjoyed reading the reports. But I had already decided to end writing for them for reasons of modesty and it shall stay this way.—

I often long for you, my dear and beloved Mother. If there was a street between us, even a long one—of course not as long as the Great Ocean—then I would have been with you again. And so, we still have to wait a little longer. My little treasure trove is not full enough with things I have learned and seen yet. But when I will return with it, then I will be a quite splendid woman, and you will enjoy that.

I don't know anything about Fanny. I shall write to her again.

I've waited so long for the children to finish their picture, and now that it's done, I don't feel like sending it after all. They've tried three times, to no avail.

I don't want to wait any longer to send this letter. My dear, dear good Mother. I hope you are cheerful and think of us now and then. I last heard from Fritz on January 4. It's terrible that I always have to wait so long.—Percy and Hertha have a severe cold and fever. I have a cough as well. The change of weather here is remarkable. The day before yesterday it was spring with blossoming flowers.—Today it's winter of the horrid sort. I wish nothing more than that you are healthy and holding me dear. Your old, faithful, dear Tilla. Mary sends her kisses and greetings. I have her on a path to recovery now.

Mathilde Franziska Anneke to Fritz Anneke
Zürich, February 26, 1862

My dear good Fritz!

Late in the evening on 02/26.

I've just received your letter dated February 6 and 7. This is terrible news, but not terrible enough to bring us down. You will do what you think is right and if you are happier as cannoneer among your men than as colonel—then I will surely be too.[85] And in the rain of bullets you can just as well be kept safe as cannoneer than as colonel. On the contrary: The stars in the military are attacked more fiercely than the common uniforms. This does not upset me. I am only worried about Father[86] who wrote me today in old cordiality and trusts me so much now that he even tells me all of his secret heartbreaks. Spare him the sad news for a bit if you can. I will keep the terrible things from him until there is a little sunshine again.

I am working as much as I can, but I cannot sit at my desk, as I have been lately, any longer, if I want to remain the caregiver of our children. Bach[87] has forbidden me to work at my desk entirely. But I can still do it. How I can keep my honor and pay the rent I owe, that certainly is still a mystery. But I still have 8 days and a little money available—I might also have 3 fr for stamps, credit for bread and meat, and Minna is in on my secret money troubles. I haven't had the harmful seizures in several days. So do not lose sleep over this. That is very foolish. But please don't make such caustic remarks to me again. As much as you must share all your sorrows with me, you must share your little joys. I hope the good Jäki[88] whom the children love like a brother will pamper you. I urgently ask him to. Why you are so defiant against our good Mary I do not know. She is a little *knownothing* but not a mean one. I have sent her "*Slave Auction*"[89] to Borkheim[90] and have asked him

---

85. Fritz had left his command of an Indiana infantry regiment because it had not afforded him frontline action. Fritz Anneke to Edwin Stanton, Columbus, Kentucky, June 28, 1863, Box 2, Folder 8, Anneke Papers; Schulte, *Fritz Anneke*, 67–69.

86. Fritz's father Christian Anneke.

87. Christoph Ernst Bach practiced as a doctor in Zürich during this time. *Denkschrift der medizinisch-chirurgischen Gesellschaft des Kantons Zürich* (Zürich: Zürcher und Furrer, 1860), xv.

88. Percy was clearly attached to Jäki (or Jäcki, perhaps short for Johann or Jacques) Kamp (also spelled Camp), who had left to fight alongside Fritz in the United States, and the family in Zürich continued to interact with Jäki's father, but Fritz and Jäki would have a dramatic falling out. We have been unable to identify these individuals who were briefly significant in the Annekes' lives.

89. "The Sclaven Auction," a fictional story featuring Gerrit Smith as a character, was first published in German in five installments in *Didaskalia* in the summer of 1862. Mathilde describes it here as Mary's work, but she got full credit for the revised German version. On the collaboration process, see Honeck, *We Are the Revolutionists*, 127–33. More generally, see Maria Wagner, "Mathilde Anneke's Stories of Slavery in the German-American Press," *MELUS* 6, no. 4 (1979): 9–16.

90. Sigismund Borkheim had participated in the Baden uprising with the Annekes and now lived in London, where he continued to move in radical circles. Heinrich Gemkow,

to find English journals for it. I especially had to entrust the money issue to him and that might be doubly good. I have been meaning to write to Fröbel[91] for weeks now. I finally did and offered my help with the feuilleton. I might be able to publish two longer works for money there. I've suspended my dream of being able to fully attend to my muse of genuinely writing fiction until you are colonel again. Isn't that so? Where will my letters reach you now? I can't wait to send this letter until I have Herr Camp's[92] response. And it doesn't change things, so I will send it tomorrow. I've added a letter from me to Jäcki's letter to his father, put it in an envelope, and it will reach him tomorrow.

Farewell my dear Fritz.

The children are healthy, only Hertha still has a pink eye.

Farewell, farewell.

Your most faithful Tilla

Mathilde Franziska Anneke to Fritz Anneke
Zürich, March 10–15, 1862

My dear Fritz!

Your last letter is dated February 9 and 11. Today is March 10, and I am looking forward to the next one with much desire. It is spring here, and I believe the community is celebrating Carnival.[93] The children are off from school, and Maria went for a stroll through the city with them. I have sent my first correspondences to the *Criminal[zeitung]* and the *Allgemeine* again. I've been outside for the first time again, but I still don't feel healthy. My head hurts because of a rheumatic cold which has spread to my neck. My teeth only hurt at night. The Kapps came by yesterday to get me out of the house by force. Their concern has done me good, more than the walk. My melancholy had gotten the better of me. We met our friends Hepp and his wife as we went for a walk. She is cheerful again—if only it would last! He is delighted like a young gen-

---

Sigismund Ludwig Borkheim: Vom königlich-preußischen Kanonier zum Russland-Experten an der Seite von Marx und Engels (Hamburg: Argument, 2003).

91. Probably Julius Fröbel, who relocated frequently after serving as a member of the left faction the Frankfurt Parliament of 1848–1849. *Julius Fröbel, Ein Lebenslauf*, 2 vols. (Stuttgart: Verlag der J.G. Cotta'schen Buchhandlung, 1890–1891).

92. The father of Jäki Kamp (also spelled Camp). See n. 88 (chapter 3).

93. The festive season preceding Lent, generally celebrated by Catholics.

tleman when he sees Mary. He was happy about the newest American news.[94] Greetings over greetings!

Where will my letter reach you this time? Have you finally found or fought for the position which will make you content and happy? I hope so. I used to believe that I needed to fight by your side for this golden goal—I see more and more how foolish that was. I was more courageous than strong. At least you might smile at my courage and let me remember my fights alone and in tears. Death is the end of all fighting.—

Your last letter arrived on March 8. We see that it usually takes 26 to 30 days until your messages reach us. The children cluster around me when I say: There's a letter from Papa. I then have to read your letter aloud and woe be to me if I halt. Hertha is a true and lovely little angel. Percy is a dear boy, but he is a little selfish. Hertha has none of that, and she is as intelligent and diligent as was little Fritz, whose day of death I marked in silence and much sadness. You will not have forgotten our weeks of suffering either. Certainly not now that you're so close to our graves. . . .[95]

As I was paying the rent (400 fr) on the first of the month,[96] I realized it was my duty to leave my apartment, and I had to do it very quickly! I was forced to do it because I don't know whether we will be able to afford rent much longer. But what should we do? Where should we relocate the family now that Percy is enjoying a school that he would not have in an inexpensive country village? I think we will cross that bridge when we get to it. It is now very dark outside, even though the spring sun is gilding everything around here. I have asked the [*Criminalzeitung*] to send me 30 doll. Schöffler is not sending anything. I was very sorry to read that Jäki was another one to disappoint you painfully. I can't even tell the children about it. They have an image of him as a person who meant so much to you. Jäki must remain the same fairy tale version of himself to them. Not that long ago, in the second to last letter I sent him the lines his father had written to him.

---

94. Union forces under General Ulysses S. Grant had won strategic victories in February 1862 with the defeat of Fort Henry and the fall of Fort Donelson in Tennessee. James M. McPherson, *Battle Cry of Freedom: The Civil War Era* (New York: Oxford University Press, 1988), 395–405.

95. The graves of their children.

96. Mathilde paid rent on a biannual basis. November 4, 1862, Heft 232, III Band, Bezirksgericht Zürich Zivilprotokoll, Staatsarchiv Kanton Zürich, Zürich.

Later. We've just now received a letter from Rome from Gerrit Smith's wife and daughter.[97] They ask us to tell them which route to take to get here from Florence. They do not want to leave Europe without visiting us. They will not find us in a good state of mind.

I will go on a walk with the children and will try to get a better picture from St. Keller.[98] The pain in my face is unbearable. My face is all in bandages, but it does not help in the least. The right eye hurts terribly and is deeper inside my head than the other.

Booth writes that he's received a letter from you in which you report to him that you haven't been paid.[99] He does not tell us more, but I do hope you will not lose your pay. He sent 3 dollars all in one letter, and luckily, the money did not get lost.

They will probably fix the story over there and the divine institution[100] will continue to exist, until it will get to the last war, which the Negroes will fight themselves. People here have high hopes for peace. Herwegh, who just peeked through the door to say hello but did not sit down with us, says that people are already guaranteeing that you will have embarked on your journey back home in 2 months already. Whoever bets on this will lose.

Schurz, the homesick *adventurer in high style*, cannot live up to his own expectations as a general and has asked to be sent to Russia as an ambassador for a change.[101] He has climbed Mount Olympus.[102]

Once again, I made little Hertha's day. This morning I took the

---

97. On Gerrit Smith, see n. 64 (chapter 3). Smith's second wife, born Ann Carroll Fitzhugh, was also an abolitionist, feminist, and proponent of temperance, and their daughter Elizabeth Smith Miller was an active suffragist. Judith Wellman, *The Road to Seneca Falls: Elizabeth Cady Stanton and the First Woman's Rights Movement* (Urbana, Ill.: University of Illinois Press, 2004), 38–41.

98. Heinrich Keller was a local art dealer. Pfister, *Verzeichniß der Bürger der Stadt Zürich*, 108.

99. Ever in search of action, Fritz had decided to travel to Tennessee to volunteer his services to General Don Carlos Buell, which may have accounted for the interruption in his pay. Fritz Anneke to Edwin Stanton, Columbus, Kentucky, June 28, 1863, Box 2, Folder 8, Anneke Papers; Schulte, *Fritz Anneke*, 67–69.

100. Slavery.

101. After serving as the U.S. minister to Spain for less than a year, Carl Schurz returned to the United States to take up a commission as a brigadier general in March 1862. Whatever rumors Mathilde was repeating, they did not reflect Schurz's plans. Hans L. Trefousse, *Carl Schurz: A Biography*, 2nd ed. (New York: Fordham University Press, 1998), 113–16.

102. Mount Olympus is the home of the gods in Greek mythology.

children to the greenhouses of the botanic garden. There in a hedge I found and plucked the first violet for you.—The children were overjoyed. They paid attention to every flower, and Hertha reveled in her ideals. I had to take a carriage back, and we got back home to Mary and Minna around 1 o'clock. . . .

I received your dear letter dated February 19 and 22 in the midst of the most terrible pain. The Kapps and Emma Herwegh sympathize with me. Beust continues to treat Percy with much venom. Whenever I could, I looked at his homework and tried hard with him. If I had another plan for him, I would take him out of the school, but all of these changes would set him back too.—He is well-behaved and good at home but lazy.

I feel ever more hopeless reading your messages, which silently exasperate me. The unscrupulous Booth is systematic in his actions. I think I will write to him again, and I will strike a different tone this time. If only I would feel better. Oh, it is so sad in our home and around us everything is in blossom and lit up by the spring sun. Only my little Hertha is smiling like the spring. The child remains cheerful.

And Amalie Struve[103] is dead too!—And so, they all go one by one. Heinrich Struve[104] informed me of her death. The two poor little children she left behind! The only thing I ask from fate is not to let me die before the children are grown.

I don't want to go into details regarding your position. Writing is getting hard for me, and I am not supposed to either. And you are already in a different position, and I hope you are happier. Don't plunge into battle hastily to sacrifice your life in discontent. Let your life be too important for that for the sake of your children. The situation in Prussia is improving. The chamber dissolved for the third time![105] The re-elections should not be any more pleasing in the sight of God. Things

---

103. A writer and radical democrat, Amalie Struve was one of the most prominent female participants in the German Revolutions of 1848 and the wife of Gustav Struve (see n. 90 (chapter 2). She died in New York at just 38 after giving birth to her third daughter. Marion Freund, "Struve, Amalie," in *Neue Deutsche Biographie* (2013), 25:601–602.

104. Gustav Struve's youngest brother Heinrich had recently returned to Europe from Texas. Heinrich von Struve, *Ein Lebensbild: Erinnerungen aus dem Leben eines Zweiundachtzigjährigen in der alten und neuen Welt* (Leipzig: Verlag von E. Ungleich, 1895).

105. The intense standoff between a series of increasingly left-leaning Prussian parliaments and King Wilhelm I would result in Otto von Bismarck being appointed minister president in September 1862. Jonathan Steinberg, *Bismarck: A Life* (Oxford: Oxford University Press, 2011), 168–78.

are moving along in Italy, and the same is true for Paris.[106] Varnhagen's book[107] has been published at an odd time, and it touches the weak sides of the Fatherland in the most sensitive way. I've sent excerpts to the [Criminalzeitung].

I now live on nothing, that is on debt. I wasn't able to pay in the pharmacies. I had to take things on credit in the little general stores, as expensive and bad as everything is there. The bills for bread are incredibly high and Frau Spörri hasn't been paid yet for the last quarter. The noble St. Booth, who had promised Mary to send money around this time, says he can't send anything but that she should not *despair* and should trust the heavens instead. When Smith arrives, then I will voice my opinions loud and clear. Our Minna has asked for 50 fr—we have already paid her over a hundred—I am quite without money.

My letter is waiting for the pictures that I have asked for in vain for days.

I do not hear a word from anyone, not from Mother, not from Fanny.

Farewell, my dear, dear Fritz.

I can't write anymore.

Forever yours, Mathilde.

Mathilde Franziska Anneke to Fritz Anneke
Zürich, March 29–31, 1862

My dear good Fritz!

I would like you just as much in a cannoneer's jacket as in a colonel's uniform. But as a fobbed off captain—I would have lost all respect for you. I feel deeply sorry for you, my dear Fritz. Again, they have found reasons to deprive you of a position that meets your interests and talents. It is a hard blow for all of us. But then the calm and resolute nature that I could feel in every line of your dear letter dated March 8, which I have received unusually quickly (on the 27th), has comforted me very much. And who knows whether the energetic Richmond won't

---

106. Mathilde was alert to campaigns for popular democracy and opportunities for working people.

107. Karl August Varnhagen von Ense's niece had just published the first volume of the well-connected German writer's diaries posthumously. Ludmilla Assing, ed., *Tagebücher von K. A. Varnhagen von Ense*, vol. 1 (Leipzig: F.A. Brockhaus, 1861).

be persistent and courageous enough to stand up for you and get you satisfaction? It seemed obvious that if not a promotion, you would still be offered the position of colonel in the army, which does not get the recognition it deserves in the States. I have to confess to you that I always have to think about the enemy Don Carlos.[108]—They will have dissolved the regiment in Wisconsin as quickly as in Indiana. But you would have been given some other kind of satisfaction in Wisconsin, I do believe that.—I am happy that you have kept your little horse, Hertha's little prince. I want you to keep it for a long time.

. . .

March 31.

This mean month that is usually so lovely is almost over. During the last few days I was only able to leave the bed for two hours a day. Today, it seems that I am a little better. Doctor Rahe,[109] who has just left me again, comforts me a lot. He said that he would have to send me to Ragatz[110] in the middle of May. I would be able to make that happen more easily than Karlsbad, if it only weren't for all of my other duties.—I am in terrible pain. And then it is so sad around me. I hardly see anyone. The Kapps are so busy, and Emma Herwegh is only thinking about Naples. And in case they don't finally receive the confirmation, she must think of a roof under which they can live starting Easter. They had already terminated their apartment lease. They will have no other choice but to stay at the Schwanen,[111] and maybe that won't even be possible. Ludmilla Assing[112] has sent them 5000 francs, but even this tidy sum was just a drop in the bucket. The Countess H. also has done her bit with great gifts and some money too. Emma though, this is for certain, is a prodigal.

---

108. Brigadier General Don Carlos Buell, commander of the Army of the Ohio, had not given Fritz the position he sought when he headed to Tennessee on his own initiative. Stephen Engle, *Don Carlos Buell: Most Promising of All* (Chapel Hill, N.C.: University of North Carolina Press, 1999), 74–76; Fritz Anneke to Edwin Stanton, Columbus, Kentucky, June 28, 1863, Box 2, Folder 8, Anneke Papers.

109. We were unable to identify this physician.

110. The mineral springs at Bad Ragaz, about sixty miles southeast of Zürich, were a popular nineteenth-century destination. K. Bædeker, *Switzerland* (Coblenz: Karl Bædeker, 1863), 332–34.

111. We could not locate the establishment called "the Swan."

112. A writer and the niece of Karl August Varnhagen von Ense, whose diaries she had just published. Ludmilla's sister Ottilie Assing was romantically involved with abolitionist Frederick Douglass. Christoph Lohmann, ed. and trans., *Radical Passion: Ottilie Assing's Reports from America and Letters for Frederick Douglass* (New York: Peter Lang, 1999), 192–93.

Later. Your letter dated Feb. 12 has come into my hands. As ill as I am—because the tiniest exertion causes new fevers—I still need to quickly tell you in how much poverty your family is. Never rely on promises that were easily made, especially if they concern the well-being of your family, and you may not have to care for me much longer. Only rely on promises for which you hold the proof in your hands. This poverty for two months now—this illness. And today the baker sent the bill and of course terminated the credit in the same letter. I regret that until I draw my last breath I seem to be destined to always cry for help in poverty. I thank you for your birthday wishes, and I am happy that you have left for Tennessee in a good mood. St. R.[113] had heard from St. Kamp[114] long before you left Indiana that he would not send money or is not authorized to. He was now able to make new arrangements if St. R. was sincere in sending us advance payments. But it has never occurred to him to even add "just a little more" to the pittance.

This poverty is dreadful—if I could take Hertha with me, I would go to the grave tomorrow rather than later. I am writing you this, so that you know how much painful sorrow is surrounding my sickbed.

Stay healthy and be happy—

Faithful unto death. Your Mathilde

---

113. Probably Otto Ruppius.
114. Also spelled Camp. Father of Jäki. See n. 88 (chapter 3).

CHAPTER 4

Transatlantic Struggles

April 1862–February 1863

FOR MATHILDE AND MARY, THE YEAR BEGINNING IN APRIL 1862 was marked by intensifying health and economic crises. Mathilde's conditions, including liver disease, were much more debilitating at this time, but Mary's bloody coughing was an ominous symptom of the tuberculosis that would soon cut her life short. Sometimes relief came in the form of a surprise payment for their writing, a gift from generous friends, a family gathering, or a trip to a resort town, but they saw more suffering than respite during these twelve months.

Across the Atlantic, Fritz's career and the fate of the Union cause seemed to mirror the women's struggles in Switzerland. Mathilde's ambitions for Fritz led her to participate in the swirl of recriminations and intrigues that surrounded the German American officers serving in the Union army. Some of the conflicts among the officers revolved around slavery or ideological differences dating back to the Revolutions of 1848, but there is no missing the role of personality clashes, jealousies, and simple misunderstandings. The absence of clear Union victories between April 1862 and May 1863 only increased Mathilde's sense of frustration, exhaustion, and even despair.

Mathilde Franziska Anneke to Fritz Anneke
Zürich, April 20, 1862

My dear Fritz!

Easter Sunday.

We sent our last letter on the 10th of this month. Since then, I was finally able to spend 2 hours out of bed yesterday afternoon with permission from the doctor. And today I am allowed to leave the bed for a while as well. If only the pain had left me altogether, and if only I could breathe some spring air outside—and if only I received a cheerful letter from you! Ten strong leeches on my head and the post-treatment bleeding during a night when Cäcilie Kapp did not leave our side have done me good. But still I first needed mercury ointment and belladonna to help ease this excruciating pain.[1]

Today is Easter. Our 3 dear children have been invited to the Kapps' house to see what the little Easter Bunny has brought them. Hertha was very enchanted, and the two girls in their Garibaldi shirts[2] and little black silk skirts looked like they were ready to pose for a portrait. Percy was successfully chasing butterflies today. His collection is impressive already. His friend Snell is in Bern[3] for 5 days. Percy misses him terribly. Percy is becoming a lovely boy. He is the little cock of the roost at the Kapps' house. They always invite him to their little Sunday balls. That has made him a bit tidy and neat. Hertha is an independent little girl. My doctor had to examine her closely. He said that an operation would be premature and should not be carried out before her gland system has somewhat changed. That's why she has a cough and a headache today. I would like to take her to the springs with me, but I need to know first how I can help myself there.—

I received your last letter from Nashville on the 14th and from the Ohio and Cumberland Rivers.[4]—If it is true what Booth reported to Mary yesterday, that Potter[5] interpellated to the war minister on your behalf, then you might still be able to participate in proper war activities. If not, then I don't quite believe in your lucky star anymore. There, you are one of the silent ones in the country anyway. You are happy adoring your *boys* and you will be a faithful friend to them. The manner in which St. Buell[6] took you in as an unauthorized adviser and was imposing himself on you was to be expected. It was indeed obvious.—

---

1. Although both mercury and *atropa belladonna* (deadly nightshade) are known for their toxicity, nineteenth-century doctors prescribed them for a range of conditions. Walter Sneader, *Drug Discovery: A History* (Hoboken, N.J.: Wiley, 2005), 45, 95–96.

2. Loose-fitting shirts or blouses inspired by the Italian revolutionary were popular between 1860 and 1865. Anne Buck, *Victorian Costume and Costume Accessories* (Bedford: R. Bean, 1984), 32.

3. The Swiss capital.

4. Fritz must have written from the confluence of the rivers near Smithland, Kentucky.

5. Likely Congressman John F. Potter, a Republican representing Wisconsin. "Potter, John Fox," in *Biographical Directory of the United States Congress*, accessed July 30, 2020, http://bioguide.congress.gov/scripts/biodisplay.pl?index=P000465.

6. See n. 99 (chapter 3) and n. 108 (chapter 3).

Ever since Herr Carl Schurz has been appointed brigadier general I rest my case! For if they do these things in a green tree, what shall be done in the dry?[7] Well, Blenker was not able to escape his fate after all![8] Schurz will likely have helped in his *escamotage*[9] to make room for himself. Schimmel[10] will be his military adviser and field officer.

These are my first lines to you again. Now I'm tired. I may add a few more lines before I go to bed.

Easter Monday. All of the medicine, the bandages, etc. have weakened me in such a way that it will take a long time until I regain my strength, even though I am free of pain now. The beautiful spring truly saddens me. I haven't been able to enjoy it one bit yet. Then the grim prospects for the future. Will I ever be completely healed?—

May 2. I haven't been able to write you more. My illness—the terrible war reports about the battle in Corinth[11] where you must have been in any case—our hopeless situation—all of that left me incapable of doing anything, especially writing to you. The doctor forbade me any exertion—and I tried to abide by the order as much as I could.

Am I now directing these lines to you, my dear Fritz? Are you among the living or the dead? Since January/February I have felt like my voice does not reach you anymore—does it now? I must not get carried away by sadness now, so as not to fall back again. For our little children—I must draw myself up for them.

I received your little letter through the *Allgemeine*. I have been wait-

---

7. The Bible (King James version), Luke 23:31.

8. Blenker, then a colonel commanding a brigade from New York, was embroiled in a controversy in the German American press over alleged financial irregularities and German nobles and princes in his service. Mathilde was speaking prematurely, but Blenker resigned in June without explanation and died on a New York farm the following year. Carl Wittke, *Refugees of Revolution: The German Forty-Eighters in America* (Philadelphia: University of Pennsylvania Press, 1952), 233–34.

9. Italian for ploy or trickery.

10. Alexander Schimmelpfennig was a Prussian officer who had lived in Cologne before participating in the Revolutions of 1848 and would serve commendably as a brigadier general under Schurz in the Union army. A. E. Zucker, ed., *The Forty-Eighters: Political Refugees of the German Revolution of 1848* (New York: Columbia University Press, 1950), 336.

11. After the Battle of Shiloh, Union forces pursued Confederates to Corinth, Mississippi, where they would lay siege to the town. Fritz, along with Buell's entire artillery, received marching orders too late to participate in either engagement. Timothy B. Smith, "A Siege from the Start: The Spring 1862 Campaign against Corinth, Mississippi," *Journal of Mississippi History* 66 (2004): 403–24; Schulte, *Fritz Anneke*, 69–70.

ing for your first articles from Nashville—in vain. I only recognize you in the piece "Pittsburg on April 3." Since then the paper has begun to boast of its military correspondent whose reports it is awaiting. So, you were at the battlefield 3 days before the battle. Won't I hope in vain and expect your message after the bloody day of the 8th? And as a *Private* in the army—I will not even be officially notified of your fate. Oh God! Ours is a sad destiny—what will become of us?

It seems that my illness is less aggressive. Of course, I felt this way 14 days ago, but then I began to suffer from paroxysms all over again and it tied me to the bed again continually. Now today the doctor has allowed me to go outside and breathe some fresh air. And suddenly there's a thunder of cannons at 3 o'clock—I'm rushing to the window to see the Polytechnic Institute in flames. What may that be? The most beautiful building of modern times. The pride of all natives of Zürich and the Sempers especially.[12]—

This is where Frau Beust[13] and Fräulein Becker[14] have interrupted me. I am anxiously searching the [*Allgemeine*] for a sign of life from you. Have you disappeared forever on me and our two children? Where can I find solace for them and for me?

Mary is spitting out blood like never before. She was feeling well and now suddenly the frightening ailment is back again.

I have written 4 lines to Booth. I have insisted with great vigor on 50 doll and later 100. I do not know what to do anymore.

I asked Mary about 14 days ago to write to St. Ritzinger[15] and ask him to let us know about the financial situation.

I very quickly received 30 doll from Lexow as payment for my correspondences. We were in the greatest misery when the money arrived. I had to pay Emma[16] back the 50 fr that she had borrowed from me because she herself was in misery again. When will my life no longer be burdened by financial worries every day?

I am endlessly sorry that I must always and always bother you with

---

12. Architect Gottfried Semper's much heralded Polytechnikum building suffered a roof fire while under construction. *Leipzig Illustrirte Zeitung*, June 27, 1863 (No. 1043), 444.
13. Anna Beust.
14. Possibly the daughter of Forty-Eighter Johann Philip Becker. See n. 29 (chapter 4).
15. Friedrich Ritzinger, a successful Forty-Eighter living in Indianapolis. B. R. Sulgrove, *History of Indianapolis and Marion County* (Philadelphia: L.H. Evert & Co., 1884), 230–31.
16. Emma Herwegh.

this—but if only I could feed the children by keeping silent. These past months have been devastating for me and now your silence after the bloody battle that you were longing for.

Your poor Mathilde

Mary Booth to Fritz Anneke
Zürich, June 4, 1862
(English original)

Dear Fritz:

This paper that I am writing on was given me by Franziska Maria on my birth day. As you will see, one letter of my name is printed wrong. F. M. has been very sick for a long time, and is kept sick by being worried to death about everything. The Dr. says she must go to Ragatz <u>immediately</u> for four or six weeks. & that she cannot expect a permanent cure until she has been there, but we might as well think of going to Ethiopia with the whole family on a pleasure trip. Dr. Hepp's family have left for an Italian tour of the summer this morning. Mrs Beüst was here yesterday, & wished to be remembered to you when we wrote.

We had a good visit last week with the family of Gerrit Smith, consisting of his wife, & only son, his daughter—Mrs. Miller, & her husband. They had a courier with them whom they took in Paris. They have been in Italy, Germany, France, Austria & Belgium, & all about—go now to Paris, from there to the world's fair, then to Scotland, Ireland, & home again by the 1st of June.

They make a regular <u>work</u> of seeing Europe, & go at it in regular <u>Steam Engine</u> manner.

They were all enraptured with Franziska Maria. Mrs. Smith said to[17] living human being ever made so wonderful an impression on her. It would have done you good to have hea[r]d them talk about her.

They wanted to know if you was <u>worthy</u> of her. I shant tell you my answer! You know better than I can tell you whether you are or not!! The young Smith said F. M. ought to be <u>Major</u> Gen. now that Shurtz is <u>Brig</u>. & that when she received the appointment he would offer himself as her Aid[e]. She took the hearts of that whole tribe completely

---

17. Mary seems to mean "no," not "to."

Studio portrait of Mathilde Anneke standing
next to Mary Booth, Zürich, ca. 1863.
Courtesy of Wisconsin Historical Society, Madison.

by storm. Mr. Fogg,[18] who wished to be telegraphed to on their arrival, could not come, owing to sickness. They called on him—went through Bern on purpose. He wished me to go to, but I would not leave F. M. She was not well enough then to ride about town with them so I went alone. We visited the grand daughter of Lavater,[19] who spent an evening here with them, & whose heart, as well as that of her husband F. F.[20] also besieged. This lady gave to them pictures of Lavater, & a whole sermon of his own handwriting for Gerrit Smith. I am also sick myself. I am not <u>able</u> to write, but I do. I hope you are not <u>half</u> killed, & that we shall hear from you soon—affectionately your friend Mary

Mathilde Franziska Anneke to Fritz Anneke
Zürich, September 21, 1862

Dear good Fritz!

The days of worry have passed yet again. Well, you have indeed waited too long to send me and your children a sign of life. From July 13 until September 2!

We have been in our peaceful rural apartment for 14 days now. The children and I like it very much—Mary only to some extent. After having to do without it for so long, we are enjoying the freedom that we have here in the beautiful Obstgarten[21]—fruit forest would be a better name for it. The owner, a kind-hearted woman, gives the children presents with true generosity. We would be sincerely content now if the furniture renter would not make such outrageous demands for money. I now feel compelled to buy us our own furniture and household utensils. The bill of exchange (50 doll.) that Gerrit Smith has given to me and Mary as a gift will be enough to pay for half of it. It arrived at exactly the right time. Another one (62 francs) finally sent by Schöffler

---

18. U.S. minister resident in Switzerland George G. Fogg. See n. 66 (chapter 3).

19. Maria Fäsi (1802–1868). Johann Heinrich Pestalozzi, *Sämtliche Werke und Briefe: Kritische Ausgabe*, ed. Leonhard Friedrich and Sylvia Springer (Zürich: Verlag Neue Züricher Zeitung, 1994), 1:132.

20. It seems likely Mary meant "F. M." or Mathilde.

21. They had moved further east from the center of the city and were living in the Obstgarten ("fruit garden") area, where today's suburb of Hottingen is situated.

will help as well. The 400 fr set aside at Pestalozzi's[22] and the 150 that I had to deposit at the court house for the Zellers[23] will help me make it to Christmas; if the full amount of the court money will be returned to me, and assuming that I will be spared the strokes of fate in the end. My health is halfway stable. I'm still suffering from neural gout[24] in the right side of my head and my lower extremities. You might see that in the little picture I'm sending you. Haven't you received the two pictures of our children that I sent you in March of last year? If you haven't received them, then I will have to have new ones made now.

You would be rejoicing if you could see Percy. Beust—whom I have paid the 50 fr by the way—is very pleased with him. Starting Easter, he will go to secondary school. In his letter, which he wrote you in the wee hours of the morning, you will see the progress he has made in his thoughts and expression. He is my pride and joy. His little study and bedroom here next to my living room is the most beautiful room in our apartment. I can see him sitting at his desk from the sofa. He is growing like a weed and constantly needs new clothes. We attribute the fact that he is walking in his sleep to his rapid growth. I have to take the greatest care of him because of that. The doctor reassures me and is looking after him in his development.—Hertha is healthy and is making great progress with her foot. The machine that she is wearing fully helps her, and her foot will be just like the other in several months. We are not considering an operation anymore. She is becoming a pretty girl and smart like no other. She is wild too, like her mother used to be. She loves horses and cows.—

Franziska surprised me last week. She came over here from Heidel-

---

22. Likely the politically active civil engineer and professor Karl Pestalozzi (1825–1891), whose great-grandfather had been Johann Heinrich Pestalozzi, the famous Swiss pedagogue. Peter Müller-Grieshaber, "Pestalozzi, Karl," in *Historischen Lexikon der Schweiz*, last modified July 13, 2020, http://www.hls-dhs-dss.ch/textes/d/D31607.php.

23. The family's first landlords in Zürich sued Mathilde for six months' rent and damages, claiming the family had destroyed the interior of the property. The claims were apparently groundless and malicious from the start, but the judge only ruled in Mathilde's favor after the case had caused her significant distress. November 4, 1862, Heft 232, III Band, Bezirksgericht Zürich Zivilprotokoll, Staatsarchiv Kanton Zürich, Zürich.

24. Mathilde's doctors apparently believed that the buildup of uric acid caused her pain, although physicians at the time debated the relationship between autoimmune diseases such as gout and what they called "neuralgia." Landon Rives, "Neuralgia," *The Western Lancet* 13, no. 4 (1852): 222–27.

berg accompanied by Schmitt.[25] Meanwhile, Hammacher is in Scotland and England. Franziska was very much her old self. She still looked quite pretty. She did not have much joy with me. I had become too earnest for her. She is probably right.—I took her invitation to go on a journey to Chur and Pfäffers[26] that lasted two days. The Tamina Gorge surprised me in such a way that I could cheer all over again. A summer stay there with my children and—if you come back to us—with you would make me happy. Mary is thinking about returning to America next year. She truly is homesick for Ella, who is ailing. I don't have any idea yet if and how she intends to realize this plan. We are furnishing the place very modestly for now in any case.

The papers reported a successful battle near Bolivar for our fighters a few days before your letter arrived.[27] I am quite good at reading the map. Percy and I pursued the idea of your helping in battle there. Your letter, dated first in Bolivar, then in Springfield, shows me that you had to leave again on the evening before the thick of the battle. And in Tennessee now, I was sure you would have the opportunity to demonstrate your war skills—but again you did not. Soon, I must admit, I will be weak enough to believe in your evil doom. In Germany, where—as Beust tells me—you will forever be blamed for leaving Rastatt[28] in that terrible moment, people are saying out loud that you will also avoid the dangers of battle in the American war. I must admit that such a view of things by former friends, such misrecognition of your true value, almost smashes me to the ground. I interpellated to Beust in this matter. I wanted to know what <u>he</u> thought. He answered that he would never have let himself be captured at Rastatt either, but he would never have taken a position like yours in the first place. He fur-

---

25. Carl Schmitt, Franziska Hammacher's brother-in-law, operated a successful bookstore in Heidelberg. Karl Schmitt, *Unsere Firmengeschichte 1841–1966* (Heidelberg: Karl Schmitt und Co. Bahnhofsbuchhandlungen Heidelberg, 1966).

26. At the small town of Pfäfers, about sixty miles southeast of Zürich, visitors could walk through a cave-like gorge.

27. Fritz's letter has not survived, but he had secured a position as a captain in the 2nd Illinois Artillery Regiment, stationed at Bolivar, Tennessee and Springfield, Illinois. Bolivar was located near where the Battle of Shiloh raged on April 6–7, 1862, ushering in the high-casualty blood baths that would come to characterize the war. Schulte, *Fritz Anneke*, 70; James M. McPherson, *Battle Cry of Freedom: The Civil War Era* (New York: Oxford University Press, 1988), 408–14.

28. The Prussian defeat of revolutionary forces at the Fortress of Rastatt in the Baden Palatinate in July 1849 ended the Revolutions of 1848. Hans L. Trefousse, *Carl Schurz: A Biography*, 2nd ed. (New York: Fordham University Press, 1998), 23–27.

ther told me that he had written to Becker when Becker and Esseln[29] brought their lies into the world and said that you, Techow,[30] and Beust fled with everyone else from the battle in Ubstadt.[31] Beust had asked Becker who his sources were, and Becker had replied that Sigel[32] had said that. Then Beust wrote to Sigel, and Sigel said Gögg[33] had said so. Then Beust confronted Gögg, and Gögg admitted that he was indeed of this opinion. To support his claims, he then said that he had met you there during this general turmoil. Beust says it's true that the three of you had been taking counsel on a hill and then had come down together. He says it is possible that Gögg was referring to that!—But—I beg your pardon!—And none of you rectified such misapprehensions when there was still time for it! It is of course too late now—now you can only make people forget about this by using your sword and not tolerating the fact that your friends are triumphing over you. I will die of grief if you can't staunch this wound. I cannot tolerate that your friends and enemies Sigel and Schurz are triumphing during your obfuscation. I have never been thirsting for glory—I swear to everything I love—I haven't! But I will not be able to endure this imminent eternal humiliation patiently—I do not want to take it to the grave. Do not rely on your virtues and merits alone—for the people do not appreciate them if they are not drawn by outer splendor as well. I also ask you

---

29. Johann Philip Becker had organized militias in the Baden uprising and went on to write about his experiences from Switzerland as well as agitating to unite Italy and working with Marx and Engels in London. Esselen (also spelled Essellen) had also fought in Baden, but he left for the United States in 1852, where he died after a brief career in radical journalism in 1859. Karl Griewank, "Becker, Johann Philipp," in *Neue deutsche Biographie* (1953), 1:717–18; Zucker, *Forty-Eighters*, 292; Johann Philipp Becker and Christian Essellen, *Geschichte der süddeutschen Mai-Revolution des Jahres 1849* (Geneva: Gottfried Becker, 1849).

30. A former Prussian military officer like Fritz, Gustav Adolph Techow had served as the chief of the general staff of the insurgent army in Baden. *Collected Works of Karl Marx and Frederick Engels* (London: Lawrence & Wishart, 1978), 10:735.

31. Fritz had favored a retreat at Ubstadt, but August Willich convinced him to stay and engage in an unsuccessful battle on June 23 and 24, 1849. Gustav Struve, *Geschichte der drei Volkserhebungen in Baden* (Bern: Verlag von Jenni, Sohn, 1849), 277.

32. Franz Sigel, who had served as a lieutenant in Baden's army before studying law, was active in the revolutionary uprising in 1848 and 1849. As a polarizing major general in the Union army, he became one of the most famous German Americans of the era. Stephen D. Engle, *The Yankee Dutchman: The Life of Franz Sigel* (Fayetteville: University of Arkansas Press, 1993).

33. Amand Goegg (1820–1897) had been a civil servant before participating in the revolutions. Markus Bürgi, "Goegg, Amand," in *Historisches Lexikon der Schweiz*, last modified December 28, 2006, http://www.hls-dhs-dss.ch/textes/d/D47638.php.

to please avoid the little personal wars. They do not bring you honor or success. Satisfaction from a fool in St. Louis, who insults you, will not make your sword look shinier.[34] I fear that your great irritability often gets you into little personal conflicts more often than necessary....

Mathilde Franziska Anneke to her mother Elisabeth Giesler
Zürich, September 25, 1862

My dear, dear Mother!

In the midst of the terrible news we are receiving from over there,[35] a lovely greeting from all of you speaks to my heart. Johanna's[36] lines and also three written by Emil,[37] then a friendly little letter from friend Zünd[38] including a supplement (bill of exchange from Schöffler). And the good news from you about the addition to your flock of grandchildren—a little son for Johanna[39]—are more or less a remedy. No news from Fritz—none—since July 13. That's a long time. He is certainly in battle with the guerillas in Tennessee,[40] and I must hope that he keeps his lucky star in war and stays alive. But is Washington already in the hands of our enemies at this moment? We are very anxiously awaiting the next telegrams.

You will have received my last letter—I wrote it to you from the springs. I think I responded to the lovely lines which you wrote to me

---

34. Fritz had engaged in a confrontation with superiors in St. Louis after he was required to conduct an investigation that showed major irregularities in ordinance requisitions. Schulte, *Fritz Anneke*, 70.

35. That summer the Union army's Peninsula Campaign to take Richmond had failed, and Confederate forces subsequently advanced north, reaching Maryland by early September. Mathilde would not yet have learned of the Battle of Antietam on the 17th or the preliminary emancipation proclamation of the 23rd, which followed the Union victory. McPherson, *Battle Cry of Freedom*, 424–27, 461–71, 524–45, 557–59.

36. Mathilde's sister Johanna Weiskirch.

37. Johanna's husband Emil Weiskirch.

38. Ernst Anton Zündt.

39. Armin Weiskirch was misidentified as Armena (female) in the 1870 census. U.S. Census, Population Schedules (1870), 7th Ward, Milwaukee, p. 48, dwelling 295, family 293; U.S. Census, Population Schedules (1920), 6th Ward, Topeka, Kansas, p. 4, dwelling 84, family 83.

40. As soon as Fritz became a captain in the Illinois Artillery, the unit was pulled back from the front. Schulte, *Fritz Anneke*, 70.

while you were staying with your good faithful friends, the Pfeils.[41] At least this is as much as I remember from that terrible time. I can feel that these mud baths have been good for me and have had a lasting effect. This terrible cure at the springs first made me even more ill. But then it seems it has truly been a stumbling block to my illness. At least I am almost free of this unbearable pain when the weather is right. Moving 14 days ago in heavy rainfall of course gave me another cold so that I am still constantly suffering from pain in my chest and in my hips. But the real gout in all its frightfulness is gone. You surely had expected to hear from me sooner. But I have been living in constant turmoil for months. First, Fräulein Ritzinger[42] came with a friend, Miss Fletcher[43] from Indianapolis, to visit me for 4 weeks. Then Franziska was here, my old, dear, eternally faithful friend. She was accompanied by her brother-in-law Schmitt, the bookseller from Heidelberg, husband of Lina Rollmann.[44] Hammacher was on a business trip to Scotland during that time. Our apartment was only scantily furnished. I am now living my dream of a Swiss idyll in a friendly modest farmhouse that looks very different from my previous elegant apartment. Franziska was happy to stay with us anyway. In all, she stayed 8 days and during that time she invited me on an excursion to the Canton of Graubünden. I saw a region that my heart did not even know existed until then. We traveled along Lake Wallenstädter and went to the Tamina Gorge, the powerful rocks that bluster out both the warm healing springs of Pfäffers, and the glacier stream of the Tamina. We watched these eternal rocks for hours as the dark granite pillars were polished by the torrential waters of the Tamina. On the right side, the Tamina

---

41. It is impossible to identify these friends with any certainty, but a successful German-born couple by the name Pfeil farmed in Milwaukee County with their children. U.S. Census, Population Schedules (1870), Town of Granville, Milwaukee County, Wisconsin, p. 45, dwelling 335, family 340.

42. Mary (Maria) Ritzinger, born in Hesse, was twenty-five at the time of the 1870 census. U.S. Census, Population Schedules (1870), 9th Ward, Indianapolis, Indiana, p. 32, dwelling 235, family 252.

43. Myla F. Fletcher would marry Friedrich Ritzinger's son, John. Her father was businessman Stoughton Alphonso Fletcher (1808–1882), a member of a prominent Indianapolis family. *Commemorative Biographical Record of Prominent and Representative Men of Indianapolis and Vicinity* (Chicago: J. H. Beers & Co., 1908), 982–83; Finding Aid, Calvin Fletcher, Jr. Family Collection, Indiana Historical Society, accessed on July 30, 2020, https://www.indianahistory.org/wp-content/uploads/calvin-fletcher-jr-family-collection.pdf.

44. Caroline Schmitt (neé Rollmann). See n. 25 (chapter 4).

devotes itself to this eternal work while it dallies with little alpine flowers on the left side. Then we traveled to the Italian border to get at least a glimpse of those skies and breathe that air. I think staying there for 8 days would have healed me completely, but we only spent 3 days there instead. We returned home to the little ones as soon as possible. Mary went on the same trip 14 days earlier, only further down to the Engadine region. She did not rest until I had at least seen a part of that. She was right. In such surroundings, one finds new courage to face life when it has dwindled a bit.

Only several weeks before, my faithful Franziska had sent me proof of her loyalty through a friend who had visited her, Cäcilie Kapp, the daughter of Professor Kapp and head of the institute.[45] She sent me a precious jewel in a ring and the message that she would come and see me. What a delight after being separated for 15 years! We immediately recognized and found each other in the crowds of people at the train station. Franziska and Mary liked each other very much.[46] Franziska's mother, Tante Rollmann,[47] has returned from Italy to her "beloved town of Warendorf."[48] Her old heart had been longing to see the big barn doors and heaps of straw there and intends to spend her last birthdays there. She is bigoted and is torturing the children terribly with her old saying-the-rosary beliefs. She is temporarily living with Lina in Heidelberg, where there aren't masses and priests enough to follow her silly desire.

—Meanwhile, I have finally received a letter from Fritz written on Sept. 2 from Springfield, Ill. I thought he was finally fighting successful battles, but then his peculiar misfortune again put him in God knows which areas. Schurz's lucky star is even shining a light on the laurels he had earned as general. At least the man does not lack the

---

45. An 1863 advertisement for "Professor Kapp's Educational Institute for Girls" explained that the couple and their daughters had run it in Zürich since 1856. *Süddeutsche Zeitung*, February 8, 1863.

46. Mary and Franziska Hammacher exchanged letters, of which about a dozen of Mary's have survived. Mary Booth to Franziska Hammacher, 1862–1864, Signatur N2105/14, Friedrich Hammacher Archiv, 1824–1904, Bundesarchiv Berlin.

47. Although Mathilde called her "Tante" (aunt), Maria Christina Elisabeth Rollmann (neé Verkrüzen) was not the sister or sister-in-law of Mathilde's mother or father. See n. 121 (chapter 1). Bernhard Koerner, ed., *Deutsches Geschlecterbuch* (Limberg an der Lahn: C. A. Stark, 1968), 148:7.

48. About forty miles east of Münster in Prussian Westphalia.

courage and skills to wriggle himself into a position where he can win and achieve anything he wants. That is the truth. I am fair enough to accept the personal courage I always thought he was capable of and which he has now proven on the battlefield as atonement for the arrogance of letting himself be made a general. His luck does not leave him in a hail of bullets. Those are gallant enough to shoot his hat triumphantly off his head but to spare his head. Fritz does not know how to take a risk and then build a good fortune on it with assurance and confidence. He is too good a mathematician, not leaving anything to chance—but everything to calculation.—I am <u>not</u> losing faith in his <u>solid military skills</u>, which the fatherland needs more than anything at this moment but is squandering. But I have never had any faith in his <u>war genius</u>. A few bold words from you would be sacred in times like today's, dear Mother. Write them down for him and send them to him. It will comfort him and elevate him.

The news from there sounds so sad that I could cry. The <u>fatherland</u> that we have chosen as such—and <u>freedom</u> in such serious danger! How are you bearing this painful thought over there? How will you bear the gravity of this fate!? Whoever can overlook this casually, does not understand, no, does not suspect <u>what</u> will come and affect every single person. The personal weal or woe in this moment becomes entirely unimportant compared to the imminent general doom. Sometimes I feel like I need to fly over there and—if only a drop in the sea—help where help is needed. But then again, I feel my own lack of power and my illness, and I should be happy to linger far away from the site of horror.

Mary, like her fellow countrymen, trusts in the blind luck of the Union. Our friend, the ambassador Mr. Fogg in Bern, is beginning to be afraid. I suspect that the troops in the West will be ordered East and that Fritz might find a more open field for action after this deployment. I ask all of you to write me often, especially in these times in which I may be far away from battle but feel the pain nonetheless. I thank you all again for the few dear lines. My health has progressed, but I haven't fully healed yet. Hertha is a true hero. Percy is growing too fast. Lili is cheerful, and Mary is also in a good mood. She got a splendid engagement for the *N.Y. Independent* and had to be industrious because of it. She is paid 10 dollars for every article that is not even a column long. But please do not mention any of it to her lovely husband because then he will take care of her even less. I don't feel strong enough yet to begin my work again with courage und vigor. My modest arrangements make our life here considerably less expensive. It is not necessary for me to think restlessly about work and not about my own health. The wonderful surroundings at our house inspire me to take walks outside and enjoy some *dolce far niente*.[49] . . .

I am sending you a sample of my portraits, which are supposedly good by the way. It would make me happy if you liked it. Above all, I would finally like to have a little picture of you and your blessed family.—

I received letters from Pauline[50] and the little children several days ago. She misses me terribly. I have just received some Prussian money. I will send it to the little children as a keepsake. When I am healthy again, then I can make them happy more often. My friend Cäcilie Kapp, who has visited them on my behalf, is full of praise of her beautiful and well-educated little children. Little Louise knits socks for Hertha whenever she can and sends them to her. They find solace in the fact that we are here.

We often receive dear letters from Gerrit Smith. How accurately this wise man has predicted the fate of the Union. If only the tattlers had wanted to listen to him in time. But they don't want to yet, and we often read about the racial hatred, or more precisely, the prejudices of the dumb masses in the correspondences of the 9th Regiment[51] in the *Banner* for example. This makes me fear that there may be many casualties because of these mischiefs. By the way, Zünd is editing the *paper* with much skill. He is writing many beautiful articles and is able to sail around the cliffs and sandbanks of the Democratic Party quite well. I do recognize which articles are written by him. If there is enough space left, then I will write to him too. If not, please give him my best until the next letter. Please send Carl Anneke and his family my greetings. I began writing letters to him a long time ago. I do not hear or see anything from Märklin, except for exquisite poetic outpourings in the

---

49. Italian for sweet idleness.
50. Mathilde's sister Pauline von Reitzenstein. See n. 79 (chapter 3).
51. The 9th Wisconsin Infantry Regiment had a large German contingent. Ella Lonn, *Foreigners in the Union Army and Navy* (Baton Rouge, La.: Louisiana State University Press, 1951), 110.

Beobachter am Hudson.[52] It seems like he hasn't sent you the *Sc[laven] Auction*.

We are indulging in an abundance of wine grapes and fruit this year. The children enjoy it like never before. They are much happier here than in our other house. It is so peaceful here—and the house owners are so much better than the previous ones. Now, dear Mother, you will say that I have been chatting with you long enough.

Farewell!

Send my greetings to your dear good friends the Pfeils and all the others.

Dear Grandmother[53]

I have plucked this little flower for you at the foot of the Jungfrau.[54] I will tell you about my alpine travels soon. Many greetings from Hertha and Lili to Ida and Alma.

Farewell and do not forget
your dear Percy.
Farewell then for today.[55]
Stay healthy and hold all of us dear
best best Grandmother
    Your faithful Tilla

Mathilde Franziska Anneke to Fritz Anneke
Zürich, September 25, 1862

My dear, dear Fritz!

I have been playing with my little Hertha all afternoon. First in the tree yard and then on the green grass—oh, how much <u>you</u> would love <u>that</u> here—and then we played war in the room. Percy has many tin soldiers and canons to simulate the American war. Lili is at little Fritz Beust's birthday party. Percy went to Mass with Mary. Hertha did not

---

52. A Sunday edition of the *New Yorker Herold*. Karl J. R. Arndt and May E. Olsen, *German-American Newspapers and Periodicals, 1732–1955: History and Bibliography* (Heidelberg: Quelle & Meyer, 1961; reprint, New York: Johnson Reprint Corporation, 1965), 346.
53. Percy added a few lines to Mathilde's letter.
54. The Jungfrau is one of the main peaks in the Bernese Alps.
55. Mathilde resumed writing.

want to leave her Mama alone, and a little thing needs to be repaired on her machine as well. Her foot is almost healthy now. Its form is almost like the other foot, and she can now use it fully. I've bought a completed winter suit for Percy. The little ones are also quite equipped, and now it is my turn—Mary has also been provided with clothes, and so we are ready for winter. I feel like a new life has begun now that I do not have the nagging worries about the large expenses. We live a simple life here, so peaceful and yet so nice. I do not want for anything except your thoughts reaching us. Now we have to try to be close to you through our pictures.—

But what will the situation be like over there at this moment? I must admit to you that the thought of the danger our chosen homeland is in is filling my soul with pain.—It seems to me that Washington cannot be saved. If Sigel indeed is this grand general[56] and if he can snatch the sword and assume control in the last minute of misery—maybe then things will take a turn for the better. I trust him more than anyone else on the Potomac River. It is my wish that you will finally be ordered out of these Western corners and that you will then get the chance to arrive at the battle fields on which the world is focusing. Yesterday afternoon the Hepps were here. He honestly cannot believe that you haven't found your right position there. These questions about your heroic deeds that the people here are waiting for with a peculiar curiosity—it pains me. When they read your nice article in the [*Augsburger*] they were satisfied—now the questioning seems to begin again.

Gritzner is leaving Zürich. He is following his son who is a consul in Oldenburg.[57] He has sold all his properties. Gr[itzner] the Younger has embarrassed himself. He has served as a tool in the hands of politicians and especially the Illinois politician Waschburne.[58] He has drawn his sword against Fremont[59] and in his laughable brochure "Fremont

---

56. In June, Sigel had received his first significant assignment in the Union army, command of the First Corps, which would become the Eleventh Corps. Engle, *Yankee Dutchman*, 126.

57. Maximilian Gritzner's son Max Carl put down deeper roots in the United States than his father, but after serving as a U.S. consul, he would return to Europe for good in the 1870s to join the family business near Karlsruhe. Helge Dvorak, ed., *Biographisches Lexikon der Deutschen Burschenschaft*, vol. 1, Part 2, (Heidelberg: Universitätsverlag C. Winter, 1998), 181.

58. Republican Congressman Elihu Washburne was an ally of Lincoln. Mathilde misspelled his name. *New York Times*, October 23, 1887.

59. Many Forty-Eighters supported Major General John Charles Frémont, who sur-

and Blenker" has tried to destroy them.[60] He adores Sigel, Schurz, and anything that concerns them. He is the quintessential imbecile, even though he is a very polite gentleman. Now we see who this German American politician truly is. The old man realized that this sharply-worded pamphlet has been a humiliating fiasco for his son. Every now and then he still tried to inspire us to rebel against the "prodigalities" and "perfidies" of Fremont's party, but we ignored him. One cannot partake in such petty and miserable persecutions when one should only be considering the grand scheme of things.—

October 4th

Your dear letter from Springfield arrived several days ago. I can somewhat feel your old *spirit* in this letter. It is necessary to be among old friends again, and the journey to Chicago has reunited you with several of them. If you shut yourself away, then you will be forgotten sooner than expected. One shouldn't hide one's light under a bushel. This is a banal truth, but nevertheless you cannot hear it often enough. I am not saying that I find it less lovely of you not to betray your true values given these most disgraceful canonists[61] of our time and their half measures. But it has been necessary always and at all times—men in ancient times knew this especially—to take every opportunity to put yourself in a good light to be able to stand up for these values.—

Butz[62] is a real poet of Westphalian character. He will likely under-

---

rounded himself with German officers when he commanded the Union army's Department of the West in 1861. Lincoln had relieved Frémont of command in November 1861 for issuing a proclamation freeing people enslaved by Confederates in Missouri. From that point on, Frémont was a rallying figure for Radical Republicans who considered Lincoln too moderate. Andrew Zimmerman, "From the Rhine to the Mississippi: Property, Democracy, and Socialism in the American Civil War," *Journal of the Civil War Era* 5 (2015): 3–37; Jorg Nagler, *Fremont contra Lincoln: Die deutsch-amerikanische Opposition in der Republikanischen Partei während des amerikanischen Burgerkrieges* (Frankfurt: P. Lang, 1984).

60. M. C. Gritzner, *Blenker und Fremont: Seinen Feinden und Versäumdern in aufrichtiger Verachtung gewidmet* ([Washington, D.C.]: [1862]). Blenker and Struve were on one side of the conflict among Forty-Eighters in the Union army and Gritzner, Sigel, and Schurz on the other. Ansgar Reiß, *Radikalismus und Exil: Gustav Struve und die Demokratie in Deutschland und Amerika* (Stuttgart: F. Steiner, 2004), 357–58.

61. Mathilde appears to be comparing Fritz's opponents to the guardians of canon law for the medieval Catholic Church, which she saw as irrational, arcane, and hierarchical. Harold J. Berman, *Law and Revolution: The Formation of the Western Legal Tradition* (Cambridge, Mass.: Harvard University Press, 1983), 199–224.

62. Forty-Eighter Caspar Butz was in 1862 a Chicago writer and Republican politician. He would go on to become one of the most beloved of German American poets. Zucker, *Forty-Eighters*, 283.

stand you, and he doesn't lack the tenacity to speak up for you in a sustained manner. I do not know Kapp[63] personally, but I know of his good reputation. And I trust that he is able to better represent the "German character" that until now has only known its one and only idol, Sigel.

I was interrupted by Jäki's father. And I will now immediately make his request known to you: "Let him know, <u>where</u> his son Jäcki is and whether he is healthy." The old man hasn't had a letter from him in ages. Tears fill his eyes when he speaks about his son. A letter that he had sent to Wisconsin in Sept. of last year was sent back to him as undeliverable in August of this year.

Well, 4 of our letters have been lost then. I wrote to you every day from Baden[64] as long as that had been possible. But I had to discontinue the health cure two times, because I was too miserable. The children visited me—you already know about this episode from Mary's otherwise very ordinary stories about the children.[65] The Countess H. virtually forced me to take 200 fr from her after she came to my bed one day before my departure and saw how much I was suffering and that the end may have been drawing near for me. Then I could depart in peace—now that I had resources enough for the family. How I have been faring in Baden—or the results of the health cure—you know about that. Zeller, as I heard later, intended to send you a telegram twice saying that I was near death. But due to my resilient nature I was close to death one day and was able to leave the bed the next day. By the way, I have only nebulous memories of that terrible time. And since you will likely not have missed all that much in these 4 letters, I'd prefer to write you nice things about our current life here, which we enjoy very much. The children keep exclaiming: "Oh, it is a hundred times nicer here than in Hofacker." And certainly, it is an Elysium[66] for them

---

63. No relation to the Annekes' Zürich friends, Friedrich Kapp was another Forty-Eighter who was better known for his nonfiction and for returning to Germany from New York in 1870 to serve in the Reichstag. Zucker, *Forty-Eighters*, 307–308; "Friedrich Kapp," *The Nation* 39, no. 1010 (November 6, 1884), 393–94.

64. Likely Baden, Switzerland, a town just 15 miles from Zürich known for mineral springs that supposedly had curative properties.

65. Mary published a series of letters for children in Booth's *Daily Life* under the pseudonym Genoa Grey. They described the Swiss adventures of "Lillian May," "Lulu Bell," and "Percy Bell." *Milwaukee Daily Life*, January 3, 1863.

66. A blissful realm of the afterlife in Greek mythology.

here. Right now (it's vacation time) they all went down to the tree yard with their friend Robert Nenninger[67] and Muralt,[68] another student at the Beust school. On the edge of this wide area blessed with hundreds of heavy fruit trees, there is a stream that drops down in cascades. This is a real *Rocky mountain territory* for their imagination. I can still see them from my windows. I hear the cheering and shouting "we are on a natural science research trip." Hertha is leading them on. Percy is out in the sun, which is so splendidly golden today for the first time in 8 days. He had a terrible cough and had to stay at home during the last few misty days. He is growing so terribly fast that I have to take good care of him when he's ill. My doctor, who visits us every week, comforts me a lot with his advice regarding the illnesses in our family. After so much suffering I am a little more worried, and since our family circle is only such a small one now, it is important to do everything we can to stay together. The little Robert Nenninger—I wrote you from Baden that N. had visited me there from Newark. He intended to put his son into a local boarding school and had chosen Wislicenus.[69] But after hearing my thoughts he sent him to Beust. B. was incredibly thankful and has since offered a conciliatory tone. Well, Robert now absolutely doesn't like it there, and it very much upsets me. As a real and independent [*illegible*], he wanted to attend a different institution and he told me that two times. I mustered all my courage and spoke with Beust to tell him my opinion on the just and equitable or unequitable in his method of education. He took it quite well, and Robert was somewhat pleased about my mediation. It doesn't seem like there is the right atmosphere at the Beust school, and if things don't change, my prognosis for the school is grim. I have now paid off Beust 100 francs of my debt. He (Beust) explained to me that Percy was ready for the canton exam. And since he will take the next step forward around Easter, I would like to hear your

---

67. Robert Nenninger, aged about 14 in 1862, was the son of a successful Württemberg-born oilcloth manufacturer in Newark. U.S. Census, Population Schedules (1860), 5th Ward, Newark, p. 255, dwelling 1633, family 2233.

68. Many Muralt men in the Zürich area filled prestigious political, business, and professional positions. Pfister, *Verzeichniß der Bürger der Stadt Zürich*, 160–61.

69. Probably Johannes Wislicenus (1835–1902), a German chemist then teaching at Zürich's college preparatory high school ("Kantonsschule"). Daniel Coit Gilman, Harry Thurston Peck, and Frank Moore Colby, eds., *The New International Encyclopedia* (New York: Dodd, Mead and Company, 1908), 20:601.

decision on whether we should send him to the secondary school or the vocational school. After all of the advice I sought, I prefer the vocational school. However, you must decide because you also know the situation here, which hasn't changed.

The day before yesterday, Gotffr[ied] Kinkel the Younger arrived.[70] Kinkel had written to me a short while ago to say that I should welcome his son warmly and in motherly style because he was such a shy boy who had never left his home before. I have done everything I could for the truly very shy young man of 18 years. He attends the university here, and I have rented a room for him. He is staying with friends of mine, Professor Schecht.[71] I have done everything in my power for him. I am always happy when I can help friends in any way in gratitude for the confidence and love they have proven to us. And so it was a pleasure to welcome the daughter of Ritzinger and the daughter of Fletcher from Indianapolis, because the former has welcomed you in his home as well.

But you have always seen things very clearly in your prognoses. Garibaldi—the hero stricken in years—was granted amnesty.[72] You were right, his game was soon over, too soon. I believe that you were right to predict the death sentence for McClellan.[73] Has he proven himself like others now that his regiment has for the first time given him a free hand? Pope and McDowell have already retreated to weapons. Halleck will likely be able to play his game for a while.[74] I certainly think you

---

70. Gottfried Kinkel's son (1844–1891) shared his name and also pursued an academic career, settling into a position in classical philology at the University of Zürich later in the decade. Katja Hürlimann, "Kinkel, Gottfried," in *Historisches Lexikon der Schweiz*, last modified October 8, 2007, http://www.hls-dhs-dss.ch/textes/d/D43467.php.

71. We cannot identify this academic.

72. In the ongoing struggle over the extent and character of a united Italy, the popular Garibaldi had been wounded and captured by the forces of the newly crowned Italian king and then amnestied. Alfronso Scirocco, *Garibaldi: Citizen of the World* (Princeton, N.J.: Princeton University Press, 2007), 329–33.

73. Lincoln would relieve General McClellan, a Democrat who opposed emancipation, of command of the Army of the Potomac on November 7 because he had not pursued his advantage after the Battle of Antietam. McPherson, *Battle Cry of Freedom*, 562.

74. Major General John Pope lost command of the Army of Virginia on September 12. His subordinate commander Irvin McDowell shared blame for the Union defeat at the Second Battle of Bull Run and received no new assignments for two years. Henry Halleck had been promoted to general-in-chief in the summer following victories in the western theater. John J. Hennessy, *Return to Bull Run: The Campaign and Battle of Second Manassas* (New York: Simon & Schuster, 1993), 451–55, 466–67; McPherson, *Battle Cry of Freedom*, 502.

were right to discipline, advise, and send messages to the *Ill[inois] Staatszeitung*, if they brought matters to a head. I hope and wish that your friends in Chicago have stayed loyal to you so that they can claim the position for you that you deserve. But to rely on the "glorious" and "bravest of the brave" hero Schurz is foolish to put it mildly.

We always receive nice letters from G. Smith's family. Yesterday the daughter let us know that she had just received a letter from Mrs. Stanton (wife of the war minister), her cousin.[75] The wise woman writes: "May the Southerners come and rob this entire nest (Washington). May they abduct Old Abe along with Seward and McClellan and take them to one of their forts and keep them there, until we have steered this ship here back on its right course."—

Mary is feeling quite well since she visited Pontresina.[76] She is currently writing her second 10 dollar letter for the *Independent*. The paper has invited her to send contributions, as I told you in my last letter. Booth sent 10 dollars again for a change. That's all. But it's enough to complete Mary's wardrobe a bit. If I get back my 150 fr from the deposit at court, then I will be able to get to December because Mary also has to contribute to the household. If you send some more resources in January, then I will make it. I myself will likely also make some money.
[*unfinished letter*]

Mathilde Franziska Anneke to Fritz Anneke
Zürich, November 24, 1862

Dear, dear Fritz!

After a few grimly cold days, the sunlight is shining through our windows again a bit. The quick and harsh change in weather announced itself when I became ill again. I am a bit better for the moment, but the doctor says that one can't be fully cured of the abnormal gout so easily. He intended to send me to Baden again this fall, but that was not possible. Now he says I should go there again for 8 days next May and

---

75. Abolitionist and feminist Elizabeth Cady Stanton was Gerrit Smith's first cousin, but Mathilde was mistaken when she said Stanton was also married to Secretary of War Edwin Stanton. John Stauffer, *The Black Hearts of Men: Radical Abolitionists and the Transformation of Race* (Cambridge, Mass.: Harvard University Press, 2001), 211.

76. A village in the Engadine region.

it will heal me. I got bedsores on my left arm. The doctor is taking extreme measures so that the gout will not spread to the lower left extremities. I am not allowed to leave the house. He forbade it. And so I asked Pestalozzi in a letter about the money. I will enclose his response in this little letter.

I did not let little Hertha go to school because it's so cold and she is not feeling quite well yet. She is sitting next to me and writing letters to her Papa. She tells me that a young lad recently said to her that her Papa certainly had been shot dead already. She responded that the soldiers liked her Papa so much that they would not shoot him dead.—A letter from you, a few lines even, are cause for celebration here. And if there is just so much as one cheerful line in your letter, just one glimmer of hope, then we are happy and content. I wonder whether you have any idea about our—or better yet—my dull existence here?

But I mustn't complain. It has always been your wish to go to battle wherever the battle horns sounded—you wanted to leave. It was your wish, and so we should respect that. I wish I had been spared this dreary illness, which will take away the last of my courage to live, for my sake and the sake of the children.

Mary has just received a letter from Booth after several weeks.— (There are 2 f[rancs] enclosed which arrive at the right moment for our household.) He writes that he hasn't heard from you directly in a long time but indirectly from various people who are in contact with General McClernand.[77] They said McClernand was full of praise for you and that you were the general's "main dependence." Well, McClellan has also been degraded. We are curiously awaiting the next events and only regret that we don't get anything decent to read from there anymore. Booth further says that a telegram announced that McClernand received marching orders to go to the Mississippi. But he doesn't yet believe it. In any case, my letter will not reach you in Springfield anymore. And if you're headed further south this winter, it will please you too. And for all the world I did not want for you to spend this winter like the last: in a linen tent and without a blanket. This dreary news you gave me in your letter back then let me sink deeper and deeper into

---

77. Illinois politician-turned-general John Alexander McClernand had just demonstrated the power of personal influence. He had just received Lincoln's permission to raise troops to march on Vicksburg, Mississippi. McPherson, *Battle Cry of Freedom*, 577–78.

misery and illness. And this anxious depression next to the terrible pain is the most difficult part of the illness.

Finally, an answer from Pestalozzi. I am sending you the first page of the letter that contains his response.[78] ... And it seems to me that we can make an <u>attempt</u> with the U.S. certificates of debt. First, because it does not make a difference whether we sell them there or here. But second, if I have them here for times of need, I only intend to sell them (in the best way possible of course) in times of need. And I can always arrange it so that I wait until the moment their value might decrease. Third, I might be able to get money loans on U.S. paper from acquaintances—friends in Germany maybe. In any case, we can somewhat make up for these losses as soon as I'm healthy enough and timely enough to get into possession of the paper and use them. But it is high time that we receive resources again. The children have very many needs, and they have all sorts of wishes during winter. I will receive my next funds from Cotta on Dec. 12. I just don't have any idea how much and how long it will last. The rest of the [*N.Y. Independent*] money that I was supposed get from Hiller[79] still hasn't arrived. I hope that maybe by Hertha's birthday I will have the chance to be able to buy her something from me and you.

Yesterday I had to answer Herr Zeller regarding the lawsuit. Fick[80] himself says that he is a vile man. I am very angry about this matter. And if he wins the lawsuit with the help of this drunken city councilman Isler,[81] who has tormented me mercilessly, then I will lose over 200 fr. I am doing whatever I can, and I hope his lawsuit will be dismissed. He is seeking 89 fr for new wallpaper and 100 fr for general repairs. Oh, that contract was unfortunate. If one must use every dime to be able to barely make a living, then being robbed of such funds is a sensitive matter. I am always so upset about losing any funds. I cannot get over this feeling of having diligently to save money, as oppressive and as humiliating it is.—And so my life is creeping by. It is full of sor-

---

78. The enclosure has not survived.
79. We have not been able to identify Hiller.
80. Possibly the legal scholar and fellow German Forty-Eighter Heinrich Fick (1822–1895). Helene Fick, *Heinrich Fick: Ein Lebensbild* (Zürich: J. Leemann, 1908).
81. J. Isler was listed as a "Gemeindeammann" for the municipality of Hirslanden in 1855. *Regierungs-Etat des Kantons Zürich für das Jahr 1855/56* (Zürich: Orel, Füßli und Comp., [1856]), 100.

row, full of sadness and tears—with no other joy than my children, no other solace than in Mary. And Mary truly has adjusted to the situation with an exemplary austerity and spirit that I never thought she had in her. She is helping me wherever she possibly can.—

I barely keep company with the Herweghs anymore. Emma comes to visit only occasionally, but she realizes that our friendship is over. She is indeed too insincere.

The poor Frau Rüstow[82] comes to visit us once a week. Her husband has returned from his triumphant journey through the Palatine region.[83] He is writing diligently about the situation in Prussia and about the military. The booksellers are scrambling to get Rüstow's works, which certainly are intelligent, but have been written in military-style. Brockhaus[84] was here himself to court her. Janke[85] in Berlin sends his wife one book after the other as a gift. Streit from Coburg[86] will come here himself to show his strengths. Herwegh owed Rüstow something for certain affairs of the "heart" and has empowered him in such a way that Rüstow is now truly reaping the fruits of the harvest.—That would be all I have to write you from our solitude. The children are healthy so far (Hertha is doing better). They think of you every hour of every day. Percy is thinking of his canton exam and hopes you will make your decision whether he should attend the secondary or the vocational school. I had asked you about this a short while ago. The papers say that Brentano is going to return to Baden.[87] Is that so? Who will become proprietor of the [*Illinois Staatszeitung*]?

---

82. Anna Katharina Rüstow (née Riedmeier). See n. 16 (chapter 3).

83. An area falling mostly in Prussia's Rhine Province at the time.

84. Heinrich Brockhaus (1804–1874) was the liberal politician who, with his brother, ran the famous publishing house his father had established in Leipzig. Annemarie Meiner, "Brockhaus, Heinrich," in *Neue Deutsche Biographie* (1953), 2:624–25.

85. Probably literary publisher Otto Janke. Karl Friedrich Pfau, "Janke, Otto," in *Allgemeine Deutsche Biographie* (1905), 50:631.

86. Feodor Streit was a German nationalist politician and publisher, who was connected to Gustav Struve and owned papers that supported Lassalle. Christian Jansen, "Streit, Feodor," in *Neue Deutsche Biographie* (2013), 25:535–36.

87. Moderate Forty-Eighter Lorenz Brentano did not in fact return to Baden, continuing instead to edit the *Illinois Staatszeitung* and remaining active in American politics. Zucker, *Forty-Eighters*, 281–82.

Mary Booth to Mathilde Franziska Anneke
[Zürich, undated, 1862]
(English original)

Pardon me, my Dear, for writing you such a miserable little note saying I was unhappy. I am indeed very happy when I think of your sweet love. It glorifies every even[ing] and illuminates the the darkest midnights. You are the morning-star of my soul, the beautiful auroral glow of my heart, the saintly lilly of my dream, the deep dark rose bud unfolding in my bosom day by day, sweetning my life with your etheriel fragrance—<u>dearest,</u> you are the <u>reality</u> of my dreams, <u>my life, my Love</u>—I have no more sorrow—<u>*I have You*</u>—My <u>dear</u> and <u>dearest</u> friend—<u>good night</u>
  Your
  Mary

Mary Booth to Mathilde Franziska Anneke
Zürich, December 24, 1862
(English original)

<u>To Franziska Maria.</u>

I have but one little thing,
Scarcely worth the offering,
Yet this little thing I hold,
Never could be bought for gold—
Not for all the pearls and gems
In the world's bright diadems.—

Though it be of little worth
It is all I have on Earth.

It may not be found, or bought,
Yet I give it all unsought.—
Take—and lay it on the shelf—
For it only is—myself!

Mary

To Franziska Maria.

I have but one little thing,
Scarcely worth the offering,
Yet this little thing I hold
Never could be bought for gold —
Not for all the pearls and gems
In the world's bright diadems. —

Though it be of little worth
It is all I have on Earth.

It may not be found, or bought,
Yet I give it all unsought. —
Take — and lay it on the shelf —
For it only is — myself!

Mary

Dec. 24. Christmas eve. '62

Mary Booth to Mathilde Franziska Anneke, Zürich, December 24, 1862.
Courtesy of Wisconsin Historical Society, Madison.

Mathilde Franziska Anneke to Fritz Anneke
Zürich, December 25, 1862

My dear Fritz!

The children are dallying under the branches of their little spruce tree. They are so happy with their modest presents as if they had received a kingdom. We celebrated the festival of lights[88] yesterday evening in our quiet solitude and much poesy—not without melancholy. There was the most delicate tree for us in the forest. We did not have many little candles and not many dalliances either. Presents: A woolen scarf for Percy, and a beautiful album that he wanted for his pictures and that his friend Snell and the other boys and little girls had promised him. The two little girls received the same presents: Each of them got a little album with pictures of Mama and Papa in it. And little wool caps. That was all. How happy and merry they were when they came running over here at Percy's signal. Percy led them by the hand. And before they ran over to the little tree, they put their little gifts in front of me. Little letters, newspapers, stitcheries, handcrafts made of cardboard, and lastly a poem by Percy. His first nice verses:

> DEAR MAMA!
>
> Dear Mama, who knew?
> We brought beautiful things for you;
> Christmas is here and we are blessed,
> and today we are all your guests.
> And may the New Year
> for you be full of cheer.
> We wish you everything on earth,
> for all you are worth.
> From your three little children.

And then the images of our dear lost ones emerged from the eternal shadows. I could see our unforgettable little Fritz at his last Christmas in front of me. I can hear the wonderful sound of his voice as he was saying: "I cannot compose songs, but Percy will be a poet." The beloved prophet! Everything that he had promised—could we see his

---

88. Germans use "Lichterfest" for a variety of celebrations. Here, Mathilde refers to Christmas Eve.

dreams fulfilled in the "little ones"? The same way he wrote the poem quietly and all by himself, he secretively made the loveliest little Swiss construction out of cardboard during the school vacation, and a castle as well. And he helped the little ones with their little letters and drawings.—And so there were we two mothers with our children. We had nothing else to give each other than once more our true friendship.

And since Percy's poem said the little group were my guests, I had to care for the well-being of my visitors. I made a steamy little bowl out of hot sugar water and spirits. Roasted chestnuts, apples, and nuts completed the meal. And so the five of us sat at our festive table. We were happy on this beautiful evening, and we raised our glasses about a hundred times. The toasts of the little "guests" were original.—But where should I start? First, they raised their glasses to the Christ Child[89]—then the mamas, then the papas. And then, much to my surprise, the little rebellious souls also started to yell: "Down with Louis Nap[oleon]!"[90] What he could have done to them that they so genuinely wished him in hell? I do not know.—

I received your letter dated Dec. 2 on the 19th already. It reported your transition to Wisconsin.[91] I wish you good luck and good fortune with that. In this letter it sounded like you were in a better mood. It wasn't bitterly hurtful like the previous one, and so I can hope that this suits your wishes better than I'd thought. But alas— it may already have all have dissolved in displeasure by now. Next to the melancholy of exile there is the worry about my loved ones who are far away!—That is how I feel from sunrise to sunset.

Mother's honest and loving spirit has had a soothing influence on you. I was deeply touched how the old woman believes she must act and influence others. I could be endlessly happy about a letter from both of you.—

And here the faithful Kapp girls[92] have interrupted me. They have demonstrated their old love for me by bringing me nice presents. Ag-

---

89. The German gift giver equivalent to Santa Claus or Father Christmas.
90. The emperor of France.
91. Wisconsin Governor Edward Salomon managed to get Fritz a colonelship in the 34th Wisconsin Infantry Regiment. Fritz would have preferred an artillery command but thought this option might give him the chance to see battle. A Forty-Eighter and good friend of Mathilde's mother, Salomon was surprised to find himself in office after his predecessor drowned. Schulte, *Fritz Anneke*, 70–71.
92. Agnes and Cäcilie.

nes and Cily send you their love. And Ottilie also recently asked me to tell you that she is thinking of you.

Franziska has sent a letter and announced that she has sent a box with presents for the children. She is still providing us with necessary clothing as usual.

We have had mostly terrible weather during the past two weeks. Snowstorms and cold weather. It hasn't been possible to warm up our living room, and so we were often close to despair. I have used the last of my money to pay for coal and wood. Cold and parsimony to the extreme: Woolen undergarments and warm shoes—all of these wishes, as modest as they may be, are unaffordable at <u>these</u> high prices. We often say to each other that terrible illnesses will be the consequence—but what can be done about it?! Any and all resources that I still had access to were absolutely necessary for our daily livelihood. I have been without any resources for several days now.—I have overcome my desperation—and I am now calmly reporting the facts to you.

You wrote to me several moons ago to ask whether I would be able to make it until January. I answered you that if we stayed very economical money would last until Dec. You had been reassured by the unreliable man Ritzinger, who had said that he had sent an advance payment my way. You further believed Booth's careless and untruthful claim that he is sending us 10 doll every week.—Neither did St. Ritzinger's money arrive, nor will Booth send us anything anytime soon. For one year now, Mary has been receiving 50 doll in bills of exchange in two parts each. The second to last was received within 14 days though. [*illegible*] Of that money, we used 40 for housekeeping and to make purchases for the children. Of course, we received a larger sum from you in August of this year. But you must keep in mind that I have been without a centime since February. (Except for the 100 doll that I received from Kamp for the rent). Until <u>August</u> with no help and this horrible illness! You further must keep in mind what was left for me after deduction of the very high percent. Now think about what we had to pay—what payments to make up for. Rent for the house and furniture 1100 per year.—Two years of payments for our maid. 250.—Percy's tuition, etc., paid in cash 250.—The lawsuits. The move. Hail damage. Taxes. Illness. Health cure, and finally the deposit of 150 fr. Now you see all that we needed to even get to this day. If I hadn't received the payment from Cotta for my November work at the beginning of this month—we would have lived in the greatest poverty. Now that is actually about to happen.—You were reassured thinking we were receiving money, but I do not have a dime.—

What can be done? My complaints probably won't reach you.—"My cry for help" will probably only be heard in several months and then in 6 months there will be lots of help. I work—every hour of every day—that is all I can do. The pharmacist's bill—the bill for bread and the <u>doctor</u>'s bill for Hertha's machine—; the doctor; they all are standing at the door like terrible visions—where—where should I get resources? Especially now that you believe we have money in abundance while up until now it was me who was supporting—nothing but supporting the family.—Oh God! Oh God! Am I just writing my letters in order to constantly and very reluctantly report our needs and our poverty to you?

We cannot stay here any longer under such circumstances, with such consuming fears and worries, and such humiliating feelings. I do not in this way want to lose the last of my power to live. In times of need, I can live in poverty. I can support our two children alone if need be. But I cannot be considered "wealthy" while I am always only struggling with poverty. If you were honest and true to yourself, then you would say that I have remained courageously and steadfastly at your side during the days of sorrow—that I have never asked anything of you that was difficult or impossible for you. I do not demand luxury—not even for a single day. We have renounced everything. But—if it is possible for you—to save us from poverty; if your resources allow it to do just a little bit for a better education for our little ones—then do it! But do it at the right moment and not when we are almost drowning, and the salvation almost does not seem to be a blessing anymore.

I am endlessly sorry that I must tell you about the blatant reality at this poetical moment of celebrating Christmas. But I cannot lose another moment. In 2 months I have to pay the rent for the house again—and so as to avoid another day of such fright, it is time, high time to remember it. And even if I tell you this today, probably in the midst of the current celebration with the other little grandchildren of Grandmother, it won't sour the mood. And even if this letter still reaches you during this festive time, it is the highest time. I just received the last 20 fr from Mary for our daily little purchases—she is denying herself the most necessary things for that. It is hard to tell you this, but we haven't been able to let ourselves be seen in public for a long time. We do not wish to attract attention to our shabby looks.

Emma Bunteschu[93] is dead. She died on Dec. 19. The *Kölnische [Zeitung]* and the *[Allgemeine Augsburger]* announced the death of the poetess Emma Emilie von Halberg.—The cause of death? I do not know.— Another gifted woman and poetess lost. I suspect that Emil will accuse her even at the graveside and say that she had seduced him—much like he did when she was still alive.[94] Oh, you poor rogues!—

—If only we poor people had never, never come to Zürich.—I had thought that Doctor Rahe would have enough decency to wait until I asked him for the bill. And then he sends it around Christmas time already. 92 visits between March 12 and Dec. 12! He expects at least 2 fr per visit because he almost always came here in a carriage—and now the pharmacy! How should I get by? Savings, and earnings of just a few centimes and francs—but demands that cost hundreds. How will I get over this disastrous year?—My arm is a big wound that hurts day and night.—The worries make my blood go to my head—I cannot work. Mary is almost always suffering from tooth pain. I had thought that I was entitled to several days of calm and peace.—I had too much confidence in myself and my lucky star.—I wish I had chosen the dark fate of a laborer in America over the bold adventure to come here.—If you can help—do it!

Yours, Mathilde.

Mathilde Franziska Anneke to Fritz Anneke
Zürich, February 11, 1863

Dear Fritz!

About eight days ago I received 3 lines from you and a treasury note of 100 dollars. In these lines you announced to me that a longer letter from you would be in the freight mail. Your lines from Jan. 26 then reached me. And it had to be on the day of mourning the loss of our

---

93. Emma Bunteschu was the married name of the poet and feminist Emilie Emma von Hallberg, whom the Annekes had met in Cologne in the late 1840s. Ernst Kelchner, "Hallberg, Emilie Emma," in *Allgemeine Deutsche Biographie* (1879), 10:416.

94. Mathilde refers to the relationship between her brother-in-law Emil Weiskirch and Bunteschu back in 1853. Fritz Anneke to Friedrich Hammacher, March 22, 1853, in *Wäre ich auch zufällig ein Millionär geworden, meine Gesinnungen und Überzeugungen würden dadurch nicht gelitten haben—: Friedrich Annekes Briefe an Friedrich Hammacher, 1846–1859*, ed. Erhard Kiehnbaum (Wuppertal: Friedrich Engels-Haus, 1998), 132.

beloved little Irla that such a letter from you had to arrive. The mood doesn't generally differ from the other letters, which I have often received from you in our homeless solitude. But it does show your blatant grimness in a way that I am the last person to deserve.

When the always longed for mailman arrives and the children only need a glimpse to read the address and can yell: "From Papa, from Papa!"—then they cling to me and look at me with hope as if their souls only wanted happy news about their father who is far away from them and who is in their thoughts and dreams. Then a flood of tears pours out of the wife's, the mother's eyes, and the poor little ones silently, and with whatever else they are feeling in their little hearts, walk away without a question, without a sound.

That is a little piece of this image of destroyed family bliss. It could be preserved through a word—a word of love—through the living voice of nature.

I have been constantly trying not to see a single little piece of paper left blank before it traveled this long way. I have tried to tell you each and every little thing happening in the dullness of our quiet life here.—I have only begged when we were in such need and sorrow and could expect help only from you. I have saved you from any other painful impression from here.—Nothing, not even the voices of love have found another echo such as the one that is in front of me in the form of your letter from Jan. 26.

There is nothing left for me to say except for rejecting these accusations that nothing would please me more than to hear about war and brave deeds. If this is to say that you think that I wish to bask in your glow, and if you think you can put words into my mouth like "Schurz is a better man, a braver soldier," etc., then I can simply respond and say that you are wrong. You don't seem to know my inner soul nor the expression of it.

I have always had too much interest in your actions and endeavors—not in the glory of it, no, only in the actual deeds.—You say it doesn't interest me anyway. It is easy to make such claims without any reason, without any foundation—and to rid yourself of a burden—and writing to us apparently seems to be one for you. I for one have drawn a lesson from that and will, as in all things, control myself when it comes to that.—

And then you brought matters to a head in that letter from J[anuary] 26 by assuming that it might interest me when finally your deepest wish has come true and a bullet will take away your tumultuous soul, etc.—If the document were not important to me because it completes my characterization of you, then I would send it back to you so that you—perhaps in the better mood that I profoundly wish for you—then you would see with what nonsense you are trying to scare me.

And by the way, I can make no secret of the fact that your wish for a deathly bullet is a very unmanly one. When your little protégé, son of the Hessian minister, the colonel's adjutant general,[95] a second version of Herr Korf[96] maybe, has taken your courage to face life, then I mourn for no one as much as my primordial healthy boy, my dear Percy.

Any father and any mother should avoid such reprehensible egoism—if this wish is not self-denial—as long as the children have the fullest right to the life and work—if not the natural love and kindheartedness—of their parents.

I would say "the poor children" if at this moment I did not feel that I <u>want to live</u>, live for them.

Mathilde.

---

95. This confusing reference is apparently to Carl (also recorded as Karl and Charles) Lachmund. As subsequent letters show, Fritz developed a close relationship to the twenty-year-old Carl Lachmund, a Hanover-born second lieutenant in his regiment. Adjutant-General's Office, *Roster of Wisconsin Volunteers, War of the Rebellion, 1861–1865* (Madison, Wisc.: 1886), 535.

96. It is possible Mathilde meant Bavarian-born Henry Orff, who had lived in Milwaukee before the war and would become a colonel and one of Fritz's many perceived enemies. U.S. Census, Population Schedules (1860), 7th Ward, Milwaukee, p. 144, dwelling 985, family 941.

CHAPTER 5
An Impetuous Colonel

April–October 1863

IN APRIL 1863, FRITZ SET OFF THE ALMOST FARCICAL SEQUENCE of events that would end his military career. As confrontational as ever, he believed that although he possessed great military talent, he was not rising in the Union army because his political connections were weak and he had denounced corruption. Fritz was especially disturbed by the solidarity that he witnessed among officers who belonged to the Freemasons, a fraternal order with distinctive secret rituals. Fritz had complained several times about one of them in particular, Colonel Isaac E. Messmore of the 31st Wisconsin Infantry Regiment, who commanded Fort Halleck, Kentucky, where Fritz was stationed. Receiving no satisfaction through the chain of command, Fritz penned Messmore a provocative personal note. Messmore responded by suspending Fritz from duty and placing him under arrest. On May 18, Fritz faced a court martial for "mutiny, disobeying orders, and escaping detention." At that point, the escape charge was a technical violation, but the process became more convoluted when Fritz did actually leave Fort Halleck before the result of the court martial was finalized. Believing his detention was illegal, he simply rode off in hopes of receiving permission to reorganize the 34th Wisconsin Infantry Regiment, his latest command. He was arrested again twenty-five miles away at Cairo, Illinois.

News of Fritz's situation humiliated Mathilde. She admonished him privately while defending him publicly. Although Mathilde and Mary's other troubles did not lift, they were lightened by some of the distractions Switzerland offered. In addition to making shorter excursions, Mary Booth had the opportunity to visit the famously beautiful Engadine region to stay with Ferdinand Lassalle's companion, Countess Sophie von Hatzfeldt. A short message that Mary sent Mathilde during this time shows the contrast between Mary and Mathilde's fulfilling relationship and the strained ones the women had with their husbands.

Fritz Anneke to his mother-in-law Elisabeth Giesler
Columbus, Kentucky, April 20, 1863

Dear Mother!

I have been meaning to write you for the longest time, and especially on your birthday. But the circumstances did not allow it. Now I have the time and leisure for it. I've been under arrest for three days now. They have put the restless spirit to rest once again. Above all, please accept my whole-hearted wishes and congratulations on your recent birthday. I doubt that you will have celebrated your birthday in such splendid spring weather as we are having here now. I'm sending you a few flowers and leaves as examples. I've been living in a house outside of Fort Halleck,[1] which has been assigned to me as my accommodation by General Asboth.[2] I have had the house painted white and now have a little flower garden in front. But first I have to tell you how it came about that I was arrested. For 6 to 8 weeks now I have been systematically tormented by bugs, fleas, and other such vermin, namely my colonels, who coincidentally are my superiors, and their hangers-on. I cannot tell you the details now because I would have to write an entire book. Behind this scandal are individual officers in my regiment and with them this Freemason fraternity.[3] All of the higher-ranking officers, except for me alone, belong to the fraternity. Of course, I have been lashing out at them. After all, I do not let anyone step on my toes, bite me, stab, and scratch me. And so it eventually came to this after I wrote the truth to Colonel Messmore[4] in strong language. Messmore is commander of the 31st Regiment and the fort, and a real rascal. Charges were brought against me, and I was put under arrest. People were so revengeful that they placed me under strict arrest. This means that I cannot leave the boundaries of my accommodation, which is a very un-

---

1. Situated just upstream from Columbus, Kentucky, which lies between Memphis and St. Louis on the Mississippi.

2. Hungarian-born Brigadier General Alexander Asboth commanded the military district of Columbus, Kentucky. John H. Eicher and David J. Eicher, *Civil War High Commands* (Stanford, Calif.: Stanford University Press, 2001), 108–9.

3. For a more positive assessment of the order's role in the Civil War, see Michael A. Halleran, *Better Angels of Our Nature: Freemasonry in the American Civil War* (Tuscaloosa: University of Alabama Press, 2010).

4. Isaac E. Messmore of Prairie du Chien, Wisconsin. Wisconsin Adjutant General's Office, *Annual Report of the Adjutant General of the State of Wisconsin* (Madison, Wisc.: William J. Park, 1863), 110.

usual measure against an officer and a colonel in particular. And my requests to these high lords whether the gravity of my crime warranted this have not been answered. General Asboth, the district commander, is a part of this noble band of Freemasons. By the way, he is—and this is between us—an old newsmonger who is most interested in keeping his position and who is for this reason flattering Americans. I feel compelled to appeal to higher authorities.—I might still get out of this entire mess by being ordered to General McClernand with my regiment. He wouldn't keep me under arrest any longer. I have recently written to him about this matter. I have so much more writing to do that I must close for today.

More soon. Warm greetings to young and old from
your faithful son Fritz.

Fritz Anneke to George E. Waring, Jr.
Columbus, Kentucky, April 23, 1863
(English original)

Col. George E. Waring jr.[5]
Com. Post Columbus.

Colonel.

I respectfully inform you that I cannot submit any longer to the exercise of a petty tyranny, which has kept me now for seven days in close confinement, because in a private letter I have in plain English rebuked the insulting imprudence of a man, who by chance—whether justly or not, I do not know yet—is placed over me as a superior. To be treated in such a way like a criminal, must revolt even a lamb. I inform you that I shall break my close confinement, and that I am ready to stand the consequences, whatever they may be, proper applications for redress to the General com. [of] the District not even having been answered.

Very respectfully
Fritz Anneke,
Col. 34th Wis. Inf. Regt.

---

5. Colonel George E. Waring, Jr., who commanded Fort Columbus, would go on to make significant contributions to modern sewage design. "Obituary: George E. Waring Jr," *The Sanitarian* 41, no. 349 (December 1898): 559.

Fritz Anneke to John A. Garrett
Columbus, Kentucky, May 19, 1863
(English original)

Col. John A. Garret[6]
President Court Martial

Colonel.

I respectfully request you to lay the following before the Court Martial for consideration.

There exists at this Post a Secret Society, composed if not entirely at least predominantly of Army Officers, who style themselves "Free Masons," and whose main object appears to be, to promote the interests of their members and to work against their opposers. I have expressed myself frequently in strong terms against any secret societies whatsoever within military organizations, as being injurious, dangerous and even destructive to such organizations, but especially against the above mentioned Society at this Post, and I can adduce proof, that they have succeeded in obtaining and enjoying high favors for their members, while non-members and opposers have been persecuted. I am ready to name several members of long standing of the ancient order of Free Masons, who join in the above assertions of mine and declare the use, which is made of the Order just at this Post, an unwarrantable misuse. To mention only one example, I state, that while I, on the 16th of April was placed in close confinement "for conduct unbecoming an officer and a gentleman," a charge, which only could be based on some expressions in a private letter written by me—Captain Ferslew[7] of my Regt., who was charged with the same offence and besides with "making a false report," never was placed under arrest at all. On the contrary, a short time afterwards, he was detached from my Regt., at a distance about a quarter of mile from my Head Quarters and was made an independent Fort Commander; while I was kept for sixteen days in close confinement, even without ever up to this day receiving copy of charges proffered against me, and might have been kept considerably

---

6. John A. Garrett was colonel of the 40th Iowa Infantry Regiment. A. K. Campbell, "Col. John A. Garrett," *Annals of Iowa* Series 1, vol. 9 (1871): 429–45.

7. W. Eugene Ferslew was the captain of Company A. Wisconsin Adjutant General's Office, *Roster of Wisconsin Volunteers: War of the Rebellion, 1861–1865* (Madison, Wisc.: Democratic Print Co., 1886), 2:526.

longer, if I would not have liberated myself by virtue of law. Captain Ferslew is a member of the Society, I am an opposed to it. I further have to state, that members of the Society often are informed beforehand of such intentions and resolutions of the higher Authorities, as usually are not divulged before their execution. Thus Capt. Robinson[8] of the 16. U.S. Infantry Rgt. on the 16. of April asserted already at 5 P.M., that I had been placed under arrest, while in fact I was two hours later. Thus, on the same day, the same Capt. Robinson knew for certain, that Lieutenant Colonel Orff[9] of the 34th Wis. Inf. Rgt., then under arrest, would be released very soon, and the above named Capt. Ferslew knew, that Lieutenant Colonel Orff not be courtmartialed, but only repremanded.

I feel certain, that members of the Lodge of Free Masons existing at this Post are prejudiced against me and cannot act as impartial judges, which is of so much the greater importance to me, as I have been systematically and even maliciously persecuted, which I shall show in the course of these proceedings. I therefore propose to challenge each member of this Court, whether he is a member of that Lodge, and to object against all those, who will answer my question with "yes," or will decline to answer.

Respectfully
Fritz Anneke,
Col, 34th Wis. Inf. Regt., D. M.

Mathilde Franziska Anneke to Fritz Anneke
Zürich, May 31, 1863

My dear Fritz!

I am close to despair at the thought of you being a prisoner for the entire beautiful month of May and of you having all this trouble. And still I cannot let the children notice anything. In general, I cannot let anyone here know. They all understand things in exactly the wrong way. How will you be faring? How will you have felt when you were

---

8. Solomon S. Robinson served on Col. Waring's staff. *Miscellaneous Documents of the House of Representatives for the First Session of the Fifty-First Congress, 1889–90* (Washington, D.C.: Government Printing Office, 1891), 255.

9. See n. 96 (chapter 4).

alone, shackled, and unarmed in the hands of your enemies—separated even from your only friend?[10]—I have pulled myself together a bit to be able to write to you. My dreadful headache is gone. The children are cheerful, and Mary is also quite healthy for the moment.

I sent you my letter yesterday as a response to your lines of the 28th. Immediately after that I received your letter from prison, dated May 5th. This morning Frank Leslie and the second pencil picture arrived from Fort Halleck. The good draftsman doesn't know how happy he has made us. Please thank him dearly on my and the children's behalf.

I hope you will be lucky again and get out of this petty fight. Your strengths and your defiance should be directed toward things other than such miserable and humiliating quarrels. Disgrace triumphs and you come out on the short end. You always get caught up in such affairs due to your irritability.—This means that you are further away from the bigger deeds, and that the miserable men who are your enemies achieve whatever they want as long as they are able to aggravate you. I think that with dignity and pride, which you have plenty of if you keep calm, and with the *smartness* that you do not have at all, such assaults could be prevented in many cases. Once you've picked fights with vermin, you are already lost.

I am endlessly sorry that you've been separated from your dear friend. Will you reunite with him? I am very worried about the dissolution of your regiment. You will have likely lost your men forever yet again. You can imagine how I wait for a message from you every day and every hour. I often wish that we had followed you when you left here. The time that we have been pulling through since then has certainly been a very sad one. I am still feeling the serious consequences of the severe illness—mercurial treatment?

"If only Papa were in the picture paper"[11] is what Hertha and Lili say to each other as they play school, sitting on their little chairs and at their little table. They sit next to each other for 3 hours every morning.—Recently, Percy has set his heart on going into the *Kadettencorps*.[12] He is only required to once he turns eleven—unfortunately, I cannot al-

---

10. Carl Lachmund. See n. 95 (chapter 4).
11. Illustrated magazines were popular at in the United States and Europe at the time.
12. Switzerland had a tradition of *Kadettencorps* that prepared teenaged boys for military service. In the 1860s, many corps were organized in high schools according to regulations established by canton governments. Their exercises and ideology bore some resemblance to those of the Turnverein. Gorden Craig, *The Triumph of Liberalism: Zürich in the Golden*

low it now, because the cost for his equipment would be prohibitive at this moment. On Tuesday, I have to get close to 60 fr for him. I have to take from Mary what she is yet to receive in the mail.—I have nothing. Herr Weiskirch[13] certainly has lied to you about that. On April 29th, he sent me a letter from Mother. But not a line from him about the money—nor the money itself. As of today, nothing has come into my hands. He is likely waiting to see whether the funds are covered, before he sends the money. You see how right I am, and how dependent I am on these funds. . . .

Mathilde Franziska Anneke to Fritz Anneke
Zürich, July 18, 1863

My dear Fritz!

About eight days ago, I received your dear letter from St. Jung.[14] This time, it was me who fell behind in writing to you. The reason was an adventurous trip that had long been our dream. That is to say that we had promised our respective newspapers to attend the marksmen's festival in Chaup de fonds[15] and report from there. We had not expected to have the opportunity to realize our dream and keep our promise. Then your letter arrives and tells me you have sent $200 to Weiskirch. Even though I was gripped by the concern that Weiskirch would again resort to the Armstrong Gun exchange method[16] and only send part of the large amount—because you know well that he sent me only 300 fr for the last 100 doll in May, which I received on June 15.

Age (New York: Charles Scribner's Sons, 1988), 129–30; Louis Burgener, *Kadetten in der Schweiz*, Beiheft zu *ASMZ: Allgemeine schweizerische Militärzeitschrift* 152, no. 10 (1986): 2–6.

13. Fritz and Mathilde exchanged money from U.S. dollars to Swiss francs through Mathilde's brother-in-law Emil Weiskirch.

14. There is insufficient evidence to identify the person forwarding Fritz's letter.

15. The Great Swiss Marksmen's Festival (das große Schweizer Schützenfest) of 1863 was held in La Chaux-de-Fonds near the French border. *Die Gartenlaube* 34 (1863), 536.

16. British engineer William Armstrong (1810–1900) had developed various different firearms and pieces of artillery that could be breech loaded or could fire shells containing many small pieces. It is unclear exactly which function Mathilde was thinking of when she chose the Armstrong gun as a metaphor for piecemeal or "scatter shot" payments. Marshall J. Bastable, *Arms and the State: Sir William Armstrong and the Remaking of British Naval Power, 1854–1914* (Aldershot: Ashgate, 2004).

Even though I was gripped by this concern, I still thought that because of the smaller payments we've earned for literary stories, Mary and I were finally entitled to rest for a change. We had therefore asked the ambassador Fogg to accompany us to Chaudefonds. It also seemed advisable to take this opportunity to see the city of Bern. F[ogg] picked us up at the train station and invited us to a splendid dinner, where we made many pleasant acquaintances. We met the wife of the American ambassador to Denmark,[17] and their daughter, a Mrs. Condith[18] from Newark, and many others. We spent the night at the Schweizerhof.[19] Mary fell ill that night, and it was so serious that I decided not to risk the arduous journey to Chaudefonds. She was feeling a little better in the morning, and in rethinking our sheer bliss, it seemed possible to see Thun, Interlaken, and maybe also Giessbach,[20] in the hopes that the fresh evening air would strengthen poor Mary again. For this reason, we sent Fogg to the marksmen's festival by himself, and set out for the mountains that were so full of charm and magnificence that I am still relishing that view. We then came home to our dear little children after three days. In my desire to have them with me, I had been thinking about them the entire time. In my imagination I would constantly see my dear and bold mountaineer Percy as the guide and the two little ones dallying and jumping next to me, happy about these beautiful surroundings. Because going on a little alpine journey by foot with the children—that is one of my ideals, dear Fritz. Oh, the children would be perfect portraits in this painted landscape! The charm of these little unruly children in the midst of the splendor of the nature! And don't be surprised that <u>when</u> this gold has run through W[eiskirch]'s hands and has safely come into mine, and <u>when</u> I have rid myself of the most

---

17. The U.S. minister to Denmark was a Republican politician from New York, Bradford R. Wood (1880–1889). "Wood, Bradford Ripley," in *Biographical Directory of the United States Congress*, accessed July 30, 2020, http://bioguide.congress.gov/scripts/biodisplay.pl?index=W000692.

18. Possibly Caroline Condit, a woman in her early twenties who farmed with her husband near New York City. U.S. Census, Population Schedules (1860), 2nd Ward, Orange, Essex County, New Jersey, p. 194, dwelling 1171, family 1672.

19. In the twenty-first century, the Schweizerhof Hotel & Spa still celebrates its history (dating back to 1859) on its website. "History," Schweizerhof Hotel & Spa, accessed July 30, 2020, http://www.schweizerhof-bern.ch/en/hotel/history.

20. Places in the alpine area around Lake Thun and Lake Brienz, to the southeast of Bern.

pressing debts with this magical cure, and when in my mind I have planned the budget for the coming months—then don't be surprised when in your imagination you can see us one beautiful morning with a fruit basket, a travel bag, and a bottle, as we leave to clamber around for three days. Now one of our favorite pastimes—Percy has school vacation and cannot go on a longer journey with his classmates, as you must know—is a gondola ride on the lake. The two little ones—always dressed like twins—are rowing, I am steering, and Percy is rowing and commanding. We attract attention because the little girls moor the gondola with such elegance and strength. If only you could see us like that!

If only we could soon learn from you how you have been faring after this outrageous court martial. You will likely be able to let us know in your next letter. Such infamy and perfidy—probably no one had to experience this before! I can't believe that you did not obtain satisfaction for this. When people ask about you, then I can only always answer that I hope you are close to Vicksburg now.[21] No one believes in you as much as I do. If I knew you to be at a certain location—then I could be sure that you've helped secure that location for the North. I often don't know how to avoid the questions anymore. "Has he not been in battle yet in two years?" No or Yes. That's what the questioners want to know. They do not have time to lend their ear to hear explanations of one thing or another. And so, I do not let them get to their questions, because they will not allow me to answer them anyway.

I thought of you and your friend at the Giessbach [Falls], wishing that both of you would be standing here with us. I can't quite say that I was very much enchanted with the Giessbach. Oh no, it was the entire landscape in which everything is just a piece of the puzzle. I climbed up all the way to the top. Then I was standing behind the falls for a long time, looking at the world through the magical mist of the waterfalls, while Mary stayed on the patio feeding a chamois that is caged there. Lake Brienz then was also delightful. At its shore I caught sight of our old friend of alpine roses, the nice chamois hunter from Stans[22] (you will surely remember him; the one who brought us these splen-

---

21. In the spring and early summer of 1863, General Grant drove to capture Vicksburg, Mississippi, the Confederacy's last stronghold on the Mississippi River. His success on July 4 was "the most important northern strategic victory of the war." James M. McPherson, *Battle Cry of Freedom: The Civil War Era* (New York: Oxford University Press, 1988), 626–37.

22. On Lake Lucerne in Switzerland.

did alpine flowers down from the mountains). He recognized me and gave me a magnificent edelweiss. And then on the tour itself we attracted many interesting people, constantly making new acquaintances. Among them was the old St. Hilaire,[23] the great French historian whom I remember fondly. I read his story 30 years ago about Josephine[24] and how she discovered Napolean. I always and always kept thinking about that anew. The old man did not want to let us go, until he finally, after trying unsuccessfully several times, had started a conversation with us. His English was just as nice as his German and French. Mary had recovered so well on the first day in Interlaken that we were able to tackle the Ruchen (2500').[25] We climbed it with ease, and from the top we could see the Jungfrau mountain.
Several days later.

Mary has left for the Engadine region. Countess Hatzfeldt wouldn't leave her in peace. She had long invited her to go on a journey with her. The stay in Tarasp might heal Mary, and now that she'd received this friendly invitation, she had to accept. Hepp accompanied us to the boat and impressed on her that she must drink from the spring of St. Moritz, and he told her that she could only get well again in that air there. The children and I took her to Rapperswyl yesterday. Once she's passed Chur, the Countess will come for her. The children were very cheerful, especially at the old castle with the court watchman, who despite his 80 years keeps watch every night and toots his horn and walks up the tower 20 times a day. We are now alone.

Today is July 21. Not a word from Weiskirch yet.—How unhappy I am with these middle-men. And you just had to put our alimony into their hands. Herr Ritzinger, Herr Weiskirch—etc. They are all the same.—Why can't you send what you have to send directly to us yourself? Booth sent 20 dollars, which I split with Mary before her departure and for our household. If only the larger sum would get here. I would leave it with our Pestalozzi and would pay the larger and most necessary sums. It would bring me much peace of mind.

---

23. Jules Barthélemy Saint-Hilaire (1805–1895) was a French philosopher and politician who opposed the Second Empire under Louis Napoleon III. *Encyclopædia Britannica*, 11th ed., 3:449.

24. The first Empress of the French, Joséphine (1763–1814), had been married to Louis Napoleon from 1796 to 1810. Henry Foljambe Hall, "Introduction," in *Napoleon's Letters to Josephine, 1796–1812* (London: J. M. Dent & Co., 1901), vii–xxv.

25. It is unclear which of the several peaks by that name Mathilde refers to here.

The little ones have studied diligently this morning. Percy was their teacher for several hours. Now they are playing and sending you their greetings. They want to send you their love soon. They also want to send you the pictures of them in their travel clothing, so that you'd be able to see them on their big journey. If only they could do everything they wanted to do for their Papa.

Mary will stay in the Engadine for 3 or 4 weeks. She sends you her love. Today, the *Telegr.*[26] announces happy news from over there. Vicksburg has surrendered.[27] Where could you be now?—I'm looking forward to the letter you promised and in which you promised to speak your mind and give me your opinion of the warfare and politics over there. I did tell several people who understand these things about your description of the court martial's defamations. A Swiss man, an esteemed teacher at the local secondary school who formerly taught in America as well, Scudor[28] is his name, a special friend of our children's who has not only visited them while Mary and I were on our trip but also went on two excursions with them, was very interested in your story. We all very much appreciate his concern for all of us. He and his young wife visit us once a week to see how we're doing. Rüstow has also visited the children and invited them for one day. They all have a strange affection for him. He often chases the children on the grass and is Hertha's friend especially.

Now I also have to tell you that Herr Zeller in his fight against us has not only brought forward false witnesses, but also fabricated bills which would bring him a criminal lawsuit if investigated more thoroughly. His lawsuit will be dismissed as Herr Fick says. And I will still have some money left from the amount deposited at court after I have paid Fick.

We are very healthy. The swelling of the gland on my neck has dissolved in the wonderful alpine air. The children are getting strong and tall. They are currently helping the owners of our house with the haymaking. Hertha is quite the agriculturalist. Please give our best to your dear friend[29] and write to your poor little family a little more often. It is disproportionate after all to write to your friend daily and to the rel-

---

26. Mathilde indicated earlier that she received issues of the *Buffalo Telegraph*, to which Fritz contributed, but perhaps she saw a copy of London's *Daily Telegraph*.
27. News of the July 4 surrender had only just reached Mathilde. See n. 21 (chapter 5).
28. We could not locate additional information.
29. Likely Carl Lachmund.

atives who are far away only once a month.—I must have followed your example or else you would have had a letter from us 8 days ago already. Farewell my dear Fritz. Yours, Mathilde.

Mary Booth to her daughter Ella Booth
Zürich, July 19, 1863
(English original)

My dear Ella: I have just returned from church with Lillian. She wants to send you the box with carved chickens on it that we brought her from Interlaken. She says it would make her the greatest pleasure of any thing in my power to bestow if I would only allow her to send it

Drawing by Lillian Booth for her sister Ella, March 27, 1863.
Courtesy of Wisconsin Historical Society, Madison.

to you. I told her that she ought to keep something herself. "What do I need?" said she, "I have every thing." And the fact is, she has <u>nothing</u>.

I expect to start to meet the Countess in the Engadin at the castle of Valpera day after to morrow. I was to have gone to morrow, but cannot "on account of my health." She will send some one to meet me. I shall probably remain with her three weeks. Madam Anneke remains here with the children. I have written no children's letters[30] for sometime because I am afraid they do not especially interest you or any one else. If you liked or cared for them I suppose you would say so. Madam A. thought I had better not write so many, but if folks like them I shall begin again. All send love. Love to all

Your aff. Mother.

Fritz Anneke to Mathilde Franziska Anneke
Columbus, Kentucky, July 27, 1863

It has been endlessly long since I last heard from you, my dear Mathilde. Your letters are roaming around somewhere in the world I suppose. . . .

My situation remains unchanged. I am under arrest—that is only suspended from duty—and I am awaiting my sentence. You can imagine how monotonous and boring my life is here. I am in excellent health. But this inaction and uncertainty are enough to drive one to despair. I have just as much uncertainty about the final result of my trial as before. Several of the hints I have received give me such an uncertain picture that I cannot make anything of it. As you must know, nothing can become known about court martial verdicts until they are published. The judges have to put an oath on it. I kept asking the judge to give me his decision and his word of honor. His diligence kept him from doing that. Since then a different judge has dropped remarks in the presence of an officer of my regiment that led me to believe that the verdict will at a minimum be dismissal from service. But then again, I received a message from Adolf Cramer[31] saying that Governor Salomon had

---

30. Publications in *Daily Life*. See n. 65 (chapter 4).

31. Likely Prussian-born Adolph J. Cramer, who worked for an insurance agency. U.S. Census, Population Schedules (1870), 1st Ward, Milwaukee, Wisc., p. 109, dwelling 726, family 889.

not been able to visit me here, even though he had very much wanted to. But the circumstances did not allow it, and he didn't think it was quite necessary because he had met two of my judges on his journey to Vicksburg and had taken from their reports that the verdict against me would amount to nothing and that I would be released from the arrest and be back in service immediately. It's not possible to make sense of this. Cramer further writes that Salomon could not be influenced by defamatory rumors and reports and that Salomon was awaiting my message and would answer right away. I did finally send him that message in form of a two-page letter; the first letter since I've been under arrest. I did not ask anything of him other than for him to use his influence so that they would not eventually keep me here when my regiment is sent back to Wisconsin for the purpose of "withdrawal from service" or dismissal. I do not have a response yet, but I am awaiting a response daily. I will write to him again tomorrow in order to—as a recently enacted law about the re-entry of officers and soldiers dictates—report for continued duty and the reformation of my regiment and to give him the number and names of my officers that I do not want to have in my regiment again under any circumstances. If they'll allow me, I intend to organize a fully equipped Jäger regiment[32] this time. Cramer wants to join my regiment as quartermaster. I won't have to tell you who would be my adjutant this time.—My dear Karl[33] was with me for several days. He was trying to get leave. Since then the lieutenant colonel in command of the regiment has done me the favor of transferring him here, and I expect him back any day now.

The story about the petition in favor of the lieutenant colonel turned out to be a lie made up by Knell:[34] I have so many assurances, both oral and written, in English and in German, that there is not a jot of truth in it, and that all the people are still as much my faithful supporters as they used to be. I now don't have a single doubt about that. It is

---

32. In eighteenth-century German Europe, Jäger regiments were composed of elite light infantrymen who specialized in skirmishing and returned to civilian life once a conflict was over. In the U.S. Civil War, the term said more about the ethnic identity of a regiment than its operational characteristics. Christopher Duffy, *The Military Experience in the Age of Reason* (New York: Atheneum, 1988), 272–73.

33. Carl Lachmund.

34. Originally from Hesse-Darmstadt, sutler John Knell was active in Milwaukee Republican politics and German American social life. After the war, he would work as a liquor salesman. John Knell Papers, Wisconsin Historical Society, Madison.

not clear to me, however, why Knell lied like that and whether the lieutenant colonel wanted him to lie or whether he knew about it or not.

Things have taken a turn for the better here recently—the first time yet that I have experienced this. The silly boy who was commander, Colonel Waring, has been replaced by a decent man it seems: Colonel Scott of the 32nd Iowa Regiment.[35] We've heard several times that we would surely get rid of rascals like Asboth. But sadly, he is still here. Messmore on the other hand, a candidate for the penitentiary, has removed himself. Apparently, to resolve the "small difficulties" that prevent his regiment from being paid. But the real reason for his departure is to avoid and flee from his soldiers, who would have taken revenge sooner rather than later. He has fallen ill somewhere on his journey to Washington. Rumor now has it that his regiment will be sent back to Washington and will be dissolved there. Several of his people now contact me every day to ask to be part of my future regiment as soon as they have the opportunity. If both regiments would be dissolved at the same time, then it would be easy for me to get half of the men from the 31st.

I have had yet another conflict, and as a result, charges have been pressed against me. It seems to be my fate to get into conflicts with every piece of villainy and meanness protected by the stripes of rank in my proximity. An individual named Adams[36] is in charge of organizing a Negro regiment here. I met this individual 14 months ago when I was chief of artillery under McClernand in West Tennessee during the "glorious" battle of Corinth, and I came to know him as a dull and dumb person. Instead of choosing the best and most capable men for the Negro regiments, honest and decent men, in several cases protégés were chosen or men who are good for nothing.[37] And this Adams is in

---

35. John Scott (1824–1903) was a colonel in the 32nd Iowa Volunteer Infantry Regiment who was elected lieutenant governor of Iowa after the Civil War. Benjamin F. Gue, *History of Iowa from the Earliest Times to the Beginning of the Twentieth Century* (New York: The Century History Company, 1903), 4:235–36.

36. Lieutenant Colonel Charles H. Adams of the First Illinois Light Artillery. *The Union Army* (Madison, Wisc.: Federal Publishing Company, 1908), 3:356.

37. In almost all cases, the officers of Black regiments (United States Colored Troops or USCT) were white. Although the USCT tried to recruit officers who were committed to supporting African Americans and the position required passing additional tests, many applicants were primarily attracted to the prospect of a promotion and raise in salary. Joseph T. Glatthaar, *Forged in Battle: The Civil War Alliance of Black Soldiers and White Officers* (New York: The Free Press, 1990), 39–43.

the latter category of men. He was the colonel of the 1st Illinois Artillery Regiment until now. As he took up my quarters, the ones where I used to live—you have a picture—this was one of the first deeds of this man: He threw the good, honest Negro family out of their house without even giving them the time to look for another place to live. I'd always had good neighborly relations with them. They lived close behind my place. But his "*ladies*" did not want to have the "*niggers*" so close by. Then he instructed his Negro servant to steal from my oats and hay. My orderly caught him stealing my hay. My dog "Hawk," a Tennessee "hound dog" and a present from Karl, got him as he was stealing my oats. The dog bit the poor devil so badly that the wound has still not healed. Then the "Negro King," as I call him, demanded from my orderly that the stables, which are also close to his quarters, be given to him. My orderly referred him to me. But he was hesitant to come to me and instead ordered my orderly to take the stables away. My orderly again referred him to me. Then the commander, Colonel Waring, came and gave my orderly the same order. My orderly referred him to me as well. The silly man responded that I was under arrest and that he could not speak to me. He then gave a captain the order to remove the stables. I teeth-gnashingly put up with this audaciousness only to avoid getting involved in another scandal. They tore down the stables and put them up again in a different location. Soon after that the Negro King relocated the camp of his people and put it up near my stables about 50 feet from his camp. And then, a few days later, he put up a chain of guards surrounding my stables. Since then my orderly has had the greatest difficulty getting from his tent and the stables to me and back to his tent and the stables. About a week ago, while I had gone to the town, my orderly saw from the fort that my horse was running around freely and that a different horse was in its place. He tried to get there, but the Negro King's guards wouldn't let him. He then ran into the town to look for me but couldn't find me. This is when I heard about this story, went to the stables, found my good fox there, who had come back voluntarily to look for his lunch, [*illegible*]. I gave him his food and then looked for the Negro King without success. After lunch I went to the stables once more with my orderly, looked again for the Negro King without success, and then started a conversation with several of his officers. At the same time, his officer du jour came to ask me who had allowed my orderly to pass through his camp. I responded to him that no one had done that and that he'd just accompanied me to look for the horse. Then the Vice-Negro King came as colonel of the regiment and asked me the same question. I gave him the same answer. He again asked what right I had to pass the man through. My answer was: "Pass through? Right? Well, I have already told you that there can be no talk of <u>passing</u> through. He just came in with me without being stopped by anyone and quite naturally because as my orderly he is responsible for taking care of my horse, as you will well know." Then the brat was bold enough to ask me: "Well, you are under arrest, what right do you have to be here?" You can imagine that I reacted accordingly given such insolence. Then the Negro King himself came and again asked the first question. My answer was the same. He then told his guard to arrest my orderly and had the audacity to tell me: "I already ordered yesterday that your stables be removed by noon today." "You, Sir, have orders for me?" was my answer. "Who do you think you are? And what's more this is a lie because I haven't even seen you in three or four days." He still insisted that he had told me that in the presence of an officer. I repeated that this was a lie. He then said that he did not want to keep having this conversation with me anymore, and I responded: "I am not even interested in a conversation with you. Just keep your mouth shut and then we will be done here instantly." Meanwhile, a mass of Black soldiers had gathered around us. They were apparently happy to see that their tyrant—people hate him like poison, have already began deserting and have been complaining to rascal Asboth that he is treating them worse than their previous "*masters*"—that their tyrant had encountered someone who was telling him the truth. The Negro King ordered the people to leave and repeated his last sentence regarding the conversation. And I gave him the same answer as before. Then he ordered me to leave his camp. I told him that according to his own instructions, officers were able to enter and leave the camp as they please and that I would not leave until he had changed his instructions. Then he did that and said that no white man was allowed to enter his camp anymore. Then I left. I found the commander, Colonel Scott, in the town and reported this event to him. I requested that my orderly be set free immediately and that the Negro King be ordered to change his line of guards in such a way that it did not surround my stables anymore. Colonel Scott accepted my request without any hesitation. Regarding the insulting behavior of the Negro King and his Vice-King I wrote a letter to each of them and demanded an apology or else they would be "*miserable, despicable scoundrels*" to me. I sent them the letters through an officer but did not receive a response. I thought they would be ready for a duel and prepared my pistols. But instead the orderly submitted the charge for "challenge to a duel." I haven't heard anything since, and I believe Colonel Scott dismissed the charge as being too silly.

I enclose merchandise for Percy. Please give my love to the children, including Mary, and all friends. As soon as I receive a letter from you again or anything important happens here, I will write to you again.

Always yours, Fritz.

Mary Booth to Mathilde Franziska Anneke
Vulpera, Tarasp, August 1, 1863
(English original)

Sweet Franziska Maria:

We are nearly all packed up, ready to send the trunks away this evening, and shall start ourselves on Monday morning for Samaden. As far as I can now see there is no prospect of our remaining there any length of time. But as I write you from day to day I shall tell as soon as I know myself. I had two letters from Miss de Ruda[38] last evening, one of which has lain here four days on account of the Postman's not knowing my name—supposed it was "May Morning" on account of your letters to me being directed so. But this post is a comic institution any way.

We shall call on Miss de Ruda on our arrival, & probably take her & her mother to dine with us in Samaden—that is if the L[39] considers the dinner a proper <u>institution</u>. We may go on Monday evening to Silva Plana,[40] & <u>may</u> not. I can't say. To day the weather is <u>wonderful</u> again, & I hope it will so continue. Miss de Ruda writes that it snowed there a few days ago.

---

38. We could not identify this person.
39. Ferdinand Lassalle.
40. Silvaplana is the name of a lake and a small municipality not far from Samedan.

Rüstow has at length spoken out and says he shall go to Lake Como[41] whether the rest do or not, so I suppose in that case, the whole tribe will go. If Lasalle does, he will not stay long, but will go on to East End where he is to make a sea-bath cure.

The Gräfin[42] will be in Zürich in time to make her nach cure[43] at Ragatz.

Rüstow is writing the most comic satirical brochure in Latin over German Politics & Politicians, &c. He and Lassalle nearly die over it. He writes evenings as a play work, & intersperses Latin poems of his own composition.

I cannot now tell you where to direct your letters to me, but will as soon as we know, and Rüstow says it is absolutely necessary he should know soon. The way that fellow works is beyond everything—all the world, nor his own pleasure, nor anything can keep him from doing what he feels as his duty towards his family, and he always will—in that—not the whole world can more,[44] or influence him.

Neither he nor Lasalle know anything about American affairs. He more a great deal than Lasalle, who knows nothing, & thinks Freedom & all ultimate Right is to revolve only round the higher European Wissenschaft[45]—a stupid idea—that is always confounded, and swallowed up in itself before it reaches the People. I find him in many of his great ideas awfully limited and contracted. But you might as well stop Niagara as to try to say any thing to him contrary to his own opinions. It tickles him that they call him the "President der Menchheit"[46] for he almost imagines himself the Creator of All Mankind!

I hope I shall have a letter from you this evening, & find one in waiting at Samaden.

In love your
Mary

The Gräfin sends love.

---

41. The lake in Lombardy has long been famous as a resort destination.
42. Countess.
43. Here, a "Nachkur" is a follow-up treatment at a resort.
44. Mary apparently means "move," not "more."
45. Science or scholarship in German.
46. President of humanity (Menschheit) in German.

Fritz Anneke to Edwin Stanton
Fort Halleck, Columbus, Kentucky, August 22, 1863
(English original)

In Prison
Hon. Edwin M. Stanton
Secretary of War.

Sir

Considering myself greatly wronged, and being unable to obtain justice of the minor Authorities I have to deal with[,] I apply to you for redress.

In order to introduce myself to you I am necessitated to make a few brief introductory remarks in regard to my former life. Having been an officer in the Prussian Artillery for about twelve years, I was dismissed from the service of that State on account of my democratic-republican views as being in contradiction with those a Prussian Officer should have. In '48 I was imprisoned for eight months for being considered a dangerous foe to monarchical institutions, and then I took an active part in the revolutionary struggle against monarchal rule in the capacity of Colonel and Chief of Artillery. Our defeat brought me and my family ultimately to the U.S., where I spent most of my time as editor of and contributor to newspapers. In '59, when the Italian war broke out, I returned to Europe, went first to Italy, thence to Switzerland. My family followed. From the very moment, when war against the seceded States of the Union appeared inevitable my only endeavor was to get back to the U.S., in order to participate in the war for the free institutions of my country of adoption. . . .[47]

On the 16th of April I was informed by one of the officers of my Rgt., that the before mentioned Col. Mesmore had used towards him language very insulting and threatening to the officers of my Rgt. I as the senior officer of the 34th Wisconsin Inf. and the natural representation of its corps of officers considered myself bound to take the matter up, and so I addressed a private note to Col. Messmore properly rebuking him and sent it over to him by a commissioned officer. A few hours afterwards I was placed in close confinement by order of Col. Martin,[48]

---

47. Fritz took several more pages to introduce himself and his situation.
48. James S. Martin was a Republican who would serve in Congress after the war. "Mar-

111th Ill. Inf., comdg. the Post. . . . Complaints about my arrest to Gen. Asboth, the District Commander, and Gen. Hurlbut,[49] the Corps Commander, never received a reply. Getting tired at last of the continuous exercise of a petty tyranny against me, I concluded to breathe a little fresh air, openly and frankly informed the Post Commander of my intention and took about one hours' ride on horseback. Subsequent to this Gen. Asboth and the post Commander promised to the Lieut. Col. of my Rgt., that my arrest should be extended to the limits of this Post, if I would withdraw the letter I had written to the Post Commander in the morning. This I did, but Gen. Asboth did not keep his promise. He acted in the same way several times, a conduct, for which an officer would be expelled in disgrace from a decent corps.

On the 2d of May, when I had been confined for 16 days, I discovered the existence of a law embodied in Gen. Order No. 91 Series 1862, which says, that the arrest of officers shall cease, if a copy of charges is not handed to them within eight days. No such copy having been served on me I reassumed command of my Rgt. and reported for duty, upon the strength of the law. Immediately after I had reported I was informed, that the above named Col. Messmore once more had used abusive language towards some of my officers and had asserted, that several officers of my Rgt. had played the part of informers to him telling him things, that were lies and calumniations. I fortwith went to Col. Mesmore, accompanied by some witnesses, as I knew the Colonel's veracity to be very poor, for the purpose of demanding the names of the calumniating officer of my Rgt. When Col. Messmore in the course of the private conversation I had with him repeatedly refused to give me the names of those officers, I told him, that <u>he</u> was a liar and calumniator, if he insisted upon his refusal. He then undertook to order me under arrest, which order I declined to obey as I considered it to be entirely illegal, a misuse of his accidental superiority over me for private revenge. A few hours later I by order of the Post Commander was

---

tin, James Stewart," in *Biographical Directory of the United States Congress*, accessed July 30, 2020, http://bioguide.congress.gov/scripts/biodisplay.pl?index=M000184.

49. Major General Stephen Augustus Hurlbut was a Republican politician from Illinois. In addition to holding many political positions, he helped form the Unions veterans' organization the Grand Army of the Republic. "Hurlbut, Stephen Augustus," in *Biographical Directory of the United States Congress*, accessed July 30, 2020, http://bioguide.congress.gov/scripts/biodisplay.pl?index=H001003.

arrested and placed in close confinement again under double guard. When I had been nine days confined in that way, the limits of my arrest were extended to the limits of this Fort, and during the progress of my Court Martial trial to the limits of this Post.

My trial commenced on the 18th of May. The charges proferred against me were: mutiny, disobedience of orders and leaving my confinement. Before the trial was opened I handed a statement to the Court relating to a certain secret organization at this Post, by which I showed the hostility of that organization against me and declared my intention to reject as my judges all those members of the Court who belonged to that organization. This paper, upon a simple remark on the part of the Judge Advocate, himself, to the best of my Knowledge, a member of the organization, was returned to me without being considered. I handed a protest against this proceeding, but my protest was treated in the same way as the statement. . . .

. . . My defence was cut short in every respect and limited to the narrowest boundaries. I however succeeded at last in gaining one foothold by ascertaining through my pertinacy in putting questions, that charges and specifications against me, subsequent to my first arrest on April 16th, had been made out, and by attaining a resolution of the Court, that those charges should be produced. They were sought for at District Head Quarters, but could not be found there, and were ultimately discovered in Col. Messmore's possession. They just as well as the second charges, upon which I was court martialed were written by one of Col. Messmore's clerks and signed by the Post Commander. When they were read, the whole Court saw at once, what a miserable fabrication they were, so miserable indeed, that the Authorities felt ashamed to bring them forward, and preferred to bury them, but to keep me meanwhile under the pretext of charges in close confinement for an indefinite length of time. Out of the letter, I had written to Col. Messmore on the 16th of April, his pettifogging genius had construed four different crimes, among them the unavoidable "mutiny." All of the members of the Court could not help smiling on such monstrous charges, in which even my words were falsified. On the succeeding morning one of the members of my Court had disappeared. Although the Court by private information knew, that he had been ordered by Gen. Asboth on a fictitious expedition, they first would not listen to my objections, because "they had not been officially informed of the absence of the member and the cause thereof." Yet I insisted, that they should procure such official information, because otherwise "they never might get it," and upon this it was elicited from Gen. Asboth. This occurred at the time, when I was right in the midst of my defence and had six of my witnesses to examine yet among them the most important ones, who were to disprove the base lies, which Col. Messmore and some of his myrmidons[50] had stated under oath. I fortwith protested against all further proceedings of that rump-court, and declared that I should not take any part in them, unless the ordered off member would take his seat again, being firmly convinced that he was sent away purposely, he being of all the members of the Court most in favor of me and convinced of the justice of my cause. The Court applied to Gen Asboth for advice and received the answer, that "although it was none of his business to give them advice, he nevertheless was of the opinion, that the Court should proceed and finish the trial as speedily as possible." I kept mute, and the trial was finished in a few hours.

There the matter rested, and I quietly waited under arrest for the ultimate decision in my case.

About six weeks ago I informed the Governor of the State of Wisconsin, that I intended immediately to reorganize my Regt., when its time of service would run out, that I intended to make it a Regt. of mounted riflemen, if the War Dept. should allow me to do so, but that I was afraid, my present Superior would keep me under arrest even after the time when my Regt. would be mustered out, and thus would prevent me from taking the reorganization in my hands. Gov. Salomon immediately applied to Gen. Grant requesting him to give his decision in my case as speedily as possible, because he, the Gov., wanted me as a good and efficient officer for reorganizing the Rgt. When the time came for my Rgt. to return home in order to be mustered out on the 15th of August, no decision on my trial had been given yet, though that trial was finished two months and eight days before, nor had a reply to Gov. Salomon's request been received, I considered, that I was entitled to return with my Rgt. to my home state, and the present Commander of this Post, Col. Scott of the 32d Iowa Inf. Rgt., was of the same opinion. Gen. Asboth however—so I was told—would not allow me to go.

50. From the Greek myths of the Trojan wars, the word means unquestioning followers. Jenny March, *Cassell Dictionary of Classical Mythology* (London: Cassell, 1988), 262–63.

Under these circumstances I concluded to go anyhow to Cairo.⁵¹ ... When I arrived there early on the 14th of August, I was informed, that Gen. Asboth on the previous day had placed Lieut. Lachmund of my Rgt., a brave, noble young officer, in close confinement, merely because he is my friend, that he had arrested one of my servants, one of my horses and my baggage and had issued an order to arrest me....

I have been about fifteen years in military service, the greatest part of that time in an army, where military order is by far stricter, discipline by far more rigid, than in our voluntary army, but I never before have seen a decent officer as outrageously treated, as I have been. I never expected, that in a republican army like ours such injustice could be done, such tyranny and despotism be exercised, as there is in parts of our army, where men, who hold a command, are unscrupulous enough to exercise the power entrusted to them for their personal objects and for most shameful suppression, and where they find protection and indemnity for their misdeeds by a connected clique of superiors.

...

In order to show who I am, I can refer you to the Governor of the State of Wisconsin, to Gen. McClernand, on whose staff I served last year, to Gen. Ross,⁵² with whom I acted as volunteer Chief of Artillery and built fortifications in Bolivar Tenn., to Gen. Willich, an old friend of mine, to all of the troops, that served under me or near me, as for instance those Wisconsin and Indiana batteries, which I organized, those batteries, which were under my command, when I was Chief of Artillery with McClernand and Ross, the 34th Wisconsin Inf., my own Rgt., the 27th and 31st Wisconsin Inf. and many more. I dare say, that they, with hardly one dissenting voice, will agree in the opinion or rather conviction, that I am a well educated officer, who fully knows and always fully does his duty, who keeps up strict order and discipline, but at the same time scrupulously cares for the personal interests and welfare of his inferiors and always acts in accordance with the most rigid

---

51. Cairo, Illinois, situated at the confluence of the Mississippi and Ohio Rivers, was an important Union staging post and refugee entrepôt. Arthur Charles Cole, *The Era of the Civil War*, vol. 3 of *The Centennial History of Illinois* (Chicago: A. C. McClurg & Co., 1922), 331–53.

52. Brigadier General Leonard F. Ross was a career officer who for a time commanded the 17th Illinois Regiment. "General Leonard F. Ross," *Iowa Historical Record* 4, no. 4 (1888): 145–83.

principles of truth, right and justice. I also might refer to the loyal German Press and in fact to the loyal German population of the United States. Perhaps I might refer, too, to Gen. Schurz, who in 1849, then a student, was my Adjutant, when I was Colonel and Chief of Artillery; but I do not like a reference of that kind.

If at the beginning of my military career in the U.S. I should have brought to bear political influence, newspaper fuss and such means, I might have obtained a brigadiership just as well as many other persons with by far less military knowledge and experience. I despise however such means, and I was perfectly satisfied with the position of a Col. of Field Artillery, by which position I expected to get an opportunity, as Chief of Artillery of an Army Corps or an Army, to show, what I could do. This was denied to me, and even as a Colonel of infantry no opportunity was granted to me to do active service in the field. Now I am prevented from reorganizing a troop, which is attached to me and from preparing for another opportunity for useful service. All I do desire is such an opportunity; and to obtain it, to obtain some justice at last, I apply to you. If it is not in your power to grant it, I respectfully request you to lay the matter before His Excellency the President of the United States.

I am, Sir with high respect

Your obdt. srvt.[53]

F.A.

P.S. Since I wrote the above, I received from the Commander of this Post a communication disapproving my application for a decent arrest. So it seems that I shall be kept and treated like a criminal for an indefinite length of time.

Mathilde Franziska Anneke to Fritz Anneke
Zürich, September 10, 1863

My dear, dear Fritz!

The *Allgemeine Augsburger Zeitung* correspondent has devastating news from "Washington" on August 25. Whether this hasty Herr Raster[54] from New York is behind the ~ sign or Herr Corvin from Washington,

---

53. Obedient servant.
54. Hermann Raster. See n. 56 (chapter 3).

who usually uses a different sign, I do not <u>know</u>. Enough. I've enclosed the piece I am referring to.

An hour ago, the old Swiss man Herr Fäsi who along with his good wife[55] has been nice to us for over a year now came by. He came here with the expression of a funeral bidder[56] and asked me to be "strong and fearless" because this would be a difficult visit.

I said: "Speak fast, my son went to school an hour ago. Did he have an accident?"

He said: "No, that's not it."

I said: "Did my husband fall in battle? Do you have news?"

He said: "When did you last hear from him?"

I said: "He wrote me on August 10 the last time."

He said: "Then it could be."

I said: "He is dead then!"

He said: "No, it may be even worse news!"

The man would have been right if he had spoken the truth. You supposedly <u>broke your word</u>—and <u>escaped</u>.—

My nerves were terribly exhausted. I still suffer from gout on the nerves. And on top of that I had fallen down the big stairs at Grossmünster Church,[57] slipping on a fruit skin. My nerves were very exhausted already—and now this coup de grâce.

But I could sigh with relief and exclaim, "This is a lie: Fritz would never break his word. He would rather lose his life than break his word and lose his honor.["] Our boy comes home and sees that I have experienced deep sorrow. I tell him what happened. And he exclaims: ["]This is a lie. Papa did not escape. He did not break his word. But he shouldn't live among such rascals any longer and risk his life while fighting with them.["] I have not yet regained my calm in order to defend your honor against such rogue—well, no, Raster did not mean it in an evil way, he has been [*illegible*]—rashness. I have not yet regained my calm to appeal openly—as your wife—to the patience of the people

---

55. Perhaps a reference to Maria Fäsi, the granddaughter of Swiss poet Johann Lavater, and her husband. See n. 19 (chapter 4).

56. Before the advent of newspaper death notices, German funeral bidders had the job of inviting people to funerals. Joachim Heinrich Campe, *Wörterbuch der deutschen Sprache* (Braunschweig; Campe, 1809), 3:86.

57. One of Zürich's landmark churches, Grossmünster dates to the Middle Ages but played an important role in the Reformation.

who want to form an opinion about you. I will wait until I am able to cast light on this dreadful allegation through messages from you.

But before I do that, I must write to the old Father, need to calm him down from all my heart, which is beating for you and our children alone.—I need to write to you, my beloved Fritz, and need to inform you that either viciously or carelessly your honor as a soldier, your honor as a man are being dragged through the mud, which plays into your enemies' hands and lets them triumph over you. I further need to write to you and bemoan our tragic fate.—No, no—not bemoan. Don't you have your dear faithful friend who helps you fight and endure— You won't—you cannot become discouraged.—But, if only I knew how you've been faring!!—How is it possible that I haven't had a message from you after the 13th? Well, naturally, you will have left for Wisconsin with your regiment on the 13th, in order to take the regiment to the governor on the 15th and be mustered out. Again, you've been legally held in contempt. You have boldly made use of your rights. But you haven't escaped. You haven't been detained on parole. Your enemy Asboth has been ordered back or dismissed from service by Grant on the 8th already (according to American news).[58] Your friend Messmore was wandering around as a dishonorable man—who could have kept you?—A thousand questions—a thousand possibilities come to mind—I don't know what to think of this.

I sent my last letter to you to Milwaukee, *care* of Weiskirch. That was on the 5th, and today is the tenth. I told you that I had correctly received the $100 in *currency*, which you had sent me directly. And also that I had received the $200 in *treasury notes* through the bank Schuchtard & Gebhard[59] in New York.—

I don't want to lose another minute to speak out against these correspondences. But I also hope every hour of every day that I will surely receive messages from you that will enable me to explain everything necessary. Tomorrow the *Züricher* [*Zeitung*] will publish the report. Poor Percy will have to listen to plenty of this tomorrow in school. Oh God, we have much, much sorrow—but we shall not despair. It is possible that you will send me a comforting letter along with a Job's missive[60]

---

58. Asboth was transferred to Florida. Eicher and Eicher, *Civil War High Commands*, 108.
59. There was a banking partnership called Schuchardt and Gebhardt. *New York Times*, July 23, 1863.
60. Refers to the suffering of the Old Testament figure Job.

about yet another incarceration. But why are you hesitating? You are not falling into despair and with your clear mind you couldn't have done anything to compromise your honor? Oh, how much I long for a letter from you! I will not send this one before Sunday. That is a long, long time. And how long until it reaches you and until I have a response from you?

In my dreams you were at Mother's. I had hoped you would maybe recover from all those troubles in Milwaukie — where could you be? Victorious over your enemies or "the defeated, imprisoned rebel?"[61]

Our little children are healthy, dear and healthy, my dear Fritz. You will be happy to hear that. Hertha says, "This is how Papa plays ball" and "This is how he shoots a ball," etc. She speaks about you as if she'd been playing with you yesterday. I wish you would see the children again soon. On September 4 I celebrated inwardly—without telling anyone—the day of our farewell. It has already been two years, dear Fritz. In all, we are not lesser people. I have refined myself—I might have gained some virtues, and I haven't lost but gained love. You might draw a more generous conclusion given this balance—but, well, that would work in my favor then. Your fortune contributes to mine. But this misfortune! If it were true that you'd been wrongly accused of desertion and of breaking your word—how could I help you bear this?—

I haven't slept tonight. In my thoughts I was always with you in your imprisonment, which must be very cramped. Dear Fritz, I think it would be good for me to come over there, but the childre—. What should we do? No other paper—I've already received the *N.Y. Demokrat*—mentions the affair. I haven't had a letter from Booth in 4 weeks. I am waiting unusually long for your messages regarding these events. Dear Fritz, if only your prison cell isn't too small. But couldn't your friend speak out if they've silenced you? Dear Fritz, I press you to my heart, and I bring you kisses from our dear little ones.

Later. Now that the *Zürcher* [*Zeitung*] has the correspondence, our dear, faithful, fatherly friend Dr. Hepp just arrived here quite breathless. He quite agrees with my counter statement that will hopefully be published in the *All*[*gemeine Augsburger Zeitung*] tomorrow. The love of this good man and his faith in you has given me much comfort. He might be the only one here we can call a friend. I reported everything to him, and

---

61. From a Georg Herwegh poem. "Essetai ämar" (1862), in *Neue Gedichte von Georg Herwegh* (Milwaukee: Karl Dörflinger, 1877), 98.

he very quickly left to give the news to his wife who was waiting impatiently. Farewell my beloved Fritz. I remain your faithful heart.

Fritz Anneke to Mathilde Franziska Anneke
Columbus, Kentucky, September 15, 1863

My dear Mathilde!

I have positive news for you today. The day before yesterday I finally received my verdict, and the first achievement is that I am now free and that I can go wherever I want. The verdict is <u>military degradation</u>, though, and this astonished me immensely at first. But after I have worked through several statute books, I found that according to American military law "military degradation" means "dismissal from service" and that a degraded officer <u>only</u> becomes incapable of becoming an officer again if that is clearly stated in the verdict. That is not the case in my verdict, and so nothing stands in the way of my reappointment. I've therefore written a letter to Madison[62] in this matter immediately. I expect my reappointment with certainty, with Cramer as my quartermaster and my friend Karl as adjutant. The only disadvantage for me would be that I would be the youngest colonel in the army again. Well, one can rejuvenate for a change! Miraculously, my verdict from June 6th was already confirmed by General Grant on the 20th, meaning 14 days earlier, even though it had to go through Asboth first, then through the corps commander Hurlbut in Memphis, and then through Grant, who himself was in battle at the time and even though all of the voluminous files had to be examined by all authorities. Extraordinarily, it took 85 straight days—from June 20th until Sept. 13th—before the confirmed verdict finally got here from Vicksburg....

More good news from Indianapolis: Herr Ritzinger wrote. He writes he "has received a letter from me" and "is very surprised that you haven't received the money yet." He ordered that the money be sent to you immediately with no interest. You will surely receive it now.

I will likely send my next letter from Milwaukee. Being greatly burdened, and with love from Karl and me,

Yours, Fritz.

---

62. The capital of Wisconsin.

Mathilde Franziska Anneke to Fritz Anneke
Zürich, September 20, 1863

My dear Fritz!

Your dear letter dated 8/25 just arrived as I enclosed a small card in Mother's letter. Your letter has given me and your friends the peace that we needed after such shameful attacks, and which we could only get through direct messages from you. Your letter has made me and the children quite happy again. Even the insidious new ambush that I have just read in another edition of the "magnanimous" *Herold* cannot dampen my spirits again. This paper is put together by fools—as I must admit irrespective of my own contributions to the paper up until now. This paper, which unmistakably bears the signature of the honorable Carl Schurz, should be ashamed of itself. I wonder whether you've read the articles? The first one was awkward and dull. The second one malicious. I don't think it needs to be said that I will not write another line for this dishonorable paper. I just want to wait to see whether you have more details and what you will do before I tell him that.

The [*Allgemeine Augsburger*] has at least done what I wanted after I sent the paper definitive information that their hasty correspondent (Raster) has only helped to spread the lie and defamation of the Washington article in question. It has published the rectification based on your statement and has published mine in a timely manner. The *Züricher* [*Zeitung*] has truly been slapped, as I hear from Beust. I will receive the articles that slapped it in the local prestige paper from Hepp.—

I just received two papers addressed to you. That means you are alive. I quietly thank the author of the Louisville article a thousand times. If it's our old Stierlin[63] then all his sins may be forgiven. I'd like to send him something from here, a picture and sign of our old friendship.—If you are in contact with him or his wife, please give them my best. Old Mother Koppel[64] writes to me often and declares her friendship in her own way. She is 83 years old. I will have written to you at the time that she lost her good son Dr. Koppel.

Dr. Hepp has been suffering from a dangerous eye infection for sev-

---

63. Ludwig Stierlin edited the *Louisville Anzeiger*. Karl J. R. Arndt and May E. Olsen, *German-American Newspapers and Periodicals, 1732–1955: History und Bibliography* (Heidelberg: Quelle & Meyer, 1961; reprint, New York: Johnson Reprint Corporation, 1965), 169.

64. We have been unable to identify the Koppels.

eral days. He was about to go on a trip to Paris with his wife when he fell ill. He is now better. He and his wife send their love.

We've had cool and foggy weather for some time now. We're not going on our little excursions anymore. The lake is too restless, and so we spend our time here in the house playing and eating wine grapes. You will likely never have seen such wonderful grapes.—I just wrote an article for the [*Criminal-Zeitung*] about the harvesting of grapes and winegrowing.

30. September. We're just back from the cadets' field day. The little heroes of the local canton gathered today. They were in a battle down at Dietikon on the Limmat River.[65] I went to the battlefield with Percy, and Mary went with us this time, accompanied by Teacher Scuder and his wife. We left early yesterday morning and took the train to the Dietikon Station and from there we crossed the Limmat to get to the Fahr Monastery.[66] Percy had great fun. In his mind he was already imagining a similar trip next year with his comrades. I collected material, and so did Mary. It was a lovely fall day and we drank much Sauser wine[67] in your honor at the monastery.—

I can see from your letter that for now there can be no talk of, as Raster put it, "desertion and breech of promise." I hope the people will get tired of their attacks. How will your friend Karl be faring? <u>What is he accused of?</u> Well, I will learn that soon enough. It seems like you haven't given up on your military career altogether. It would not be surprising if you had had enough—less surprising than that it was made impossible for you.

Herr Orff, the "good comrade," is surely playing a game, and as far as I can tell from afar he will play it until the end.

I like Meßmore's soldiers if they have actually <u>declared</u> only to continue service in a regiment led by you. Your "boys" are a bit weak or else they would have told the papers their opinion or one of them would have written faithful letters like Jäcki instead of not sending you a message in 4 weeks. Does Märklin have a different opinion than you? Why isn't he telling you about it? Oh, it is the basis of all American life:

---

65. A municipality just west of Zürich.

66. A Benedictine nunnery. Hélène Arnet, "Fahr," in *Historisches Lexikon der Schweiz*, last modified November 1, 2017, https://hls-dhs-dss.ch/de/articles/011606/2017-11-01/.

67. Federweißer or incompletely fermented wine.

everyone for himself. It's supposed to be different in New England, but I don't know.

Is it possible to find a place to like on this earth? "Where everything is beautiful, only the people aren't."

I like my little people. Our children are kind, and I often wish you the refreshing feeling of scuffling and romping around with them on the grass. Hertha is the wildest and most athletic one. She climbs every tree. Her most original innovation, however, was building homes in trees. Lovely hidden places that I recently found as I was looking out the window at the wonderful nut and fruit forest and the gorge of waterfalls and then heard chatter and humming in the air close by—but not above and not below me. "Where are you now?" was my question. "Here." "Where?" "In the elderberry trees?" But now at the border of the little garden that is located between us and the fruit forest are gigantic elderberry trees and slim bushes that spread their branches in every direction. It is not possible to see the big birds in there if you're not standing right under the tree. And so, I went downstairs to look at this original beaver's lodge. There they were sitting in the branches with 3 or 4 playmates too: Percy, Lili, Hertha, Bella, Albert, Emil, and the others. For more comfort, not only did they build stairs up to their asylums, no, they had also turned the floors above the branches into comfortable air-castles with boards and slats. Even their dolls had beds there, and in one tree they had a kitchen with kitchen utensils. It looked so inviting that I would have gladly taken up quarters there if I were more agile. There was no better place for them throughout the fall than in the elderberry trees on the same level as my window. Two little white sparrows, rare birds themselves, lived with them in the trees.

Our stay here in this rural area has been endlessly good for the children. They have enjoyed the fresh air outside as never before. They have had freedom and happiness they haven't found elsewhere before. Naturally, we had to be very careful here. There are very rough and uneducated people around us. That's also why I only left them for 4 days one time as I was making my *escape* to Interlaken. (Apropos Interlaken: I wrote nice alpine scenes, 4 or 6. The brilliant *Herold* was smart enough to tastelessly combine them all in one correspondence. Well, I don't want to be angry about this Milwaukie anymore.—And in the same edition this ambush on you!)

Herr Booth has stopped communicating with Mary altogether. Not a sign from him in 2 months. The requirements for raising the children and for Mary are growing daily. Mary has never stopped working for his *Daily Life* even for a minute. He would have let her starve if it hadn't been for us. I haven't bothered with him since last year. Mary has constantly written reports for the *Herold* in N[ew] York. He has sent her the 5 dollars on time so far. That's all. I cannot tell how it will end.

If only he would give the child a proper education. No, this lack of character and ignobility of these Americans I have the honor of knowing directly or indirectly—they are all the same. And still—one doesn't want to give up on this land with its foundation of freedom. . . .[68]

Assistant Adjutant General Jas. A. Hardie to Fritz Anneke
Washington, D.C., October 1863
(English original)

Sir,

The secretary of war directs me to acknowledge the receipt of your communication of the 22d August last, covering statement of alleged facts in connection with your trial and imprisonment on the charge of mutiny and appealing from the sentence; and in reply to state that your argument does not present sufficient grounds for the reversion or modification of the sentence awarded you.

Very Respectfully
Your obedient Servant
Jas. A. Hardie[69]
Assist. Adjutant General[70]

---

68. Letter continues with an installment written on October 2.

69. New Yorker James Allan Hardie held many senior positions. Eicher and Eicher, *Civil War High Commands*, 279.

70. An administrative position within the War Department. Finding Aid, Record of the Adjutant General's Office, National Archives, accessed July 30, 2020, https://www.archives.gov/research/guide-fed-records/groups/407.html.

CHAPTER 6

Separation

February 1864–January 1865

THE CONCLUSION OF FRITZ'S TRIAL AND MARY'S DECISION TO return to the United States made 1864 a year of transition. Fritz had to relinquish his dreams of becoming a Civil War hero and search for another source of purpose and income. He was disillusioned with the Republican Party, which countenanced cronyism and corrupt practices in the Union army. Along with many Forty-Eighters, he opposed Lincoln's renomination in 1864, partly because he considered the president insufficiently committed to emancipation.

While Fritz lost a political party, Mathilde lost Mary. Mary longed to reunite with her older daughter, Mary Ella, who was living with Mary's mother in Connecticut, and she placed what little hope she had of recovery in experimental treatments funded by friends in the United States. Mathilde expressed her sorrow at Mary's departure at the end of June 1864 in letters that reveal the significance of their five-year relationship.

After Mary and Lili left, living in Zürich no longer held the same appeal to Mathilde. Like Fritz, she reevaluated how she could best earn a living and revisited the perennial question of what place to call home. As had always been the case, those decisions were intertwined with her aspirations for her children. Hertha and Percy were Americans in her mind, but she preferred European schooling and thought they should be able to speak French and German. As Mathilde considered her situation, another friend became more influential in her life. She grew closer to Cäcilie Kapp, the talented adult daughter of her old friends the Kapps.

Mathilde Franziska Anneke to Fritz Anneke
Zürich, February 9, 1864

My dear Fritz!

Admittedly, I have just sent you a letter via Bremen, but it reflects my discontent and absent-mindedness and will likely not please you. And so, I hurry to answer your lovely last letters, which have taken a long time to get here, and I will tell you as much as possible about us. There were 50 doll in your letter dated Dec. 28.

The political developments in this country are taking such a turn that you may already be thinking of coming back here at this moment. But maybe not, because you usually have a good eye for political things, and you see right through this imperial-royal game of scoundrels more than anyone. It may be that if England interfered in the German cause and France also played its hand, then Germany could play a different role. But up until now it seems to be the strategy of imperial-royal diplomacy to amuse the nations with war dances.[1] You are still likely not coming back here, at least not until you know whether you will be able to be of serious use in the field. You are waiting over there for your moment to arrive, and you think it will arrive. So, you are not one of the 5,000 who will accompany Herr Kapf[2] on his way here from New York. That is my opinion.—Assuming that you would come either as a soldier or as a private citizen, you would in any case encounter as many if not more difficulties here than you have ever encountered there. Raster's slander has not been retracted—has not been avenged.[3] Admittedly, the press hasn't taken much notice of it and in general people did not believe the lie. But as soon as you were here yourself and got

---

1. During the 1860s, Prussia moved to consolidate the German Empire under its control. In 1862, Minister President Otto von Bismarck had argued that "blood and iron," not liberalism, would effect unification. He proceeded to rule without a parliamentary-approved budget and pursued armed conflict, including a war with Denmark over Schleswig-Holstein, which started about a week before Mathilde wrote this letter. James J. Sheehan, *German History, 1770–1866* (Oxford: Clarendon, 1989), 880–83, 890.

2. Newspapers reported that Württemberg Forty-Eighter Eduard Kapff, an officer in the 7th New York Infantry Regiment, planned to lead German Americans to fight with Prussia and Austria against Denmark in the Second Schleswig War, but there is no evidence he did. A. E. Zucker, ed. *The Forty-Eighters: Political Refugees of the German Revolution of 1848* (New York: Columbia University Press, 1950), 307; *Minnesota Staats-Zeitung*, March 5, 1864.

3. A reference to continued fallout over the court martial.

in people's way and became their rival, then you would have to, as you rightly say yourself, go to war to defend your honor. Not only that—to use your own words—"the great undiscriminating mob judges based on success." No, it is impossible that the people here will ever truly understand the situation over there. I had to experience this quite bitterly when I defended you against these shameful defamations. I was truly devastated for a while. So, you are not coming here, unless a social fight[4] erupts. In that case there would be no question but that you would come here.

I'd like to stay in Europe perhaps as much as you would. I love the nature here more than there. I only love one single place there: below the cypress tree where our children—our unforgettable children are buried. If it were not for them—for you—for my Fanny and my old Mother over there—I would <u>never, never</u> return. I would bid my eternal farewell to Mary, my beloved Mary, and I would live out my life here in silent rural modesty.

What pulls me over there is just <u>ideal</u>, I know that. What I leave behind is <u>real</u>. But I cannot escape my fate. I must follow an inner urge that is not fully developed in me. And so, I will once again embark on a journey across the ocean with our two remaining children as soon as you call us.

But <u>where</u> will we have our permanent residence? Where will we go in the vast country over there? I love the East the most, not only because the nature there attracts me more, but also because one is not so cut off from civilization. But I also love the West in its wildness. I love having my Mother and Mary close by. I will just never go to Lansing.[5] I'll go anywhere where I can find a modest but secure home, but I will not go there. If you want my reasons, then I will give you my reasons. And I have no doubt that you will find them right and proper. Other than that, I will accept any of the choices that you inform me of. The best opportunity for the education and advancement of our children can or must of course tip the balance as we decide on a location.

I very much lament the fact that our dear Percy will once more be pulled out of these strongholds of education. Despite still being so childlike, he is so hungry for knowledge. He has assembled a nice little

---

4. Unless the war became connected to class struggle.
5. Home to Fritz's brother Emil Anneke, where Fritz stayed before moving to St. Louis.

treasury of knowledge for himself. He would be a cadet here come Easter. He would still like to get to know the beautiful Switzerland better, which he is beginning to love as much as his parents.

Hertha, that clever girl, would also still like so much to attend the "Hottingen school," which only costs 15 rappens in fees every other month and still teaches so much more or so many nicer things than the elaborate teaching system of Herr Beust. Hertha would also still like to learn so much more music. She has made a start—a valuable start—on that, and now this achievement will be lost and gone. She would like to stay here longer, but for all in the world she would like again to be with her Papa, whom she has not forgotten for even a moment. She would also like—yes, she <u>wants</u>—to go with Mary and Lili. She maybe doesn't suspect yet that a separation—even if we go our separate ways over there—is imminent. Our family life in these past years has been the most wonderful you can imagine. We had incredible heartache and pain. But the harmony, the love, that has graced our life together—we will never again have that. Hertha and Lili, always dressed like twins, pretty and clever, well-behaved, too well-behaved in the beginning, like no siblings ever could be; they were always pleased about their little Mama who taught them all kinds of nice things and who taught them an appreciation for the arts that will stay with them for the rest of their lives. They only started with it because I made up little fairy tales for them and arranged the most necessary things for their games together. Percy often acted as their guardian and even as their teacher.

Mary and I have solely been pursuing our intellectual endeavors and our further education during the past years. Through this, we have ultimately sought to achieve an easier position. We have worked as tirelessly as you can probably barely imagine. We have both published a lot, really a lot. We have found recognition, but we have only slightly bettered our situation. Since our endeavors to this end were fruitless, we have come to understand that a temporary separation for the benefit of our families is inevitable. A "<u>temporary</u>" separation: In all probability I need to consider it an eternal one.—Why? A separation is a separation—and a separation from her who is so ailing and weak and will embark on such a long journey—is eternal. The imminent separation and change of climate may delay her death a while longer—but she will die in the course of not too long a time. In Mary I have come to know a beautiful and dear female soul who is so great and noble as to be called venerable. She may have her minor faults and weaknesses. But those are more part of her nationality and education than herself.—I am not letting her cross the ocean all by herself without deep heartache—and not without worry. But what must be, must be.

If we can and do travel together, then that will ease my worries. Her departure date has not yet been determined, but I think she's selected the month of July for it.—

But first the question arises: Will <u>you</u> not want to go and see the European battlefield, depending on how things develop over the course of the year and have us <u>here</u> rather than separated and far away from you once more? Then I will spend the waiting time here alone with the children and will use it to bestow the benefit of European education on them a while longer? Will I be able to depart as a lawful and honest woman at last, who is free of all debts that I as your successor here owe the doctor, the pharmacy, the teachers, Linke, Dr. Hepp, Schabelitz, Duden,[6] etc. for you and for me? Will Mr. Booth reach out and help? Mary has faithfully put her efforts into it. She believed that through her fabulous diligence she had accomplished what had been necessary for it. How can she be shielded from betrayal?—What else could we do that we haven't done already?

Mary's entire possessions at this moment are 30 dollars. 20 will have to go to the bank immediately and we will get 30 francs for them.—I <u>only</u> have a loan of 300 francs on my bonds. Will we be able to cash them in at the right time? Other than that, I have the 50 doll that you sent last and several more. But selling them at this time would not free me of the shoemaker's *bill* and the bread *bill*. We must pay all the others first! We live more than just modestly. We live very, very much in poverty—but if we were simply healthy and had the most necessary things, then we would be content and happy. As soon as I receive my fee from Leipzig—the correspondences are long finished—I will be able to buy the most <u>necessary</u> things for us, but I will not even get rid of half of my debts....

---

6. On Thomas J. Linke and Johann Hepp, see n. 58 (chapter 3) and n. 3 (chapter 3). Mathilde probably also refers to Swiss publisher, bookseller, and communist Jakob Schabelitz and the Dortmund native who settled in Zürich in 1851, Friedrich Ludwig Wilhelm Carl Duden. *Karl Marx, Frederick Engels: Collected Works* (New York: International Publishers, 1982), 38:667; J. Caspar Pfister, *Verzeichnis der Bürger der Stadt Zürich im Jahr 1861* (Zürich: Friedrich Schultheß, 1861), 45.

Mathilde Franziska Anneke to Fritz Anneke
Zürich, April 19, 1864

My dear Fritz!
The black ink is so thick that I'd rather use the watery red one. I am so distressed because of Maria. The heart spasm I wrote you about was followed by severe coughing up of blood on the second day, which threatened to turn into a literal rush of blood. We fetched a doctor as fast as possible, who took care of her following homeopathic guidelines and it seems with much understanding. She is very ill and weak, even though the rush of blood is over, according to the doctor. I will hear his prognosis on the consequences this afternoon. It feels to me like I myself am—ascending to Him—as if I am dying myself. I am telling you about my misery and my worries about my beloved friend with trembling heartbeats. I will also report what the doctor says immediately, so that you can inform Booth of it. I still dare to hope. I have spent half of the nights since that horrible night at her little bed. She only sleeps while whining and groaning, and I am always scared that the dreadful spasm—worse than the worst death struggle—will return. If I had to bury her here, if she would not see her dear Ella again, and her homeland, which she so desperately longs for—what would I do?

Percy is very busy with his preparations as cadet and well-known student. I have already paid the debt of 60 fr for the uniform. Now I have to buy books and a drawing set and pay the tuition of 30 fr. I have hardly used my pen to write at all in this month—it's a serious time again: The garnishment case is not over yet. If it weren't for the children, I would try to get Mary over there myself as quickly as possible. But it can't be that I neglect my duties and care for the children in this decisive moment. Hiller has not sent anything. You will have realized by now as much as we have that this individual has shamefully stolen from us. The consequences of it are heart-breaking. We know that the *Herold* has accepted all correspondences, and we know it pays more than any other paper in New York. Now, see what you can do, and then with your energy in such matters, stop the scoundrels' devilry for the sake of other people like Carl.[7] As soon as we have resolved the matter, I will inform Lexow. I will now take Percy to the tailor—and will

---

7. Carl Lachmund.

go to the doctor. Dr. Schilling[8] says the imminent danger is now over, the burst blood vessel seems to have closed again. The seizure was of the worst kind. There can be no talk of her traveling alone with poor little Lilli. She has a strong desire to see Ella. She hopes the air of her homeland will help her recovery.—She already has an expansion of the heart. Free of all sorrow and all emotional distress, which cause cramps, and if she were taken care of very thoughtfully and would rest for a little while, then she might live several years yet. But a journey home in those first weeks after the cramps would kill her instantly. I have lavished care on her like on a child—may Booth do his part now. She considers the years that she has spent with me the most wonderful of her sorrowful life. I can say the same. It is almost midnight, dear good Fritz. Mary has been asleep for a while now, but she is very restless. Percy has been feeling quite well again for several days. Hertha is not coughing anymore either. She drew and colored the nice flower all by herself.—Mother has sent several lovely lines. Well, it was a long letter in fact.

Sunday morning. It was a quite peaceful night for Mary. Only Lili made me leave my bed several times. The child is so feverishly excited. Percy went to his painting lessons, which he was taking during the school vacation and can now only take on Sunday mornings. He paints for three hours with the greatest pleasure. If only these private lessons weren't so shamefully expensive. You won't believe just how I have to fend for myself. The children's education is my main focus, and I am more capable in achieving that goal than I had thought myself. We had to defer payment for the music lessons for six weeks—each lesson costs 3 francs or 1 dollar. But they are diligently practicing their melodious string music and making us quite happy with their nice tunes. The weather is bad again. I am not hopeful for the summer, even though it would be so important for our health. The Hepps are faring well. Father H. was ill again but is now happy and healthy. I received every issue of the Sunday paper except the last one.—Would Brentano like to have a novella that is four times as long for 100 dollars? *Uhland in Texas*? It is exciting and interesting. Has the *Geisterhaus* arrived

---

8. We have been unable to identify Mary's physician.

on time? I am awaiting a response from Sauerländer.[9]—Farewell, dear Fritz. Give my best to your friend and the relatives.

Your faithful Tilla.

Fritz Anneke to Mathilde Franziska Anneke
Lansing, April 26–May 2, 1864

My dear Mathilde!

Sadly, I need to modify if not entirely withdraw the favorable news about Mother[10] that I gave you in my last two letters. I am enclosing Emil Weiskirch's letter, which I received several days ago, so that you see things clearly. If it is at all possible, I will travel to Milwaukee next month to see for myself what Mother's condition is like and—if it can't be any other way—at least to see her one more time.

I still cannot give you specific details about the resources for your journey here. I do not hear anything from my paymaster and my commissioner in Detroit. This commissioner, a personal friend of Emil's,[11] is the most reliable man in Detroit. We haven't been able to continue traveling with the fox and showing it to people for some time now. We can't think of selling it before the weather is reliably better.

May 2.

I have left this letter unfinished for so long, partly because I was waiting for more news from Milwaukee, and partly because I was hoping for letters from you, and partly because I thought I would finally, finally receive my salary. All of these hopes and expectations have been illusive. Emil's friend writes from Detroit that the paymaster has money now, but that he hasn't been able to examine his papers. There is nothing I can do about it when the vermin keep stalling me a while longer, not even when they don't pay me at all. *Such is American liberty*. The freedom of roguery, villainy, and malice is one of our main liberties.

---

9. The major Swiss publishing house printed Aarau's liberal *Schweizerbote* newspaper. Corinne Leuenberger, "Der Schweizerbote," in *Historisches Lexikon der Schweiz*, last modified November 27, 2012, https://hls-dhs-dss.ch/de/articles/043036/2012-11-27/; Patrick Zehnder, "Sauderländer," in *Historisches Lexikon der Schweiz*, last modified February 16, 2011, https://hls-dhs-dss.ch/de/articles/024705/2011-02-16/.

10. Mathilde's mother, Elisabeth Giesler.

11. Fritz's brother Emil Anneke.

I am not clear on what the near future will bring us in regard to politics and the military. All the machinery has been set in motion to get the mule Lincoln into power again. The entire military and civil machinery of the government is basically mainly working toward that goal. I do not see the remotest possibility of appointing another candidate. And if it were a possibility, where would one find a decent candidate? A candidate of character with a good education who is energetic, honest, and has a sharp eye? Our former ideal Fremont is also a real crook who is being led by scoundrels and frauds.[12] Butler[13] is an archrogue. Banks, whom I thought of highly for a long time, is not only a *knownothing*,[14] but has also proven over and over again that his energy and his talent aren't nearly matching his roguery and malice. His military operations are rash. His agents treat the poor Negroes worse than their *masters* and people in his *department* are stealing more than ever. Things are looking sad in our republic.

The military successes of this year have all been on the side of the rebels so far. We have suffered a couple of difficult defeats, and with parts of our army we have made senseless and inefficient efforts that are tantamount to a moral defeat. I wrote you before how little trust I have in the lucky fellow Grant. He now wants to try and suppress the enemy with numerical superiority on the blood-soaked battlefield in Virginia. It is possible that luck will be on his side again like so often before. But it is also possible that Lee will rip the false laurels off his head.

Here in Lansing everyone is very interested in the nominations for the next state elections. Emil especially is very preoccupied with it. Each political blow makes him ill. But once he is reappointed as can-

---

12. Lincoln's opponents among the German American Radical Republicans wanted to nominate John C. Frémont for president, but Democrats with quite different views also participated in the abortive Frémont movement. Jorg Nagler, *Fremont contra Lincoln: Die deutsch-amerikanische Opposition in der Republikanischen Partei während des amerikanischen Bürgerkrieges* (Frankfurt: P. Lang, 1984), 208-18.

13. The Democrat-turned-Radical Republican Major General Benjamin Butler profited from war contracts, but Fritz was probably commenting on Butler's opportunistic politics. Chester Hearn, *When the Devil Came Down to Dixie: Ben Butler in New Orleans* (Baton Rouge, La.: Louisiana State University Press, 1997), 23-25.

14. As Republican governor of Massachusetts, Nathanial P. Banks had supported a state constitutional amendment denying naturalized citizens the right to vote for two years. In 1864 he was serving as a major general in the Union army. James Hollandsworth, *Pretense of Glory: The Life of General Nathaniel P. Banks* (Baton Rouge, La.: Louisiana State University Press, 1998), 37-38.

didate for his office,[15] then I believe he will soon have fully recovered. In case of his reelection he wants me to be his "*deputy*," an office that would bring me about $1,800, but with the help of speculations could bring me in several thousand.

Brigadier General Willich, whom I have sent a longer letter in accordance with his wishes, has not deigned to answer me yet. He has left Cincinnati again to reassume control over his brigade. The 35th regiment under Colonel Orff has marched off to St. Louis and will unite with the army of General Steele[16] in Arkansas from there.

Other than that, and except for newspaper articles, I almost don't hear any of what is going on in the world.

At the end of the month, I will go to Milwaukee in any case to see Grandmother.

Karl[17] sends his love. He is about to fall in love with a very pretty, tow-colored, very German-looking American little girl who is studying at the local "*academy*" (girls' boarding school). Emil and Friedi[18] also send their greetings. Give my best to Percy, Mary, and our friends, not to forget Cäcilie Kapp.

Yours, Fritz.

Mathilde Franziska Anneke to Fritz Anneke
Zürich, June 9, 1864

Dear Fritz!

Mary's suitcases are packed. But as yet no ship contract, which Booth said would be here ten days ago. And no bills of exchange over about $100 yet. Mary is in critical condition. Poor Mary. I feel like my heart is breaking. The sanguine requirements to have the ambassador or even the consul as companion are simply ridiculous. Booth doesn't know anything about Mary's condition. Mary is like a child who knows noth-

---

15. The Republican Party renominated Emil Anneke for the position of state auditor general, and he won the election. *Report of the Pioneer Society of the State of Michigan* 14 (1889): 57.

16. Career officer Major General Frederick Steele. Eicher and Eicher, *Civil War High Commands*, 705.

17. Carl Lachmund had accompanied Fritz to Lansing.

18. Presumably Emil's oldest child, Frederick. U.S. Census, Population Schedules (1860), Lansing, Michigan, p. 66, dwelling 504, family 511.

ing about life and the world. She can naively indulge in one moment and then stoically remain in silent sorrow and resignation the next, until a truly loving hand helps her out of it. I was anxiously awake last night and at her side because it seemed to me that attacks of spasm were coming again. I will not have any peace of mind letting her travel to Havre alone. Ottilie[19] will take care of our children—even if it requires sacrificing the last of my energy, I will take this journey.

Your dear letter has just arrived, announcing that I now also have the resources allowing me to accompany Mary. It is too late for that now. I mustn't leave here in a rush. I need to get things thoroughly in order here, and finally also because of Percy's education, I have to consider the departure seriously. I have resigned myself to the fate of being far away from Mary or even losing her altogether. My life with her was a beautiful fragment of my life. And since life in general is not a harmonious entity—and rather consists of fragments or epochs, it is crucial to end them properly and string the fragments together so that they form a whole. Our children are faring quite well again. I hope the summer will support the care of their as well as my health. I have been so constantly worried about Mary that I haven't had any time to think about myself. It is finally necessary that I myself also get care. Despite the "victory reports" from over there,[20] I am not in the mood for victory cheers. I don't know whether it's the dreadful butchery or the anticipation of a disastrous end.

I cannot and will not read the reports anymore. . . .

I am sending these lines as a diligent greeting. I have hope of getting your messages from Milwaukee and hearing about my good mother.

    My dear Fritz, farewell.
    Yours, Mathilde

---

    19. Likely Ottilie Kapp. See n. 71 (chapter 1).
    20. Union Major General William Tecumseh Sherman was pushing toward Atlanta, and General Grant was slowly moving south through Virginia. James M. McPherson, *Battle Cry of Freedom: The Civil War Era* (New York: Oxford University Press, 1988), 725–31, 743–49.

Mathilde Franziska Anneke to Mary Booth
Zürich, undated, 1864

Marie![21]

My heart is now silent, like the dreamful lake in front of me; it is dark and serious like the blue mountains before my eyes; the scent that fills the air around them is you, Marie, with your wonderful smile and the hope of rays of light in the realm of shadows.

You want me to open the book of my past, the book of my varied life! Take it as it is and as you wanted it to be: honest and true. In the presence of the eternal Alps, which with their pure and sparkling white radiance might lighten my dark cell again tomorrow, I will write down what I have experienced and endured: May they be my silent witnesses.

It is for you only, Marie!
Franziska Maria.

Mathilde Franziska Anneke to Lili Booth
Zürich, July 9, 1864

My dear Lili!

How happy I was to receive your nice little letter from Paris! And Herthali[22] too, and she's already written many letters back to you, but I can't find them at all right now.—The white kitten has suddenly disappeared, but the gray one is almost always sitting on my desk as if to tell me how much its little mama loved it. Herr Weiß[23] sends his best and Herr Terry[24] and the little children from the school as well.

I will send you longer letters in the future. But I am ill right now. I have a fever.

Adieu my dear Lili. Give my best to Ella, your grandmother, and all of your aunts from
your faithful Mama
   M. F. Anneke

---

21. Another German variant of Mary's name. This "letter" served as a preface for an unfinished autobiography that Mathilde wrote in Zürich at Mary's urging. Mathilde Anneke, "Unpublished Autobiography" (1862), Box 5, Folder 1, Anneke Papers.

22. The Swiss version of the diminutive form of Hertha's name.

23. Possibly a teacher in Zürich.

24. Probably another teacher.

Mary Booth to Mathilde Franziska Anneke
New York City, August 6, 1864
(English original)

Sweet Franziska Maria: You are a beautiful female! You ought to be ashamed of yourself, and be sent to the "Ancient Henry"[25] beside. What on Earth is the matter with you? Not a divil of a letter have I rec'd from you since my arrival in America—nearly three [weeks] ago! What can be the reason of such a course I should like to know? I hope and trust that you are not sick—as I have been—but am now getting better under Dr. Bronson's[26] treatment. Yesterday I went up to Hartford after having been here a week & a day. I came back in the boat last night—arrived early this morning. My artist[27] went with me, & was enchanted with the beauty of Jane, & also Ella, whom he says is more handsome far than Lilian, & that there is the most beautiful zauber[28] in her whole face, manner, and atmosphere. That she is the living expression of poesy. I wanted to bring her here with me but she was too sick to come. She can never live & I look & think on her with the greatest sorrow. I was greatly disappointed in not finding a letter from you. There were twelve waiting me—from everybody inviting me to visit them. One, first of all, from my Uncle Robert,[29] saying he was at Saratogo[30] when I arrived in N. York or should have visited me. That he was then going to a Bathing place—being sick. I hope to see him yet, as I shall remain here a week longer. Mr. Booth is anxious for me to come West as soon as I can, of course.

There was a letter from Gerritt Smith inviting me to come there & stay a week, & saying he would send his carraige for me. I think I shall

---

25. A reference to Satan similar to "Old Harry." I. W. Scribner, *Rozella of Laconia; Or, Legends of the While Mountains and Merry-Meeting Day* (Boston: James French and Company, 1857), 113; "Harry," in OED Online, Oxford University Press, accessed July 30, 2020, https://www.oed.com/view/Entry/84383.

26. Possibly New Haven, Connecticut physician Henry Bronson. *New York Daily Tribune*, November 27, 1893.

27. Mary's letters include numerous references to a "Mr. Wüst," possibly the Frankfurt-born artist, illustrator, and caricaturist Theodore Wüst, who worked for the *New York Daily Graphic* in the 1870s. Theodore E. Stebbins, Jr., Kimberly Orcutt, and Virginia Anderson, eds., *American Paintings at Harvard*, vol. 2, *Paintings, Watercolors, Pastels, and Stained Glass by Artists Born 1826–1856* (New Haven, Conn.: Yale University Press, 2008), 454.

28. Magic.

29. We could not find a likely Robert Corss or Robert Humphrey, but perhaps he was a more distant relation.

30. Saratoga lies about 190 miles north of New York City.

go. There was also a letter from Mrs. Gray[31] asking me to come now that her husband is at home, & inviting me to visit her in Washington this winter. I am received everywhere with the greatest love—more than you can imagine, and far more than I deserve or am worth, as you, who <u>know</u> my <u>nichts</u>[32] worth can know. [A]lso a letter from Myla's[33] sister, which I will enclose for you, & as you will see, her husband is dead. I have been writing her just now. Mr. Booth and Mr. Rose in Hartford,[34] says my poems have cost <u>awful</u>. They have to be sold for a <u>dollar & a half</u> each in order to pay the cost—& <u>that</u> only pays without a cent's profit. The duties & express charges were dreadfully high. Mr. Lippencott[35] in Philadelphia has written to Mr. Booth about the book in terms of the highest critical praise, & as I should think, wants to republish it. Several publishers wish to do it - & I am to have offers from a firm here about it I here.[36] Every one is charmed with the poems, & want to have more original in the next edition. I have said very decidedly that no American Publisher must do it, but they say it <u>cannot</u> be done in Europe for here because it would never pay as it is - & whoever <u>should</u> do it here would pay me well. Tell me what I ought to do. In my next I shall tell you of the offer I shall have before that time—it is proposed by a publisher in N.Y. to get it out in blue & gold for Christmas. Ought I to let him do it?—I do not wish to do wrong against Mr. Schmitt[37]— to whom I am so much indebted[.] I shall see what can be done about having my children's stories in a book.

Mr. Plumb has mailed to Kinkel[38] in Heidelberg Mrs. Farnham's wonderful work of "Woman & her Era."[39] He will find it the greatest

---

31. Although there is little evidence here, Mary possibly spoke of Jane Lathrop Loring Gray, who assisted in the botanical work of her politically active husband Asa Gray at Harvard University and visited Washington, D.C. regularly. A. Hunter Dupree, *Asa Gray: American Botanist, Friend of Darwin* (Baltimore, Md.: Johns Hopkins University Press, 1959), 177–89, 403, 413.

32. Nothing.

33. Probably Myla Fletcher. See n. 43 (chapter 4).

34. Probably Abraham Rose, a Hartford bookseller. U.S. Census, Population Schedules (1870), 2nd Ward, Hartford, Connecticut, p. 6, dwelling 51, family 49.

35. Joshua Lippincott was Mary's U.S. publisher. See n. 18 (chapter 3).

36. Mary means "hear," not "here."

37. Carl Schmitt, Mary's German publisher and Franziska Hammacher's brother-in-law. See n. 25 (chapter 4).

38. Gottfried Kinkel. See n. 72 (chapter 1).

39. In 1864, prison reformer Eliza Wood Farnham published *Woman and Her Era*, which argued women were superior to men. W. David Lewis, "Farnham, Eliza Wood Burhans,"

thing of the sort he ever heard of. It is in two volumes. Mr. Plumb is to publish a monthly magazine called "The Friend of Progress"[40] for which he has engaged me as contributer. He says he shall have the best of writers & pay them good prices, & if the magizine cannot sustain itself on that basis it can die, for that he shall accept no free trashy things whatever. The "Herald" used only <u>half</u> of my last letters, it was so crowded with war news & so owes me but for 8 correspondences. The "Independent" paid me—Mr. Tilton[41] himself, who is lovely, without even a question. He says he will speak a kind word for my book as soon as it comes into his hands.[42]

Mathilde Franziska Anneke to Fritz Anneke
Zürich, September 6–12, 1864

My dear Fritz!

Your last letter is dated August 20. I received three letters from Mary this week. She tells me about every step that she takes. But I do not become aware of how her inner life keeps in step with her outer life. Otherwise you will see her now or have seen her already because Booth was there recently to *lecture* her and then take them with him.[43] She only wanted to stay 14 days and then return east to stay in New York as the doctors have advised. It may well be the best for her in some respects. I trust that <u>attentive</u> friends—because this lovely child finds friends everywhere—will take care of her. It seems like she is a little more aware of her condition. I've maintained deep silence because I feared saying the word would kill her. As you must know, Mary has epilepsy. I say that only to <u>you</u>; (Booth might know as well). The word is enough to give you the entirety of her and our suffering. She did not know about it when she left me. Only the doctor and I knew. Now it seems to me that the doctor over there has informed her about it. She

---

in *Notable American Women, 1607–1950: A Biographical Dictionary*, ed. Edward T. James (Cambridge, Mass.: Belknap Press of Harvard University Press, 1971), 2:598–600.

40. C. M. Plumb published the spiritualist monthly for less than a year.

41. Poet and abolitionist Theodore Tilton edited the Congregationalist *New York Independent*. Richard Wrightman Fox, *Trials of Intimacy: Love and Loss in the Beecher-Tilton Scandal* (Chicago: Chicago University Press, 1999), 179–212.

42. The letter either ended abruptly or the final pages have not survived.

43. Mary never in fact returned to Milwaukee.

avoids the word with me, not telling me anything, but I can tell.—I couldn't have endured carrying that suffering with her even one day longer.

I am faring quite well now with my dear little ones. Admittedly, we don't like it here in Obstgarten anymore, where we cannot buy fruit, not for love or money. But we are hoping to finally find a modest shelter for us closer to the city. In all, we are very *homesick*. No "cheerful" news from you—you are becoming like a fossil in your secret circle. It makes me so sad when I see you fight with and against these miserable people and their maiden treatises. It's nothing but people always harping on the same old string, and they will continue to harp on until everything finally breaks down. I now let them harp on. I feel ridiculous even trying to oppose them. And to tell you the truth about this shamefulness, the majority of books that Percy needed to buy in first class were the Bible, a book about the history of the Bible, songbooks, etc. He had to learn God knows what kinds of church songs rather than a ballad. Would it help me to wage war on this? His school masters would maybe feel sorry for the boy as a victim of the "foolishness of his mother," but in the end he would have to partake in it. The most terrible nonsense is obligatory here as well. *Nevermind*. I won't be tilting at windmills anymore. May it stay as lovely and holy as it is.—Little Hertha again has much to say: "I don't know why you are always laughing about God. All other people speak highly of Him and the books are full of Him." When I told her that her school masters—whom she has the highest opinion of since they are indeed quite diligent—only give her schoolbooks that mention God, and so she couldn't possibly know the other books that say the opposite. Now she is more than curious to see those. At this moment she is writing a letter to you that is too funny for words. All of her ideas are her own and original. Her imagination is as vivid as her will is strong. How the children will adjust to the situation and completely different demands over there this time, I do not know.—How will I fare over there after having settled back into European life and having held my "ground" here? How will <u>you</u> halfway accept the situation over there despite opposing it?—those are all questions that need to be considered soon. The image you have depicted in the last years of the situation and the people there is a very dark one. You are not resilient enough to take irreversible things lightly, forget about them, and start anew with joyful courage.

Remember Platen's[44] words:

> Yet if one loathes whole-hearted what is base,
> It will pursue him from his heritage,
> If there 't is honored by the populace.
> To flee one's fatherland is far more sage
> Than still to bear among a childish race
> The yoke of the unthinking rabble's rage.[45]

If I knew anything about your inner life, which you have kept completely from me for a long time, and if I knew anything about your plans for the future, then it would be easy for me to help you with suggestions, etc. It was to be anticipated that your relationship with your good, weak brother in Lansing and the carnal soul of his wife would make you discontent, yes unhappy, in the long run. It has always been my misfortune that you have put mean characters above me and have always underestimated me, while very, very much overestimating them. Whenever more beautiful people than me have loved you more than I have and have honestly appreciated and seen you, then I always stepped back voluntarily and without any of the jealousy that you wrongfully accused me of. But whenever I saw your errors in judging people for what they were, whenever I saw you spellbound and in shackles unworthy of you, I was very unhappy and miserable. That has ended now. I can be at your side lovingly and admonishingly, but I cannot sacrifice my pride and allow you to put others before me who are not worth it. You will naturally keep doing that and keep judging me wrongly and harshly. You will never take into account my individuality, which is more highly developed than is ordinary after all. And I would not be able to do anything, anything at all, even if I did try to divest myself of my entire oddity—but I won't and don't need to allow you anymore to do what makes me anonymous and miserable. In me you still have the old faithful heart that knows you, loves you, and highly regards your character traits, the good ones. But this heart after a long time of probation has finally re-

---

44. German poet and dramatist Karl August Georg Maximilian, Count of Platen-Hallermünde (1796–1835), famously clashed with Heinrich Heine and other Romantic poets and spent much of his life in Italian cities. Max Koch, "Platen-Hallermünde, August Graf von," in *Allgemeine Deutsche Biographie* (1888), 26:244–49.

45. The English here follows Reginald B. Cooke, trans., *Miscellaneous Sonnets Translated from the German of Platen* (Ithaca, N.Y.: Andrus & Church, 1921), XIX.

gained its independence and I will from now on seek to keep it for the sake of your freedom and mine. . . .

I wish that in this moment you could listen to the loveliest zither[46] playing of our Hertha. She is playing the "May Breezes"[47] with such confidence and clarity and such skill that you would be surprised. In general, I think that Hertha is acting much more pleasantly and has become more lovely since Lili's departure. Percy too is so brave and kind. I went to see Principal Jetschton[48] myself a few days ago to probe the causes of certain complaints, but I have quite convinced myself of their unsustainability. Character, knowledge, all of that was praised—just the many misdeeds, such were the complaints. But where do they come from?—As I could conclude after this closer inspection—they depend on the mood of his teachers and also quite a bit on his forgetfulness and negligence when it comes to certain things. Other than that, I couldn't be more satisfied. Everyone likes the boy very much, also because he has such a beautiful appearance. Also, the oldest son of the Kapps was here, Cäcilie's brother. He literally doted on him.—Now that you don't want to go to battle anymore, it doesn't make sense anymore that you further deny yourself the happiness of having your children with you, isn't that so? . . .

Your old Mathilde.

Cäcilie Kapp to Mathilde Franziska Anneke
Undated, 1864

Saturday, 11 o'clock in the morning

Your letter is here—why did you write it?

I do not understand it—it made me shiver with cold. I've not been able to stop shivering since 7 o'clock when I first read it.—But I will try to overcome this because what is there that a person can't do?—A per-

---

46. A flat stringed instrument without a neck.

47. "Mailüfterl," composed by Joseph Kreipel (1853), German words by Anton von Klesheim. James M. McLaughlin, *Intermediate Song Reader* (Boston: Ginn and Company, 1904), 70; Alexander Rausch, "Kreipel (Kreipl), Josef," in *Oesterreichisches Musiklexikon Online*, last modified May 6, 2001, https://www.musiklexikon.ac.at/ml/musik_K/Kreipel_Josef.xml.

48. The principal is not identifiable.

son learns to live without the most and least valuable things in life—defeated by the vast hours.—Life is now cold and colorless. Just recently life glowed in the most intense colors. "And never, never again you will be unjust to the one—nevermore, not even in thought."—God forbid—no, by God, not unjust.—If "the one" is Mary, so be reassured—you have never been unjust to her with me—and never unfaithful—not even on your way to being unfaithful.—If you'd like, I'll pledge this to her with several holy oaths. <u>She</u> is the lucky one!—

And "expected to?"—No, you are not ["]<u>expected to</u> buy my heart"—you are not <u>expected to</u>—if you don't like and want. You <u>mustn't be expected to</u>. You are not <u>expected to be expected to</u>. I think the love—your love would poison me if you thought you ought to love me because you don't have anyone better at the moment. Delve into Mary's heart—ah, has it ever loved you like—but no—I don't love you and I will not come to you anymore unless you call me.—

Cäcilie Kapp to Mathilde Franziska Anneke
September 21, 1864

You are always in the same harmonious mood! Always the same graciousness that knows no fatigue and no shadow. I've been envious of it for 4 years and will never get there. What came over me today and has held me captive? Your interesting reflections and our tempestuous past perhaps? The memory of all the love I have given you and the love you have taken from me?

No, all of that captured me more than anything can capture me—it was what I have often described to you—an extreme sadness surrounding me like a dark cloud.—And why? Because you are so beautiful—as pretty and decorated and magnificent as any woman on earth has ever been. Your heart often pours out such a narcotic smell on mine that I feel like I'm dying because all my love will not be enough to get to you and hold you tight and make you happy.—That is the extreme sadness I have never felt before, perhaps because I was brave and proud and victorious and never had time for being extremely sad. Let me cry, Mathilde, and take my head into your hands—I think I am ill—I am not saying heal me—because you can't be a diffcrent person than who you are: divine and unique and calm and so enchanting that no human could ever be lovelier. I only say: Have patience!—Good night—the tears are flowing as a soothing relief—I wish it were the blood of my heart that I could shed for you. Dear Mathilde, dear beloved Mathilde!

Fritz Anneke to Mathilde Franziska Anneke
St. Louis, December 19, 1864

My dear Mathilde!

Still nothing new nor old, or maybe lost or delayed, from you.

Today, I'm sending the secondary part of the 640 fr in bills of exchange. I sent the primary part in my last letter via Prussian mail. I can only send you one page of the essay because I was too occupied finding an occupation, and I am now too busy with the one I've finally found. I cannot give you all the details about all of this running around. And it wouldn't be interesting enough for you either. . . . I have now been busy for 10 days collecting census information for a small district in the city of St. Louis. They pay 1½ cents for every name. But apart from the name I also need to note nationality, age, occupation, skin color, address, for children whether they attend school, and further naturalization or not, etc. I've found another occupation in an engagement writing military articles for the *Neuer Anzeiger des Westens*. Dänzer[49] is owner and editor. The paper is the most stable in St. Louis, but it is a very "*Copperhead*"[50] paper. . . . Dänzer would have liked to have me as co-editor, but it goes without saying that that's not possible.[51]

No answer from Mary yet. Kapp[52] writes that the new paper in New York would not be published before March or April of 1865. I have

---

49. Baden Forty-Eighter Carl Dänzer resurrected St. Louis's *Anzeiger des Westens* (briefly the *Neuer Anzeiger des Westens*) as a conservative Unionist newspaper in 1863. In editorials, he accepted emancipation as a fait accompli but resisted other efforts to support African Americans and neutralize Confederate sentiment. Alison Clark Efford, *German Immigrants, Race, and Citizenship in the Civil War Era* (New York: Cambridge University Press, 2013), 95; Zucker, *Forty-Eighters*, 285.

50. A derogatory term for the northern Democrats who wanted an immediate end to the Civil War, which would have allowed slavery to survive. Jennifer L. Weber, *Copperheads: The Rise and Fall of Lincoln's Opponents in the North* (New York: Oxford University Press, 2006).

51. Perhaps because Fritz did not have money to invest in the newspaper or because he held different political views.

52. Friedrich Kapp. See n. 63 (chapter 4).

nothing to do with it. Cluseret[53] says he is already engaged as military editor and when the time comes would keep in mind that I've expressed interest. In the same mail with the letter to you, I'll send "a dramatic poem by Friedrich Schnake"[54] to you which has received positive reviews. I did not have time to read it. . . .

More about that soon. I'm sending greetings and kisses to my dear children.

Yours, Fritz.

Mathilde Franziska Anneke to Fritz Anneke
Zürich, January 24, 1865

My dear Fritz!

After a long period of longing and waiting for them, I finally received two letters at the same time. The one dated December 19 with the splendid photograph of Carl and Emmy[55] and the secondary part of the bill of exchange and the letter dated Jan. 4. Thank you for delivering me from distressing darkness. How can you think that your decision regarding my plan and suggestion would embarrass me? Only in so far as my hopes of a betterment of our situation are fading with it—but if my hopes were baseless then I can be only happy that after thor-

---

53. A French military officer who was active on the left and participated in nationalist uprisings around Europe. He briefly served as a brigadier general in the U.S. Civil War. Alban Bargain-Villeger, "Captain Tin Can: Gustave Cluseret and the Socialist Left, 1848–1900," *Socialist History* 46 (2015): 13–32.

54. Friedrich Schnake, *Unabhängigkeits-Erklärung der Vereinigten Staaten von Amerika: Ein dramatisches Gedicht* (St. Louis, Mo.: Christian Fr. Lammers & Co., 1864). Schnake was an almost unknown German American author who served in the Union army in Missouri. Rudolf Cronau, *Drei Jahrhunderte deutschen Lebens in Amerika* (Berlin: Dietrich Reimer, 1909), 496; U.S. Census, Population Schedules (1880), St. Louis, Missouri, p. 411, dwelling 66, family 209; U.S. Census of Union Veterans and Widows of the Civil War (1890), Omaha, Nebraska, p. 3, dwelling 312, family 343.

55. Carl Lachmund and Emilie or Emily ("Emmy") Schmidtill, the daughter of Fritz's sister, whom Lachmund was about to marry. The two had met while Fritz and Lachmund were staying with the Schmidtills together on first arriving in St. Louis. Some writers have misidentified Emmy as Fanny, but that that was the name of Lachmund's second wife. "St. Louis Marriage Records, vol. 12 (1865–1867)," p. 8, *FamilySearch*, accessed July 30, 2020, https://familysearch.org/ark:/61903/3:1:3QS7-898M-BQBF?cc=2060668&wc=ZMYJ T38%3A352318101%2C1583592801; Henriette M. Heinzen and Hertha Anneke Sanne, "Biographical Notes in Commemoration of Fritz Anneke and Mathilde Franziska Anneke," 1940, unpublished manuscript, Box 8. Folders 1–2, Anneke Papers.

ough examination and consideration of the plan you are making a decision. I've always been happy to defer to your sober judgement and have never acted one-sidedly. You will admit that. And it is like that this time as well, dear Fritz. I give in and will dwell on thoughts and new ideals.

I haven't read the ending of your essay, which has an interesting beginning, because I'm answering you instantly. I will send it to the *Allgemeine* today. I am very much looking forward to your military articles—you know I've always enjoyed listening when you told me about your area of expertise. Now that I can't listen to you, I'd like even more to read them. The papers (I mean the American papers with the mail via Bremen) have not been delivered yet. The poem by "<u>Friedrich Schnake</u>"—I have long seen its announcement in American papers—but I haven't been able to find out whether it's written by our old Ahasuerus.[56] He was in Münster when I was there. But of course, in the few hours I spent there I did not see him. He was furious about that. I'm eager to read the poem. Even more so because I've collected American material for an epic poem. I now want to devote my attention to fiction more seriously again, if you and a better fate may not allow me that the terrible correspondence work will give me my quietus. I want to shout for joy at my *Sturmgeiger* again and promise completion. People here are beginning to have high hopes for me. I received a letter from Countess Hatzfeldt yesterday. She is repeatedly asking me to send her an obituary (a poetic one) for Lasalle[57] for the book that she and her friends are dedicating to him and that is supposed to elucidate the last few days of his life. It will attract much attention because people are eagerly awaiting it. But exactly because it will create a spectacle, and I am a shy singing little forest bird—or rather my muse is—I will hold my peace. She insists that my name be among the names of his friends. I have held the thinker in high regard—I've read his last 12 works for the most part. The Countess is calling upon my friendship to dedicate the next months to her. Surely, I am supposed to stay at baths with her—she would like that. But I can't. She is calling all good spirits and is

---

56. The name associated with the "wandering Jew" of legend from about 1600 on in German Europe. George K. Anderson, *The Legend of the Wandering Jew* (Providence, R.I.: Brown University, 1965), 50.

57. Lassalle had died on August 31, 1864, from wounds sustained in a duel he had initiated after a woman rejected him in favor of another suitor. David Footman, *Ferdinand Lassalle: Romantic Revolutionary* (New York: Greenwood Press, 1947), 230–39.

begging me not to go to America during the war for the well-being of my children and a more thorough and better education for Percy. But I must leave Zürich. I need to see different things and breathe different air so that maybe my body will recover. I am ill. The gout has spread in my entire upper body, and will I ever be freed of the gout? I have had terrible nights and days. The sun is shining today, and I'm feeling better. We had 2–3 feet of snow last week, and I was feeling quite terrible then. I suffer inwardly. Of course, I am not consulting a doctor. I warm up my chest with hot stones, and that helps at times. My arms often feel as if they were benumbed. Smart people will claim that this will change with the years. Certainly! When your letters arrived, many others did too. Cäcilie especially sent a letter beseeching me to please leave the awful Zürich at once. Throughout the entire winter she has tried to convince me to come to her[58] for my own benefit and the benefit of the children. She is in a boarding school, an institute consisting of various buildings. There are none but elite people in the one building, mostly women who are working and who are not taking care of their own households. The actual boarding school is a boys' school with 120 students. Cäcilie is full of admiration for it and things it would be very much suitable for Percy, especially since I would not be separated from the boy if I took her advice. She believes that she would be able to arrange a fruitful stay for him there at reduced cost, say 20 to 25 fr per month for him and 68 a month for me. And at reduced cost for Hertha.—Cäcilie is now in a comfortable situation. She teaches and looks after the daughter of one Duchess of Riviere[59] six afternoons a week and earns 140 francs a month for it. She now desires an occupation for the mornings so that she can increase her pay. She only asks to have me nearby so that she can take care of me like she did with so much love when I was ill 2 years ago. She kept watch at night. Now she demands a decision about whether I will come to Paris or not. If not, then it would be her unwelcome duty to come back to Zürich out of love for me. You are not against this plan in your letter, but I'd like to hear your thoughts regarding Percy before I make a decision. What influence will the impressions of that major city have on him? Will they impede his

---

58. In Paris.

59. Possibly Stéphanie de Riffardeau (née de Crossé), wife of the Duc de Rivière, although her children were approaching adulthood. M. Borel d'Hauterive, *Annuaire de la noblesse de France* (Paris: Bureau de la Publication, 1857), 137.

intellectual education in its more noble, pure direction, or will they be beneficial? Or is that not a question that needs to be considered regarding this enclosed institute? On which *department* should he mainly focus? The industrial or the commercial? The Christian for now? I am standing here in silence and don't know what to do. First, I will let Cäcilie draw up the exact budget and then make plans for our departure based on that—since right now a few rooms will become available next month. How I will deal with the creditors here, I do not know. . . .

But then this anxiety creeps up on me about being in Paris with the children and without Mother. Here, I am used to that and basically, I have much trust in the people here, especially in the community of Hottingen, where I have the right of settlement. But the fog and Cilly[60] are chasing me away from here. And the children too—other than the benefit of their education and broadening their minds—ask to get out of this one-year rural solitude for a change.—I have become so timid and indecisive. Above all, I don't want to do anything that is not for the benefit of the children. I blame myself if we even lose one day for them and even spend one cent unnecessarily.

You should see our handsome, blooming Percy, a fine figure in his blue uniform jacket with shiny silver buttons—and now with his watch—as proud as a king! He has the loveliest way of expressing himself. Both in the world of words and in the clear expression of his thoughts. In arithmetic and math, he must be ahead of his classmates in the second grade. He has grown taller than most of the professors. He is top of his class and therefore called "Colonel Anneke." Little Hertha is a truly smart, dear child who is hungry for knowledge and Cäcilie's favorite. She has consequently been trying to learn French all by herself for weeks. She has learned the English script so well that it is a joy. When she doesn't write the letters in their full beauty and thinks they are still far from how mine look then she gets angry at herself. You couldn't get enough of the children. It always pains me when I have to justify myself to Percy when it comes to sciences that are completely unknown to me, like physics and such, and when I have to admit that I do not know about things like that. I could avoid that in Mons[ieur] Carre's Institute[61] though. But what should I do? Yes, I ask, and by the time you answer, I will have already decided. But Cäcilie says "try it for

---

60. Cäcilie Kapp.
61. Possibly the Institution de Carré-Demailly on the Rue du Rocher, less than a mile

a month"! I am slowly approaching the Atlantic journey, and that is for the best.

I've made a mistake in calculating my obligations and then borrowing money from Pestalozzi. For one item I was now given a loan of 203 instead 103 fr. In all, we have borrowed 2,103 fr now.—Will we be able to keep our funds, and do you have hope that the finances will settle so that we have enough resources for our journey back?—I hope it was comfortable for you to receive the *currency* instead of the 10/40s. . . .[62]

Hertha is plucking the strings and with her happy folkdance she is chasing the musty spirits away. You should hear her play one day. I will lament losing her expensive but excellent music teacher.

On another day. The storm is howling, and I have been lamenting trying to keep up with the storm this night. There can be no thought of getting any sleep.—The matter of how to make a living in Paris—and the more difficult one—the matter of our debts here make me so miserable that I do not know what to do. I cannot make a decision—but it is time—and I will need to be courageous. Oh, and I am courageous whenever I am free of this pain—now the papers have arrived. I recognize you in two military articles: "Vandalism" and "200,000 more!" The dramatic poem isn't by our Schnake. He is happily hiking in Germany, from one part to another. The author lives in St. Louis. I've been meaning to find him.

Greetings to the whole family. Our children are healthy and very kind. They send greetings and kisses to their Papa.

Do you think the gold price will stay at the same steady high price for a while? I haven't spoken with Pestalozzi yet to see whether he wants to keep the sum or not. But I cannot go outside in this rain and snow. It would be very dangerous.

Is Ida[63] always quite healthy? Emmy's little face is incredibly dear and pleasing. Carl looks different based on the picture. Congratulate them for me.

I haven't had news from over there in weeks. And now everything all

---

from the Champs-Élysées. Didot-Bottin, *Annuaire-almanach du commerce, de l'industrie, de la magistrature et de l'administration* (Paris: Didot Freres, 1859), 1161.

62. In 1864 Congress authorized the issuing of 10/40 bonds, which would pay 5 percent in coin when redeemed between ten and forty years in the future. *New York Times*, April 22, 1864.

63. Fritz's sister Ida Schmidtill.

at once. Thank you for every letter. Mary also wrote me a very dear letter after the excursion that she made on Dec. 23 to visit Fanny.

Farewell, farewell.

Yours, Mathilde.

Greetings to my Mother

CHAPTER 7

Endings and Beginnings

February–August 1865

FOR FRITZ AND MATHILDE, THE LAST YEAR OF THE CIVIL WAR brought definitive endings, but also new beginnings. Late in 1864, Fritz had moved to St. Louis and accepted a position with the (*Neuer*) *Anzeiger des Westens*, which took him in a new political direction. The newspaper set itself in opposition to most Forty-Eighters by editorializing against African American rights and Republican measures to control Confederate sympathizers. Mary and Mathilde, on the other hand, did not lose their commitment to the Republican Party and Abraham Lincoln's leadership.[1] Mary was visiting Mathilde's adult daughter Fanny in Newark when she described the celebrations in honor of Lincoln's second inauguration, but she spent most of her final months living in private New York clinics surrounded by male admirers.

The news of Mary's death on April 11, 1865, devastated Mathilde, but she had already begun to look to the future. From February to August 1865, Mathilde, Percy, and Hertha lived with Cäcilie Kapp in Paris. Kapp worked as a governess and the children continued their educations, while Mathilde began making plans to open a private girls' school with Kapp in the United States. Milwaukee's Töchter-Institut (or Daughters' Institute) became one of Mathilde's best-known achievements. It offered innovative instruction to a small group of girls, most from well-off German American families. Because female academies empowered girls, Mathilde's educational work aligned with her conviction that social conventions held women back from achieving equality with men. As she settled back into Milwaukee, she resumed her work campaigning for women's right to vote and began her rise to become Wisconsin's leading woman suffragist.

---

1. Mathilde to Franziska Hammacher, January 17, 1864, in *"Ich gestehe, die Herrschaft der fluchwürdigen 'Demokratie' dieses Landes macht mich betrübt...": Mathilde Franziska Annekes Briefe an Franziska und Friedrich Hammacher, 1860–1884*, ed. Erhard Kiehnbaum (Hamburg: Argument Verlag mit Ariadne, 2017), 202.

Mathilde Franziska Anneke to Fritz Anneke
Paris, February 14, 1865

My dear Fritz!

You will have received my last letter (with 50 dollars in *currency* and a letter for Mary). I told you that we would immediately send word to you about our move. We have been within the walls of Paris since Saturday. We traveled in the wee hours of the morning—it was hardly three o'clock when we left our *"home."* Frau Müller, our landlady, took care of us with a warm breakfast. She kept us warm during a sudden snow flurry and gave us her best blessing to take along the way. And our maid also showed us her touching loyalty. The children were very cheerful about their move to Paris. In front of the Hauenstein[2] they again expressed their love and admiration for the beautiful Swiss valleys and "snow mountains." The snow-covered landscape was lovely, as you must know. Then we took the French railroad through the ghastly tunnel and then to Basel to finally get into sad and dull France. Percy's opinion of France and his astonishment at the entirely neglected *Kultur* here, his reflections on the institutions in an empire and a republic—the obvious fact to him that a wretched emperor is not doing anything for his country and its people, his fresh humor—all of this would have made you endlessly happy about our dear boy. We were traveling in a heated railroad car in Switzerland. But not in this sad France where we traveled in the cheap class. The children were suffering terribly from the cold, but I kept them warm and took good care of them with wine, sausages, eggs, and bread. And then around noon the sun shone into our little cell—we had the railroad car to ourselves throughout the entire journey. Percy acted as the master of ceremonies and we then happily arrived at the train station de Strasbourg[3] in Paris, where the good Cilly awaited us. She immediately took us to the boardinghouse, where we found our little shelter to be quite good and comfortable.

---

2. A pair of mountain passes in northern Switzerland.

3. Now known as the Gare de Paris-Est. *Harper's Guide to Paris and the Exposition of 1900* (London: Harper and Brothers, 1900), 50.

The boardinghouse of the Carré family consists of a boys' and a girls' institute. I moved into the latter with Hertha. It is a spacious house in between gardens and trees and is connected to the schoolhouses. In the main house where I live are the dining rooms for the young girls and the apartments of several quiet women and teachers. The daughters of the family and a young woman named Frida and several teachers oversee it. The boys' institute is one street away from here. Herr and Madame Carée are its dignified directors. There are more than 100 boys and our teachers there. Percy started school immediately and with much joy. Hertha instantly joined her class. Naturally, she is staying with me and not with the rest of the girls in the dormitories. Other than that, she partakes in everything. She speaks English and German with the various children and teachers and is very proud to have written in French for two days now with the teacher praising her and giving her a big "tres bon." The children are discovering a new world. I will tell you more about the educational material and Percy's studies after I've had my first consultation with the director today.

I need to tell you the following about our finances. We are to pay 67 francs per month in advance for Percy and 150 for Hertha and me. Everything is included: the apartment, food, and wash. I can end this contract any month on the 12th of the month: You will now have to see, dear Fritz, how you will send us these monthly resources. After first consideration, examinations, and searches, I was not able to find anything more suitable for me and the children anywhere.—I have paid for the month, but I do not have our equipment yet, for which I do not have money anymore. Before I can think of working, I need to rest a while yet. I need to try to be free of the gout first and need to devote my attention to the children. Cäcilie also has her school in this building, but she goes to the Duchess Riviere and the Marquise Beaufort[4] every day to teach two daughters there. She has quite a nice little income and comfortable position, but it's not long-term.

I now hear Hertha below my window playing and dancing with the sweet little French girls. It is play hour. How happy the child is again

---

4. Perhaps the wife of Charles-Napolèon Brandouin de Balaguier, Marquis of Beaufort d'Hautpoul (1804–1890), although he had no surviving children. C. d'E.-A., *Dictionnaire des familles françaises anciennes ou notables à la fin du XIXe siècle* (Évreux: Charles Hérissey, 1907), 6:362.

among other children! She does have a tendency for melancholy after all.—And now that her eagerness to speak French and learn how to read English is satisfied, she is very happy. And Percy too is presented with a different life goal. In Zürich, apart from good things, he definitely gave in to such things that would have soon transformed his character. And given my constant illness I could not handle him. He was always fighting with the girls. He gave them commands and no matter how much he likes them, annoyed her and Hertha—he was a boy of both good and boorish behavior. Now he needs to adjust to order and obedience for a while.—I hope and wish, dear Fritz, that you not only approve of my actions—but will be as happy as I am about this happy coincidence. Imagine my dear Cilly here, my little Hertha here and still in a good institute, and Percy close by and diligently working toward his goal.—

You are now obligated to send the money, to prevent us from losses as much as possible. You cannot quite count on me for that now, dear Fritz. I will work and earn as much as I can. (I have published another novella in *Der Bund*[5] and received a decent payment for the last one.) But this is the time that must be devoted to our children.

But above all, please tell me the direction Percy should be taking in his studies. In the meantime, I have selected the *French* and English languages and history, which also supports the study of language, as well as math. I think we will leave it at that until we hear your decision.
Wednesday

We have been here for three days now, and I can already tell you this much: The institute here is the most suitable and best that we could have chosen. It will have the best influence on the physical development of our two. The food is so perfect for children. They are so content and happy about the plentiful good meat, jam, and fruit they get here. Hertha is sitting among the little girls and is being flattered. She speaks English to most of them.

Please write to me at once. I must rush to a close because the mail is leaving, and I want this letter to be on the next *steamer*.

Percy is off tomorrow afternoon and is allowed to be with his little sister and with us. I don't have any more money. The boxes will arrive in the next few days.

---

5. A liberal newspaper in Switzerland. Ernst Bollinger, "Der Bund (Zeitung)," in *Historisches Lexikon der Schweiz*, last modified, September 7, 2019, https://hls-dhs-dss.ch/de/articles/024773/2019-07-09/.

Farewell, dear Fritz, and give my best to all our loved ones.

Cilly is very kind and like an angel with our children. I am supposed to tell you that she would also take good care of me. Write to her too soon.

Adieu, Adieu.

Yours, Mathilde.

Mathilde Franziska Anneke to Fritz Anneke
Paris, February 1865

My dear Fritz!

Percy is beginning to speak French quite nicely, while Hertha is keeping to her English and German with stubborn persistency. The teachers at the institute all speak English in addition to French—and she also chose the English-speaking children—and so she keeps with that. "Well, I am an American child after all," she says, "Why should I learn French?"—I cannot abandon my native German either. Cäcilie and I went to a lecture by Alexander Dumas.[6] It was more out of my curiosity to see the man than thirst for knowledge. He spoke about the topic of the day: Julius Caesar.[7] I did not understand a word, but I did understand more of the enthusiastic social speech given by a flaming young socialist about the eternal topic: *la femme*. When I saw the prologue of the imperial work, which hasn't been published yet,[8] I translated the strange document at once and sent it to the [*Illinois Staatszeitung*]. A bold challenge indeed—I wonder whether the author isn't afraid of the Ides of March[9] and whether his soothsayers haven't warned him? This country of France would have to put up with too much humiliation if it were to endure this! . . .

---

6. The prolific and popular French author was in Paris only briefly during the period when he traveled around Europe, especially the Italian lands, where he supported unification. Claude Schopp, *Alexandre Dumas: Genius of Life*, trans. A. J. Hoch (New York: Franklin Watts, 1988).

7. Louis Napoleon was famously finishing a book appropriating the legacy of the Roman emperor. E. Richardson, "The Emperor's Caesar: Napoleon III, Karl Marx and the History of Julius Caesar," in *Graeco-Roman Antiquity and the Idea of Nationalism in the 19th Century: Case Studies* (Berlin: De Gruyter, 2016), 113–30.

8. See previous note.

9. March 15 was the date of Julius Caesar's assassination.

I am always alone during the day. During the breaks—which are at 10 in the mornings and from 12–2 and at 4 o'clock—Hertha visits me. If I get too bored, I often take her out of her classes too. She doesn't like to leave her lovely teacher, who has learned German a bit, but in the end, I win the day.

At 10 o'clock Cäcilie leaves already to go to her marquises and dukes to teach her lessons. She comes home only after 6 o'clock. Working as a private teacher in the streets of Paris is not an enviable fate. She earns 200 fr a month. That about covers the wash and food. An institute in America is the goal of her striving. You haven't given further notice. If we are to depart this year and if we plan on the month of August, then might I still see my mother alive?! She writes me that Milwaukie is very suitable for a daughters' institute at this moment. Cäcilie is a highly educated teacher. The people of Milwaukie could congratulate themselves for being so lucky.—

I am very happy to have her as a friend and that she likes me enough to follow me across the ocean. I was invited to a soirée the day before yesterday. I met Bamberger,[10] whom you know well from 48, his wife, and Szarvady,[11] the well-known journalist and his wife. Bamberger sends his best. They have invited me to visit, and I will go in order to spend some time with trustworthy Germans. I know you respect him as such.

Hertha just jumped out of her class. She said she learned the French musical notes in a heartbeat, and I should ask you whether she could have piano lessons too now. I would let her start immediately, if the finances didn't worry me so much. She is playing her zither to everyone's enjoyment. It is too bad she can't get zither lessons here. The children are strikingly thirsty for knowledge and education, Hertha especially. . . .

Unfortunately, once our financial crisis is over so too will be the time and opportunity to make the necessary changes to the upbringing and education of the children. And then I will eternally regret it. Maybe

---

10. The German economist had been a republican in 1848 but was beginning to embrace Bismarck's nationalism. Theodor Heuss, "Bamberger, Ludwig," in *Neue Deutsche Biographie* (1953), 1:572–74.

11. Author Frigyes Szarvady (1822–1882) was a Hungarian Forty-Eighter émigré close to Lajos Kossuth. Robert R. Ivany, "The Exploited Émigrés: The Hungarians in Europe, 1853–1861" (PhD diss., University of Wisconsin–Madison, 1980), 144–47.

when the worries are over you will think it is appropriate to stay here in Europe with them for another year or half a year. I am awaiting your decision on this, which you will be able to make more easily since this letter will reach you at a time when events will have progressed. I have finished half of my novel Uhland in Texas. If only I knew how to send the manuscript? I hear the Sunday edition of the *Staatszeitung*[12] lashed into the *Geisterhaus* quite a bit. Mary wrote to me. Mary has a very good engagement for the publication of her poems with Lipincott in Philadelphia. She writes that too. I wonder how things are between her and her "artist"?[13] If her health should return and if she has hope, then maybe she will get married? I think so. It has always been her plan. As a fatalist, she has always claimed not to be able to escape her fate. If it only makes her happy, then that is all fine. Her naive soul-searching with individuals who've crossed her path has been very painful for me. She may have the right to do that. She can ask for much from these people in return for her humbleness and sweetness.—This certainly is a view that is not usually commonplace—but which one can come to achieve when having a different view of things from what is ordinary. It is such terrible weather here that I can barely find an hour here and there to go outside. The children aren't much luckier with their free periods. I need to buy a new suit for Percy. Despite the fact that I still have enough clothing for him, it won't do as he certainly is growing like weed.—The sleeve of his uniform—he is still wearing the cadet's uniform—barely covers his elbow & I cannot stand it any longer. I must take 40 fr into the Palais Royal district[14] where supposedly one can buy the cheapest suits. Cheaper than in Zürich, where I always paid 60 francs at least.—

We are looking forward to tomorrow, Sunday, when Percy will be with us as soon as 8 o'clock already. He wanted to bring me a little note for you.—Then I will send you these lines. Now I will attend to the *Illinois* [*Staatszeitung*] and write the bills for my articles.

Farewell, farewell.

---

12. Probably the *New-Yorker Staats-Zeitung*. See n. 89 (chapter 2).
13. Theodore Wüst. See n. 27 (chapter 6).
14. This area north of the Louvre was home to covered shopping arcades in the nineteenth century. Jonathan Conlin, *Tales of Two Cities: Paris, London and the Birth of the Modern City* (Berkeley: Counterpoint, 2013), 74–75.

I am feeling better. I lit a nice fire in the fireplace. I hope that you are faring well. Greetings to our folks.

Yours, Mathilde.

. . .

Cäcilie sends her love.
Cher papa, je t'embrasse de tout mon coeur.[15]
Hertha.

Mary Booth to Mathilde Franziska Anneke
Newark, March 3–4, 1865
(English original)

Sweet Franziska Maria! Going to bed, but must first say you good night, and tell you how I happened to be here.—Dr. Greves[16] brought me from New York this afternoon to consult a very distinguished clavoyant female physician, whose husband is also a Dr. and I did not know but I should have to stay here in boarding a few weeks under her care, and so I came prepared accordingly, but it will not be needful. She finds me very sick indeed, and says if I go on as I now am, and stay in this climate with my present health, I shall die in the month of May—but she said it was not need[ed]—and that Dr. Greves must magnitize[17] me always every day. He told he[r] he lived too far away, and had not the time, and she said he must <u>steal</u> the time, because he <u>must</u> do it—it was his <u>duty</u>, and he said it would. I told her Dr. Bronson was a magnitizer, and lived in the house, but she said he would never do at all, and that he must not touch me. She said I must get out of this climate <u>quick</u>, and told the Dr. it was his <u>duty</u> to take me to Calafornia.—He did not see how he could afford it this time, but she said that was not a question—he must—that he would be a richer man a year sooner by doing so, though she could not see clearly <u>how</u> still it was so, and he said he had already <u>wished</u> to do it, & now, should, if he possi-

---

15. Hertha wrote in French: "Dear Papa, I kiss you with all my heart."
16. We have not been able to identify this physician.
17. The practice of supposedly healing someone by manipulating their magnetic field by touch. Also called "animal magnetism" and "mesmerism," it originated in Germany in the eighteenth century. John C. Gunn, *Gunn's Domestic Physician* (Cincinnati, Ohio: Moore, Wilstach, Keys & Co, 1861), 349–63.

bly could. She said, as all the Dr.'s do, that I was coming to the <u>turn of life</u>, & I am much too young. It is <u>three months</u> to-morrow since I had a "period," and it has been very irregular since I left you, & I have the most dreadful nose bleeds. Last week I had again two fits in one night. They were only half an hour each. Mr. Wüst was alone with me in the first, and the Dr., & the whole family in the second, which was at morning. They also come from this trouble with my age. Dr. Greves is truly an angel to me—he is wonderful, and I am astonished more and more with him. He brought me here to Fanny's. She is just getting up from a sickness of loss of blood—from both ways. She looks as pale as I, and cannot speak loud. She had two Dr.'s—one American, & one German. Dr. Greves said she would now get up soon—that all she wants is strength, and happy society, and he said he was glad for her sake and health to have me stay a couple of days. He was much pleased with her as well as the children. I told him I thought I would go home Sunday evening, and he said if he could not come for me he would have Mr. Wüst come, or someone from the house. Fanny is very happy that I came. She says I shall give you her love. Good night—Your

    Mary

<u>March 4, 1865.</u>
<u>Saturday morning</u>. To day is the day of the Presidential Inauguration. Fanny says she feels a great deal better and stronger to day. I have been cooking oyster pancakes for our dinner, which both Fanny and I enjoyed very much. It is horrid how that awful old woman has plagued her with her lies. I wish you could see the young Paula,[18] who is just the perfect image of yourself, and so, of course, a most beautiful child. I wish she was yours, as she ought to be. Everybody would be satisfied. The others are not a comparison, yet Mathilde is wonderful good, and very pretty. The boy is nothing especial, though very pleasant and good natured, and makes no trouble. Mathilde thinks of nothing save when Lillian will come again, which will be in her vacation soon after her birthday.

My dear Mama[19]

    Mary will have told you about my illness. This time, I barely escaped death. I

---

18. Fanny's daughter Paula died in 1866. Mathilde to Franziska Hammacher, April 8–June 5, 1866, in "*Ich gestehe, die Herrschaft der fluchwürdigen 'Demokratie' dieses Landes macht mich betrübt*," 236.

19. Mathilde's daughter Fanny Störger wrote a paragraph in German in the middle of Mary's letter.

had such a terrible rush of blood that the doctors said they had rarely seen such a thing and could not understand what has kept me alive. But I am quite well again, only very weak. I can barely walk, and the good Marie has to go on a ride with me. Marie and I are enjoying each other's company. You would be glad to see us like this.

Dear Mama, I can't write anymore!
More tomorrow.

...

Mathilde Franziska Anneke to her sister Johanna Weiskirch
Paris, March 30, 1865

Dear Johanna!

Our good mother will barely receive these greetings in time for the most beautiful of spring celebrations. Oh, I have missed the celebrations of her children for years, and it would almost comfort me to know that she almost won't miss me anymore, if I did not have hopes of maybe seeing her again this summer. Yes, the children and I are drawn to our homeland again, which in our minds has always been at Lake Michigan.

I won't go into detail but want to let you know that I cannot consent to Fritz's proposal to go to St. Louis. My liver illness would kill me there. I wish to settle independently in a city where I can work and secure my livelihood together with Cäcilie Kapp. This would be possible for me in Europe. Only for the benefit of the children, who should not be under the curse of rootlessness like their mother, I am returning to their fatherland. I am returning because there I have my dear living and my unforgettable dead. Will and can you assist me with advice on my future position that I hope to establish for myself together with Cäcilie Kapp, possibly in Milwaukie. The <u>founding</u> of a "*Ladies' Academie*" would be Cäcilie's task, and I would only support her wherever I would be of help. In any case, we would have our "*home*" together. I would continue my literary writing on the side, and after providing for Percy, I could afford the necessities of life for Hertha and me. You will certainly be so kind as to answer my questions regarding the institute as quickly as possible. You can of course make suggestions of how to support this institute, which is of public benefit. You mothers should all be very interested in donating. I ask you to give the enclosed letter to a former acquaintance of Cäcilie, Frau Quentin,[20] yourself if possible. This is to spark the woman's interest—and I do not know her, but as a well-to-do woman, she will likely be influential—and in fact assure her support and immediate response.

Cäcilie has the most noble skills. Not only is she very fluent in all three languages: English, French, and German, but she also speaks Italian, plays the piano, in short is an impressive woman and moreover an experienced educator. The people of Milwaukie would be proud to be able to get her. The reason why I prefer to be in the background of this endeavor is that my radical views might not be helpful. But Cäcilie is practical and smart enough to take a moderate path. She is by no means a heathen, like me. In fact, she is fairly religious, but in a way that doesn't bother me when it comes to our close friendship.

The reason that I moved here from Zürich was first of all so that Percy could learn the French language. The child makes me very happy. Yesterday, the director of the institute let me know that he has never had an alumnus who so thoroughly, so quickly, and so purely learned the French language as a foreigner. He will be done with it in a few months.—All my hopes lie on getting Percy into a practical career <u>at once</u> so that he will not start dreaming and philosophizing about unlucky stars, etc., etc. Perhaps, when the path is in front of him and everything is ready, Fritz will not be against it. But maybe—and probably likely—Fritz will not allow Percy to enter a practical profession like an American. It would be terrible for me if I had to part ways with the lad insofar as the academies in St. Louis are being praised and in case his father would insist on letting him take the path of a theoretical education. His inherent character traits would not develop positively under the regime of Fritz. I would then consider my big worries and efforts regarding Percy's education if not entirely in vain, then surely as very ineffective.

Hertha also has a true Anneke nature. However, she can be quite kind. She is incredibly advanced for her age. I haven't gotten to know Paris much yet. There is such raw weather that one doesn't dare to go

---

20. Likely Charlotte Quentin, the wife of Johann Christian Carl Quentin, a former Prussian government official. He immigrated to Milwaukee in 1851, where he invested in German American businesses, became a state senator, and wrote travel literature. Rudolph Koss, *Milwaukee* (Milwaukee: Schnellpressen-Druck des Herold, 1871), 315.

outside. Since I've left Zürich and its foggy surroundings, I have been freed of the gout which has nearly killed me throughout the entire winter. My liver illness is better also.

I could secure a living here in Paris better than anywhere else. But I couldn't give the children what is necessary for their education. Fritz is leaving me high and dry in that regard. What does it help me that he claims to earn 100 and more recently $150 a month, when he expects me to do the impossible? In July of last year, I received 500 dollars from him which I leveraged for 500 francs, only to keep that capital. And since I've only received 500 francs from him since but would have needed 250 francs a month for a halfway decent life and education of the children, you will see what I had to earn myself.—

And I would increase my salary here more and more. But with regard to Percy's future, I must not even think of postponing returning any longer. Don't you agree?—Will you think about this and immediately let me know your thoughts and conclusions about Cäcilie's prospects and my own?

But keep my letter to yourself. I do not want the *Jobsiade* singer[21] to gossip about this. I know you know what I mean.—

The questions regarding the institute are:

What are the prospects for founding an institute for the education of the daughters of German and English families?

Would such an institute be viable solely as a <u>Daughters' Academy</u> for external students or also for internal students (meaning female students living in the building)?

Would it be welcome to put a large focus on the French language?

Or would it be advisable for Cäcilie to join an existing English American academy or even expand it? Who would be our points of contact for this?

Take this to heart, dear Johanna, and help support an endeavor that might be beneficial for your daughters and granddaughters.

And I just remembered that our esteemed teacher Frau Költgen[22] has gone off to the realms of shadows. Consumption carried her off.—

---

21. With "Jobsiadensänger" Mathilde was referring to a 1784 satire of student life that mocked German philistines. Carl Arnold Kortum, *Die Jobsiade: Ein grotesk-komisches Heldengedicht in 3 Theilen*, 8th ed. (Leipzig: Brockhaus, 1857). She seems concerned that people would mock her plans in the same way Kortum had derided his characters. It is unclear here whether she has a particular person or a type of person in mind.

22. *Das Institut der Fräulein Költgen* is now the Annette von Droste-Hülshoff-Gymnasium,

You will also let me know your ideas about an apartment and a location for the institute.—Please answer soon because we are leaving soon.—What do you think of Cincinnati, which has been recommended to us because of the protectorate of Stallo and Willich?[23]

—Farewell, dear Johanna. Please do not consider my requests to be egoistical. As soon as I am on solid ground again, I will be a different person. If there is need for any course subjects, then please let me know. Then we could hire teachers accordingly. Farewell, dear Johanna. Rest assured of the love of your old Mathilde.

Mathilde Franziska Anneke to Fritz Anneke
Paris, April 10, 1865

My dear Fritz!

I haven't written to you in a long time. You may think that this is because the city of Paris holds all kinds of distractions for me. I didn't have any external distractions. And I still have so few impressions of Paris that I can barely say that I live here. Until April 4 we had the most unpleasant cold. We barely knew how to protect ourselves from it. In the end, I had to buy warmer suits for the children. And now it has suddenly become a nice and blooming spring.

Our children, our only joy, are healthy and are striving toward progress and education with the rarest diligence. Since we've been here, the past Sunday was the first one on which the weather could be praised. We seized the day and went on a little Paris trip, much to Percy's delight. Cäcilie and I took the children to the beautiful Luxembourg [Palace].[24] On Sundays, one can visit the coronation halls and art galleries at a lower cost. We were all delighted. Tired and thirsty we then ven-

---

a high school in Münster, Germany. Wolfgang König and Jürgen Sprekels, eds., *Karl Weierstraß, 1815–1897: Aspekte seines Lebens und Werkes—Aspects of His Life and Work* (Wiesbaden: Springer, 2016), 29.

23. Mathilde would have been politically aligned with Willich (see n. 81 (chapter 2)) and jurist J. B. Stallo, who were influential German American leaders in Cincinnati. Jürgen Kessel, *Johann Bernard Stallo (1823–1900): Ein deutsch-amerikanischer Jurist, Schriftsteller und Diplomat* (Oldenburg: Oldenburgische Gesellschaft für Familiekunde, 2016).

24. A seventeenth-century royal residence that became a legislative building, the palace south of the River Seine was known for its gardens. Arthur Hustin, *Le palais du Luxembourg* (Paris: P. Mouillot, 1904).

tured to go to a restaurant for the first time—even though all the ladies of Paris do it—it was still the first time we dared to sit down and drink beer and seltzer. While Hertha is now approaching adolescence a bit— she is growing and gaining much weight, Percy is the mildest and kindest boy—a true dear little paragon—as Cäcilie claimed. He has all of the integrity that characterized our unforgettable little Fritz. On Thursday I took both children to the lovely Parc Monceau,[25] which is very close by. You should have heard him cautioning his little wild sister not to touch the new plantings with her feet. "There aren't any signs on the trees," he said, "but for this reason we need to be all the more careful." The faithful Cäcilie gave me the most beautiful potted flowers and bouquets for my birthday. Percy's visit should have been the happiest hour of celebration—unfortunately I was waiting in vain because the rules of the institute did not allow for this exception.[26] That made me quite sad.

You will have seen from my letters that I fully agreed with you on all things. I also thought of the stay in Paris as a transition for Percy from one continent to the other and only had the eased language study in mind. I calculated that 6 to 7 months would suffice for Percy to learn this important language. We would still have arrived to be with you starting around August. . . .

Since I have always aimed not to keep the children from you any longer, as you can imagine, I don't want to lose any more time than is absolutely necessary in realizing my deepest wish. As soon as I have paid the most necessary of our debts and as soon as I have earned what is most necessary for our travels, or better yet have cash in hand, I will embark on the journey across the ocean with Cäcilie and our children.

I still have to get a few things in order in Zürich and, for the sake of our reputation, should not depart before I have done what is in my power. I could make quite a decent salary here little by little—but like you, I think that the future and the homeland of our children is over there. I've only seen the *Augsburger Allg[emeine]* sporadically since I left Switzerland, but I did see an article by you from Missouri. Of course, I haven't seen your articles about the schools in Michigan, but I have sincerely asked the editors to make an exception to their rule and send me back the manuscript if they are not going to use it. I do not doubt

---

25. A park three blocks west of the Rue du Rocher.
26. Apparently, Percy's school did not allow him to skip class to celebrate Mathilde's birthday.

for a moment that they used it for one Cotta journal or another.[27] I also had articles in the *Allgemeine* from here. In the *Berliner [Börsenzeitung]* as well.

I was sorry to read, my dear Fritz, that you are working so hard. I was as well. But it is not right. One cannot achieve everything through <u>hard work</u>. One is so very excluded from the world of enjoyment and in the end does not fit in anymore into that world, even though as a writer that actually is <u>necessary</u>. I hope to find a field of work over there. But like here—not without difficulty.

You will not expect me to move to St. Louis. You know how much I have suffered and am still suffering from my liver illness. The climate in St. Louis would be the death of me. But I also don't believe that it is the right place for you long-term. Joining the quite chaotically led Democratic paper[28] would not be satisfying for you long-term.

April 10, 1865.

My brother, my one and only beloved brother dead[29]—my Mother is approaching her last days on earth—my Fanny has barely recovered from a severe illness—Mary may be dying—You are without peace and happiness—oh God! oh God! How much pain is in these lines, how much misery! That's quite a return home. Graves, graves—I am so tired and faint from all the crying. My dear Julius—perhaps no one loved and understood him more than me, except for his poor wife! Your lines from March 20 arrived this morning and bear the sad news of Julius's death and Mother's weakness.—Where is Julius's wife? How many children does he leave behind? Are they taken care of? I can't write any more.

Stay healthy! I will let you know soon when I can depart, unless you have other suggestions or have made other decisions. I do not know anything, not which boat, not which line—oh, I am very helpless and sad. Percy will not hear about the death of his good uncle until the day after tomorrow. I don't want to bring the sadness into the walls of his institute. Hertha is doing very well and making good progress,

---

27. On Cotta publishers, see n. 20 (chapter 3).

28. The *Anzeiger des Westens*.

29. Captain Julius Giesler of the 3rd Wisconsin Cavalry Regiment died on March 12, 1865, from wounds sustained skirmishing with Confederate guerillas in Arkansas. Wilhelm Hense-Jensen, *Wisconsin's Deutsch-Amerikaner: bis zum Schluß des neunzehnten Jahrhunderts* (Milwaukee, Wisc.: Germania, 1900), 1:195; *Soldiers' and Citizens' Album of Biographical Record* (Chicago: Grand Army Publishing Company, 1888), 1:501.

much to the astonishment of all of her teachers. Percy's grades, which he brings me every week, are very good.

Farewell, dear Fritz. Cäcilie and the children send their greetings.

Yours, Mathilde.

Mathilde Franziska Anneke to Fritz Anneke
Paris, May 15, 1865

My dear Fritz!

My beloved Mary is no more. Dr. Rufus Brown,[30] who supported her until she drew her last heavy breath, announced her death to Mathilde Kriege,[31] who then in true old friendship sent me the message from Berlin. Other than that, I have heard from neither Booth nor Mary's mother. My poor little Lili wrote to me on my birthday on April 3rd. Mary herself enclosed her last lines, which were written to Cäcilie asking her to tell me about my dear brother's death and to do so with her loving sensitivity. The child's description of her mother's condition informed me that she only had hours left to live. On her birthday, April 8, I wrote to the faithful, already-broken heart one more time. I enclosed a silken ribbon that I'd bought here as a sign of my love.—But I am sure now that it will arrive too late—too late. I do not know on which day she sighed out her broken flower of a soul into the spring. Everything is silent now. Poor, poor, faithful Mary!

How much I have been suffering from all the strokes of fate in the past month, I do not want to describe to you.

What should I do now? Your wish was for me to be ready for departure in May. I am ready. But you have left us entirely without the means for daily living—and so this year my savings are almost all spent.

Your calculations from Dec. of last year are not accurate anymore after almost half a year.

When I told you what I had saved to reassure you, I did not do it so that you would make us spend these savings but so that you would send us the necessary subsidies. I told you about my savings so that you

---

30. We have been unable to find further information.

31. Mathilde Kriege was a teacher and English-to-German translator who would later move to New York. Helmut Heiland, *Fröbelforschung heute: Aufsätze, 1990–2002* (Würzburg: Königshausen & Neumann, 2003), 47.

would let me use them for the journey and to pay the debt I had carelessly made with my good credit during the times of pressure, which you knew yourself. I later made debts in order to save the American notes.—

I had to spend some of those so-called savings at the beginning of this year, because I was earning less myself and because you left us without resources.

The Hammachers did not want to leave me in this terrible misery and offered to give me what I would need for the American obligations. They did so with great discretion, which they preferred to openly and directly offering financial support. I accepted that and asked for 100 th[alers] per 100 doll. Hammacher himself made no money with this. He sells the obligations for the daily price and gives me what I want— the 100 th[alers]. He isn't rich himself either, as people say. They have all they need for a simple life—but they have plenty.

I have used our time here for the education of the children, as much as our resources allowed. You will have to hand it to me that I have been economical and diligent. I have rarely received a word of encouragement from you, even though you could have known how much I needed it.

As soon as you send a little money—provided that it happens soon because otherwise even a large sum won't help anymore—I will be able to determine the day of departure. You will imagine how much I am on tenterhooks. I have calculated this for you down to the last cent!

The children are growing very splendidly. Hertha is overjoyed under the big almond trees with her graceful little French friends. She often plays for them on the zither. Percy used his Sunday afternoon yesterday to travel to Saint-Cloud[32] and see the waterworks. He was delighted when he came home. It was his first journey that was a little longer and he went all by himself.—We spend every hour that he is not in school with him.—

Gerrit Smith's daughter, the dear Mrs. Miller, is the only one from over there who remembered my grieving heart. She has informed me of Mary's death in a compassionate letter. Poor, poor Mary! If only you could have seen her and spoken to her one more time. It was on her birthday that I wrote her last—I sent a little keepsake in the letter—of course she will not receive that anymore.—What will my poor Lili do

---

32. A Paris suburb.

now? Poor, poor child! Hertha is wailing for her. The children have shed tears over Mary.

<u>Later</u>. Unless we get other directions from you, we will depart on the 10th or 12th of June.—This certainly sounds peculiar. Depart? Last year I needed to stay because as an honest woman I wanted to first pay off my debts. I paid off a small part of them. 200 fr to Linke alone, as you know. I promised to have paid off the other debts by now! Instead, I am leaving. Is that right? Leaving without keeping my word? But my Mother wants me to come. Percy is getting older and must go back if he wants to love and know his fatherland as an American.—I did what was in my power.

Send my letters to Lexow in New York. The French steamers ask for 500 fr from <u>here</u> to New York in second class for each seat. I will see now what the German line asks for[.] I do not know what I should do and still—given the state of things, I cannot exist here longer with the children. Well, you had promised to at least send us the money for the boarding house! We have been here for three months, and I haven't even received half from you.

The children and Cäcilie send their love.

Yours, Mathilde.

Mathilde Franziska Anneke to Fritz Anneke
June 13, 1865

My dear Fritz!

The reason that I hesitated for several days to respond to your last letters was that I had to have answers from different people before I could make more detailed plans regarding our departure. I have asked the General Direction of North German Lloyd[33] for reductions in the price of passage because of my correspondence for American and German journals. I had to discuss the rest of my resources with Hammacher and had to wait for business letters from different people. Lloyd responded very politely to inform me that the decision of their board of directors was that they would charge for first class what they usu-

---

33. The enormous Bremen shipping line founded in 1857. Edwin Dreschel, *Norddeutscher Lloyd, Bremen, 1857–1970: History, Fleet, Ship Mails*, vol 1 (Vancouver: Cordillera Publishing Company, 1995).

ally charge for second. While that certainly does not make any difference for my finances—(since second class itself would have been good enough anyway)—however, it does make a significant difference for my comfort. Now that we have completed the calculations, and now that Hammacher has actually cashed the commercial papers for 550 [dollars], he has proven himself to be nothing but a noble friend. There will be time enough to tell you more details about all of this in person. Corresponding at such long distance often creates more misunderstanding than understanding.—I hope to still get seats on the *America*, which is sailing on July 1. If not—I have written a letter about that today—then I must board the *New York*, which is sailing on July 15. In my next and last letter from here, I will let you know with certainty. I have received the bill of exchange in the amount of 615 fr I used it to make the last rent payment for the boarding house and to make purchases that absolutely have been necessary to travel halfway across the ocean safely. I will carefully use the rest to pay off our debts in Zürich. Hertha's little indisposition has also prevented me from working. The child is so delicate. I sat at her bedside for two days. Today however, she is sitting at my desk next to me and is writing. Percy is well and kind.

I am not clear on our near future in America. You haven't given me any picture at all. When I gathered from your letters that your staying in St. Louis would be problematic, I made you aware that I could not get used to the thought of living there. You well know that I do not know the climate there from my own experience because I have never been there, as you know. You and everyone else knows that it is a climate that people are afraid of, especially those with fevers and liver illnesses. And then the old slave state of Missouri does not tempt me either. The Mississippi on the other hand very much so. I would be happy to see Ida and her family again. I have faithfully kept the love and respect for both Ida and Schmidtill that my heart had to pay in silence.— Now that until now it had seemed very questionable to me whether you would find a suitable and sufficient sphere of activity there, I have set my eyes on different terrain in the meantime. Namely, my imagination had an important foundation in Gerrit Smith—as you must know, his entire family loves and cares for me—the family will <u>await</u> me when I arrive in Peterboro,[34] as well as our friends in New York (Fritz Kapp, Lexow etc.). I would preferably build my future *home* in or near New

---

34. Gerrit Smith's home town near Syracuse, New York.

York. All other places in the United States would always be unsatisfactory to me. But first of all, I cannot pay any heed to all the wishes I might have because I have the urge to see Mother on her deathbed. She will be expecting me with tears in her eyes at the beginning of July. When stretching out all of the question marks about our near future, I had also asked Johanna when she gets the chance to start making preparations for the founding of an institute according to the wishes of Cäcilie. For the beginning, it seems unavoidably necessary to make Milwaukie the first stop in our new American life so that we can collect our belongings, and our library, which Reverend Richmond has been entrusted with, and so that we can realize the plan for Percy.—

I will eternally be wishing myself back to Switzerland. Even if the liberal institutions there all need to be improved significantly, one can live a modest life there when working and living solidly. And finally, the nature there recompenses us for many a deprivation. The children's future and their need, their desire to see you again were chasing us away from there.

I am now very much longing for a suitable and viable occupation. Will I have the opportunity again to find one over there like I had here?

Yesterday, a certain Dr. Lipperheide,[35] until now editor of the widely popular *Berliner Bazar*, asked me to work for his newly established paper *Frauenwelt*.[36] It will be concurrently published in Leipzig and Berlin in German, in Paris in French, in Madrid in Spanish, and in London in English. I will also contribute to the *Börsenzeitung* in Berlin from over there; it published an article of mine for 16 th[alers]. I haven't been able to get other engagements despite my efforts. We will find in our check what the *Augsburger Allgemeine* will pay you for your articles it published. The article "<u>Missouri</u>" was yours.—

From time to time I meet with the old faithful socialist father Heß.[37]— He and his wife send you their love. I will recommend Heß as correspondent to the *Staatszeitung* in Chicago.—

The current views of the *Anzeiger des Westens* suit me much better. I

---

35. Working with his wife Frieda, Franz Lipperheide would become a famous publisher committed to preserving the history of fashion. Gretel Wagner, "Lipperheide, Franz Freiherr von," in *Neue Deutsche Biographie* (1985), 14:655.

36. Lipperheide began publishing *Die Modewelt* in 1865. Ibid.

37. German Jewish socialist who helped found the *Rheinische Zeitung* in 1841 and would become Paris correspondent for the *Illinois Staatszeitung*. Edmund Silberner, "Hess, Moses," in *Neue Deutsche Biographie* (1972), 9:11–12.

cannot deliver a judgement about its politics, because I have become a little uninformed right now. I like the calm tone. The scolding about the "ribald Lincoln" in previous editions was too outrageous.

Where will I find Fanny with her little children? I will have to look for her in some corner of the sad Newark that is left for the poor proletariat that works there. We have experienced nothing but worries, misery, and pain in Newark. She had two rushes of blood, and when Mary wrote me last, the threat was still not over. Störger was in Cuba, and he was in a position to send sufficient resources for the family from there.

Haven't you thought of your friendship with the poor Luise Giesler[38] anymore or reminded yourself of it now in her unspeakable grief? I hear Emil Weiskirch has ministered to her needs. She has three children and is so far away from everyone else.

Hertha is only thinking about Lili and how she can see her again. No one has given me an authentic report about Mary's last moments in life. Neither the dreadful mother nor the husband have thought it was necessary to even inform me of her death.

Cäcilie, the good faithful Cäcilie, who would rather leave everything behind in the homeland than leave me, sends her love. Today, Percy has his free periods, when he's allowed to visit me and Hertha. But his letter will be here too late to send it with this one. Cäcilie's classes will end this week. So we still have to get things in order and pack so that we will be ready come July 1. I hope to get letters from you before then or at least find some at Lexow's or Kapp's in New York.

Stay healthy and with a heartfelt thank you and greetings from your—

Mathilde.

Mathilde Franziska Anneke to Fritz Anneke
Milwaukee, August 1865

My dear Fritz!

I received your second letter while I was busy with our departure from New York. The difficulties of landing and departing from there exceeded anything we experienced during the ocean travel. The costs

---

38. Widow of Mathilde's brother Julius.

were immense and drained all my savings. I had to pay 39 d alone for the journey across the ocean. A terrible scoundrel the Great Western.[39] We were welcomed here with much love from the Weißkirchs, and we have been able to breathe the air of the homeland again. We arrived yesterday morning in the Milwaukie harbor.—We did not find you here. I assume that Dänzer has not returned yet and that this is what keeps you there.

I did not go to Hartford! I passed Hartford, the silent place where my Mary rests, with a bleeding heart. But I did see where she died and where she still fought and suffered on during the last days of her life....

Working with Cäcilie in her future institute will be impossible for you and for me.[40] Cäcilie is certainly not free of religious prejudices. I can still live but not work with her.—I cannot say anything about the situation here. What will the future bring?—I do not know. I will faithfully use my strengths. I have begun a new engagement with the [*Belletristisches*] *Journal*. If I am healthy and diligent, I will make some money from it. I am also writing for a Stuttgart paper, the *Lyra*.[41] I wish to complete my three-volume novel here. Everyone thinks our children are lovely. We are having a lovely family celebration, and Grandmother is surrounded by 12 grandchildren and great-grandchildren.

I am very tired, but I rush to inform you of our happy arrival as fast as possible. Let us know soon when we can expect you here. Hertha says thank you for the sweet Cannon-Fritz.

Farewell, dear Fritz. I do not have more to write you, and I do not have the peace for that now.

    Yours, Mathilde.

Weiskirch's house, Sunday morning

    All of us here are sending you our love.

---

39. Perhaps a reference to the cost of the rail journey from New York to Milwaukee.
40. Mathilde would in fact work with Kapp for several years.
41. We have not been able to the locate details of this newspaper.

Select Bibliography

Archival Sources

MADISON, WISCONSIN

Fritz Anneke and Mathilde Franziska Giesler Anneke Papers, 1791–1884. Wisconsin Historical Society.

MILWAUKEE, WISCONSIN

Sherman M. Booth Family Papers, 1818–1908. Wisconsin Historical Society —Milwaukee Area Research Center. University of Wisconsin–Milwaukee Libraries Archives.

ZÜRICH, SWITZERLAND

Familienarchiv Beust, 1817–1899. Stadtarchiv Zürich.
Baugeschichtliches Archiv. Amt für Stadtbau. Stadt Zürich.
Graphische Sammlung und Fotoarchiv. Zentralbibliothek Zürich.
Bezirksgericht Zürich Zivilprotokoll, 1862. Z 826.32.3. Staatsarchiv Kanton Zürich.

BERLIN, GERMANY

Friedrich Hammacher Archiv, 1824–1904. Bundesarchiv Berlin.

MARBACH AM NECKAR, GERMANY

Cotta-Archiv. Korrespondenz von Mathilde und Fritz Anneke mit dem Cotta-Verlag (Letter Correspondence of Mathilde and Fritz Anneke with their publisher Cotta-Verlag). Deutsches Literaturarchiv Marbach.

MÜNSTER, GERMANY

Nachlass Droste-Hülshoff/Sammlung Droste-Hülshoff. Universitäts- und Landesbibliothek Münster.

RASTATT, GERMANY

Schloss Rastatt, Erinnerungsstätte für die Freiheitsbewegungen in der deutschen Geschichte (Rastatt Castle, Museum Commemorating the Revolutions of 1848).

SPROCKHÖVEL, GERMANY

Archiv der Mathilde Franziska Anneke, 1817–1884. Stadtarchiv Sprockhövel.

Works by Mathilde Franziska Anneke, Fritz Anneke, and Mary Booth

Anneke, Friedrich. *"Wäre ich auch zufällig ein Millionär geworden, meine Gesinnungen und Überzeugungen würden dadurch nicht gelitten haben—": Friedrich Annekes Briefe an Friedrich Hammacher, 1846–1859.* Edited by Erhard Kiehnbaum. Wuppertal: Friedrich Engels-Haus, 1998.

Anneke, Fritz. *Der zweite Freiheitskampf der Vereinigten Staaten von Amerika.* 2 vols. Frankfurt am Main: Sauerländer, 1861.

Anneke, Mathilde Franziska Giesler. *Des Christen freudiger Aufblick zum himmlischen Vater: Gebete und Betrachtungen.* Wesel: Bagel, 1839.

———. *Damen Almanach.* Wesel: A. Prinz, 1842.

———. *Die gebrochenen Ketten: Erzählungen, Reportagen und Reden, 1861–1873.* Edited by Maria Wagner. Stuttgart: Akademischer Verlag, 1983.

———. *Das Geisterhaus in New York.* Leipzig: Hermann Costenoble, 1864.

———. *Der Heimathgruß: Eine Pfingstgabe von Mathilde von Tabouillot, geborene Giesler.* Wesel: Bagel, 1840.

———. *"Ich gestehe, die Herrschaft der fluchwürdigen 'Demokratie' dieses Landes macht mich betrübt . . .": Mathilde Franziska Annekes Briefe an Franziska und Friedrich Hammacher, 1860–1884.* Edited by Erhard Kiehnbaum. Hamburg: Argument Verlag mit Ariadne, 2017.

———. *Der Meister ist da und rufet dich: Ein vollständiges Gebet- und Erbauungsbuch für die gebildete christkatholische Frauenwelt.* Wesel: Bagel, 1840.

———. *Memoiren einer Frau aus dem badisch-pfälzischen Feldzuge.* Newark, N.J.: Buchdruckerei von F. Anneke, 1853.

———. *Producte der Rothen Erde.* Münster: Coppenrath, 1846.

———. "Das Weib im Conflict mit den socialen Verhältnissen." Cologne: Self-published pamphlet, [1846–1847]. Box 6, Folder 7. Fritz Anneke and Mathilde Franziska Anneke Papers. Wisconsin Historical Society, Madison.

Anneke, Mathilde Franziska Giesler (lyrics), and J. Remington Fairlamb (music). *"Entblättert!" The Faded Rose, Op. 28.* New York: Wm. A. Pond & Company, 1865.

Anneke, Mathilde Franziska Giesler, and Friedrich Hammacher. *"Bleib gesund, mein liebster Sohn Fritz—": Mathilde Franziska Annekes Briefe an Friedrich Hammacher, 1846–1849.* Edited by Erhard Kiehnbaum. Hamburg: Argument Verlag, 2004.

Anneke, Mathilde Franziska Giesler. *Mathilde Franziska Anneke in Selbstzeugnissen und Dokumenten.* Edited by Maria Wagner. Frankfurt am Main: Fischer-Taschenbuch-Verlag, 1980.

———. "Mathilde und Fritz Anneke: drei unbekannte Briefe aus dem Jahre

1848." Edited by Michael Knieriem. In *Beiträge zur Heimatkunde der Stadt Schwelm und ihrer Umgebung*, Neue Folge 32 (1982): 85–92.

Booth, Mary H. C. *Wayside Blossoms*. Philadelphia: J. B. Lippincott & Co, 1865.

———. *Wayside Blossoms among Flowers from German Gardens*. Heidelberg: Bangel & Schmitt; Milwaukee: S. C. West, 1864.

Selected Secondary Sources

Baker, H. Robert. *The Rescue of Joshua Glover: A Fugitive Slave, the Constitution, and the Coming of the Civil War*. Athens, Ohio: Ohio University Press, 2006.

Bank, Michaela. *Women of Two Countries: German-American Women, Women's Rights and Nativism, 1848–1890*. New York: Berghahn Books, 2012.

Barton, David and Nigel Hall, eds. *Letter Writing as a Social Practice*. Philadelphia: John Benjamins Publishing, 2000.

Bilić, Viktorija. *Historische amerikanische und deutsche Briefsammlungen: Alltagstexte als Gegenstand des Kooperativen Übersetzens*. Trier: Wissenschaftlicher Verlag Trier, 2014.

Bus, Annette P. "Mathilde Anneke and the Suffrage Movement." In *German Forty-Eighters in the United States*. Edited by Charlotte L. Brancaforte, 79–92. New York: Peter Lang, 1989.

Butler, Diane S. "The Public Life and Private Affairs of Sherman M. Booth." *Wisconsin Magazine of History* 82, no 3 (1999): 166–97.

Ecker, Diana. *Der Freiheit kurzer Sommer: Auf Mathilde Franziska Annekes Spuren durch die pfälzisch-badische Revolution von 1849*. Ubstadt-Weiher: Verlag Regionalkultur, 2012.

Efford, Alison Clark. *German Immigrants, Race, and Citizenship in the Civil War Era*. New York: Cambridge University Press, 2013.

Etges, Andreas. "Erziehung zur Gleichheit. Mathilde Franziska Annekes Töchter-Institut in Milwaukee und ihr Eintreten für Rechte der Frauen." *Zeitschrift für Pädagogik* 40 (1994): 945–62.

Faderman, Lillian. *Surpassing the Love of Men: Romantic Friendship and Love between Women from the Renaissance to the Present*. New York: William Morrow and Company, 1981.

French, Lorely. *German Women as Letter Writers, 1750–1850*. Madison, N.J.: Fairleigh Dickinson University Press, 1996.

Gebhardt, Manfred. *Mathilde Franziska Anneke: Madame, Soldat und Suffragette*. Berlin: Neues Leben, 1988.

Hanschke, Annette. "Frauen und Scheidung im Vormärz: Mathilde Franziska Anneke. Ein Beitrag zum Scheidungsrecht und zur Scheidungswirklichkeit von Frauen im landrechtlichen Preußen." *Geschichte in Köln* 34, no. 1 (1993): 67–98.

Heinzen, Henriette M., and Hertha Anneke Sanne, "Biographical Notes in Commemoration of Fritz Anneke and Mathilde Franziska Giesler Anneke." Unpublished manuscript, 1940. Box 8, Folders 1–2. Fritz Anneke and Mathilde Franziska Giesler Anneke Papers, 1791–1848. Wisconsin Historical Society, Madison.

Henkel, Martin, and Rolf Taubert. *Das Weib im Conflict mit den socialen Verhältnissen: Mathilde Franziska Anneke und die erste deutsche Frauenzeitung.* Bochum: Verlag Égalité, 1976.

Hockamp, Karin. *"Von vielem Geist und großer Herzensgüte": Mathilde Franziska Anneke, 1817–1884.* Bochum: Brockmeyer, 2012.

Hockamp, Karin, Wilfried Korngiebel, and Susanne Slobodzian, eds. *"Die Vernunft befiehlt uns frei zu sein!": Mathilde Franziska Anneke: Demokratin, Frauenrechtlerin, Schriftstellerin.* Münster: Westfälisches Dampfboot, 2018.

Honeck, Mischa. *We Are the Revolutionists: German-Speaking Immigrants and American Abolitionists after 1848.* Athens, Ga.: University of Georgia Press, 2011.

Horsley, Joey. "A German-American Feminist and Her Female Marriages: Mathilde Franziska Anneke (1817–1884)." *Fembio*, http://www.fembio.org/english/biography.php/woman/biography_extra/mathilde-franziska-anneke/. Accessed July 30, 2020.

Horsley, Joey, and Luise F. Pusch. *Frauengeschichten: Berühmte Frauen und ihre Freundinnen.* Göttingen: Wallstein Verlag, 2010.

Kaufmann, Wilhelm. *Die deutschen im amerikanischen Bürgerkriege.* Munich: R. Oldenbourg, 1911.

Killa, Susanne. "Wach geküsst von der Poesie: eine Strategie weiblicher emanzipation in der westfälischen Provinz." *Bürgerkultur im 19. Jahrhundert* (1996): 53–65.

Krueger, Lillian. "Madame Mathilda Franziska Anneke, an Early Wisconsin Journalist." *Wisconsin Magazine of History* 21, no. 2 (1937): 160–67.

Levine, Bruce. *The Spirit of 1848: German Immigrants, Labor Conflict, and the Coming of the Civil War.* Urbana, Ill.: University of Illinois Press, 1992.

Linnhoff, Ursula. *"Zur Freiheit, oh, zur einzig wahren": Schreibende Frauen kämpfen um ihre Rechte.* Köln: Kiepenheuer und Witsch, 1979.

"Mathilde Franziska Anneke." *Lexikon Westfälischer Autorinnen und Autoren, 1750 bis 1950.* https://www.lexikon-westfaelischer-autorinnen-und-autoren.de/autoren/anneke-mathilde-franziska/. Accessed July 30, 2020.

McFarland, Robert B. and Michelle Stott James, eds. *Sophie Discovers Amerika: German-Speaking Women Write the New World.* New York: Camden House, 2014.

Mikus, Birgit. *The Political Woman in Print: German Women's Writing, 1845–1919.* Bern: Peter Lang, 2014.

Möhrmann, Renate, ed. *Frauenemanzipation im deutschen Vormärz: Texte und Dokumente.* Stuttgart: Reclam, 1980.

Ortlepp, Anke. „Auf denn, Ihr Schwestern!": Deutschamerikanische Frauen-vereine in Milwaukee, Wisconsin, 1844–1914. Stuttgart: Franz Steiner, 2004.
———. "Deutsch-Athen Revisited: Writing the History of Germans in Milwaukee." In *Perspectives on Milwaukee's Past*, edited by Margo Anderson and Victor Greene, 109–30. Urbana, Ill.: University of Illinois Press, 2009.
Paepcke, Fritz. *Im übersetzen Leben: Übersetzen und Textvergleich*. Edited by Klaus Berger and Hans-Michael Speier. Tübinger Beiträge zur Linguistik 281. Tübingen: Narr, 1986.
Piepke, Susan L. *Mathilde Franziska Anneke, 1817–1884: The Works and Life of a German-American Activist, including English Translations of "Woman in Conflict with Society" and "Broken Chains."* New York: Peter Lang, 2006.
Rainer-Wilson, Stephani. "Mathilde Franziska Anneke (née Giesler) (1817–1884)." In *Immigrant Entrepreneurship: The German-American Experience Since 1700*. Edited by Hartmut Berghoff and Uwe Spiekermann. Washington, D.C.: German Historical Institute, 2016. https://www.immigrantentrepreneurship.org/entry.php?rec=204#_edn5. Accessed July 30, 2020.
Ruben, Regina. *Mathilde Franziska Anneke: Die erste grosse deutsche Verfechterin des Frauenstimmrechts*. Hamburg: R. Ruben, 1906.
Scherer, Andrea. "Politische Aktivitäten und Verfolgung von Frauen um 1848: zum Beispiel Mathilde Franziska Anneke." *Jahrbuch/Malwida von Meysenbug-Gesellschaft* 6 (1999): 42–49.
Schmidt, Klaus. *Mathilde Franziska und Fritz Anneke: Eine Biographie aus der Pionierzeit von Demokratie und Frauenbewegung*. Köln: Schmidt von Schwind, 2000.
Schulte, Wilhelm. *Fritz Anneke: Ein Leben für die Freiheit in Deutschland und in den USA*. Dortmund: Verlag des Historischen Vereins Dortmund, 1961.
Sinha, Manisha. *The Slave's Cause: A History of Abolition*. New Haven, Conn.: Yale University Press, 2016.
Smith-Rosenberg, Carroll. "The Female World of Love and Ritual: Relations between Women in Nineteenth-Century America." *Signs* 1 (1975): 1–29.
Stahl, Enno. *Mathilde Franziska Anneke Lesebuch*. Bielefeld: Aisthesis, 2015.
Stuecher, Dorothea Diver. *Twice Removed: The Experience of German-American Women Writers in the 19th Century*. New York: P. Lang, 1990.
Venuti, Lawrence, ed. *The Translation Studies Reader*. 3rd ed. London: Routledge, 2012.
Vermeer, Hans J., and Katharina Reiß. *Grundlegung einer allgemeinen Translationstheorie*. Tübingen: Niemeyer, 1984.
Vicinus, Martha. *Intimate Friends: Women Who Loved Women, 1778–1928*. Chicago: University of Chicago Press, 2004.
Wagner, Maria. "Mathilde Anneke's Stories of Slavery in the German-American Press." *MELUS* 6, no. 4 (1979): 9–16.

———, ed. *Mathilde Franziska Anneke in Selbstzeugnissen und Dokumenten.* Frankfurt am Main: Fischer, 1980.

Wallach, Martha Kaarsberg. "Women of German-American Fiction: Therese Robinson, Mathilde Anneke, and Fernande Richter." In *America and the Germans: An Assessment of a Three-Hundred Year History—Immigration, Language, Ethnicity*, Vol. 1, edited by Frank Trommler and Joseph McVeigh, 331–42. Philadelphia: University of Philadelphia Press, 1985.

Wiegmink, Pia. "Antislavery Discourses in Nineteenth-Century German American Women's Fiction." *Atlantic Studies* 14, no. 4 (2017): 476–96.

Zimmerman, Andrew. "From the Second American Revolution to the First International and Back Again: Marxism, the Popular Front, and the American Civil War." In *The World the Civil War Made*, edited by Gregory P. Downs and Kate Masur, 304–37. Chapel Hill, N.C.: University of North Carolina Press, 2015.

Zucker, A. E., ed. *The Forty-Eighters: Political Refugees of the German Revolution of 1848.* New York: Columbia University Press, 1950.

Index

abolitionists. *See* Booth, Sherman; Glover, Joshua, jailbreak; *and specific individuals*
Adams, Charles H., 178
African Americans, 125, 179–81, 205
Allgemeine Augsburger Zeitung, 108, 112, 161, 188; Fritz Anneke's work for, 111, 133, 236–37, 242; Mathilde Anneke's work for, 110, 123, 193; mail forwarded by, 132, 218
American Party. *See* Know Nothing Party
Americans, criticism of, 76, 90, 201. *See also under* United States
Anneke, Carl (brother-in-law), 21, 27, 31, 50; family of, 21, 44n96; pharmacy of, 36, 66, 83
Anneke, Christian (father-in-law), 77, 122, 190; attempts to see, 39–40, 43, 50, 52, 63, 98; conflicts with, 58, 83, 43
Anneke, Emil (brother-in-law), 50, 199n5, 204–6
Anneke, Henriette (sister-in-law), 44, 66, 88n78
Anneke, Hertha (daughter), 22, 35, 74; as adult, 13, 15, 52n121; behavior of, 65, 85, 90, 124, 214, 145–46, 169; development of, 137, 214, 212, 220; excursions of, 125–26, 131, 171–72, 174 195; in Paris, 225–28, 233, 236, 237–38, 239–40, 244; schooling of, 48, 51, 200, 225; separation from Fritz Anneke, 59, 75, 82, 107, 152, 154 162, 174, 191; writing and art of, 77, 121, 152, 212, 220. *See also* Christianity: children and; Civil War: children's response to; Kapp, Cäcilie; music: children and; *and under* illness and injury
Anneke, Percy (son), 22, 90, 120; behavior of, 64–65, 75, 76, 85–86, 124, 145; birthday of, 97–98; cadet corps and, 169–70, 194, 202, 220; development of, 48, 76, 117, 131, 137, 149, 229; excursions of, 171–72, 174, 195, 235–36; on France, 224; illness and injury, 121, 149; schooling in Milwaukee, 32, 33, 34, 38, 48, 82–83; schooling in Paris, 225–27, 233, 236, 238; schooling in Zürich, 110, 124–25, 137, 149–50, 154, 199–200, 212, 214; schooling plans, 219, 220; separation from Fritz Anneke, 65, 82, 107, 154, 162, 174, 229; writing and art of, 51, 121, 157–58. *See also* Civil War: children's response to; Kapp, Cäcilie
Anthony, Susan B., 12, 25n22
anxiety. *See* depression; grief; worry
Arnold, Jonathan E., 45, 49, 53
Asboth, Alexander, 165, 166, 178, 180, 190; court martial of Fritz Anneke and, 184–87, 192
Assing, Ludmilla, 96, 127n107, 128
Aston, Louise, 4

Baden, 154, 154n87; participants in 1848–1849 fighting, 25n23, 47n106, 58n142, 90n81, 92n91, 112n55, 122n90; during Revolutions of 1848–1849, 1, 7, 22–23, 24–25, 138–40, 183
Baden, Switzerland, 42, 148–49, 151
Bad Ragaz, Switzerland, 128, 134, 182
Bakunin, Mikhail, 6
Balatka, Hans, 66, 69
Bamberger, Ludwig, 228
Basel, 41–42, 98, 99, 224
Becker, Johann Philip, 133n14, 139
Berliner Börsenzeitung, 237, 242
Bernays, Karl Ludwig, 60, 114, 116
Beust, Anna von, 42–44, 58, 76, 133, 134

Beust, Friedrich von, 36, 42–44, 138–39, 193; school of, 91, 109–10, 126, 137, 149, 200; trip to Samedan, 54–55, 59
Biedermann, J. A., 33n54, 35, 48
birthdays: of children, 59, 61, 97–98, 106, 145; of family members, 31, 70, 120, 129, 165, 236; of friends, 84, 92, 134
Black Americans, 125, 179–81, 205
Blenker, Louis, 92, 108, 111, 132, 147
Blind, Karl, 84
Booth, Lillian May, 22, 25, 33–34, 56, 231; behavior of, 56, 74, 90, 106; Mary Booth's death and, 238, 240; excursions of, 68, 75, 79; German language and, 74; in New York, 93–95; in Paris, 208; writing and art of, 69–70, 77, 175; in Zürich, 110, 145, 195, 200, 202. *See also* child and spousal support; Christianity
Booth, Mary Ella, 22, 54, 68, 91, 114, 209; letters to, 68–70, 74–75, 93–95, 106, 175–76; in Milwaukee, 26; separation from Mary Booth, 106, 138, 202–3. *See also* child and spousal support; parenting
Booth, Selah, 68n18, 69n19
Booth, Sherman, 8; incarceration in 1860–1861, 62–63, 79–80, 81, 83, 85, 86–89; jailbreak in 1860, 94–95. *See also* child and spousal support; marriage: Sherman and Mary Booth; seduction trial
Borkheim, Sigismund, 122, 122–23n90
Börnstein, Heinrich, 41n86, 43, 47, 60
Brandis, Hermann M., 52, 60
Bremen, 95, 97, 98, 198, 218
Brentano, Lorenz, 157, 203
Brown, John, 87, 115n64
Buell, Don Carlos, 125n99, 128, 131, 132n11
Buffalo Telegraph, 73, 79, 174n26
Bunteschu, Emma, 161
Butler, Benjamin, 205
Butler, William F., 49n100, 53
Butz, Caspar, 147

Cairo, Ill., 164, 187
Carnival, 123
Carré Institute, 219, 225–26
Chicago, 147, 151
Chicago Illinois Staatszeitung, 41n86, 67, 112n56, 154, 242; Fritz and Mathilde Anneke's work for, 41, 47, 71, 151, 227, 229
child and spousal support, 4, 49; from Sherman Booth, 152, 173; Sherman Booth's failure to provide, 82, 89, 109–10, 114, 126, 127, 159, 195–96, 201, 126
children. *See* birthdays; child and spousal support; Christianity; Civil War; death; grief; illness and injury; music; parenting; *and specific names*
Christianity, 202; Mathilde Anneke's opposition to, 4–5, 19, 212, 233, 244; children and, 26, 68–69, 70, 74, 212. *See also* churches
Christmas, 100, 118, 157–61
Chur, Switzerland, 56, 138, 173
churches: in Milwaukee; 53, 68, 70, 74–75; in Zürich, 106, 145, 175, 189. *See also* Christianity
Civil War, 148, 205–6; Fritz Anneke's service in, 97 108–9, 113, 119–20, 124–25, 140, 152, 158; Mathilde Anneke on, 118, 125, 143–44, 150–51, 174, 207; Mathilde Anneke's judgments of Fritz Anneke's service, 127–28, 131–33, 138–40, 142–43, 146; Mathilde Anneke's support for Fritz Anneke's service, 111, 121–22; Mary Booth on, 143, 182; children's response to, 145, 152, 189, 190; Europeans on, 114, 182; transnational dimensions of, 8–10, 188. *See also* court martial
Cologne, 6
Cook, Caroline, 34n55, 45n99, 45n101, 53, 54n128, 56, 69n21. *See also* seduction trial
Corinth, Miss., 132
correspondence. *See* letters; *and specific publications*
Corvin, Otto von, 112, 188
Cotta publishing house, 101, 108n41, 153, 159, 237
court martial, of Fritz Anneke (husband), 164–66; absconding from custody, 187, 189; Mathilde Anneke's response to, 168–69, 172, 189–91, 193; newspaper response to, 190–91, 193, 194, 198–99;

protest of, 166–68, 183–88; trial in, 176–78, 185–86, 192, 196
Cramer, William E., 38, 47
Criminal-Zeitung und Belletrisches Journal, 50, 92, 110–11, 123–24, 127, 194
Crounse, Lorenzo L., 45, 54, 80n51, 85

Daniels, Edward, 24, 68, 86–88, 95
Dänzer, Carl, 216, 244
Daughters' Institute. *See* Töchter-Institut
death: of Mary Booth, 202, 223, 237, 238, 243, 244; of children, 8, 21, 232; contemplated, 129, 152, 162–63, 228, 230, 242; of individuals, 39–40, 91, 126, 161, 218n57, 237. *See also* grief
debt, 27, 38, 71, 89; to Friedrich von Beust, 110; honor and 122; settling, 239, 240, 241; to Gerrit Smith, 115; in Zürich, 127, 133, 153, 201, 220, 221
Democratic Party, 144, 205n12, 216n50, 237
depression, 123, 127, 133, 153, 159–61, 190–91. *See also* grief; worry
Detroit, 26–29, 41, 66, 84–85n70, 90, 204
Detroit Michigan Journal, 59, 85n70
Deutsche Frauen-Zeitung, 8
Dietikon, Switzerland, 194
divorce, 4, 33
doctors. *See* physicians
domestication, 14, 17
domestic staff, 102, 107, 122, 124, 127, 224; rape of, 53–54, 56. *See also* Cook, Caroline; seduction trial
Domschke, Bernhard, 41n87, 47n107, 88
Doolittle, James R., 89
Dortmund, 6, 28, 98
Droste-Hülshoff, Annette von, 6
Duden, Carl, 201
dueling, 6, 181, 218n57
Dumas, Alexandre, 227
Durkee, Charles, 86, 89

Easter, 131
education. *See* Anneke, Hertha; Anneke, Percy; Beust, Friedrich von; *and specific educators and institutions*
election of 1860, 102
Engadine, Switzerland, 54n131, 120n84, 142, 164, 173, 174

Engelmann, Peter, 34n34, 38, 83
English language, 13–14, 30, 50–51, 69, 70; instruction, 8; skills, 23, 24, 50, 51, 233. *See also* translation
Esselen, Christian, 139
Europe, as home, 58, 82, 98, 99, 243. *See also* fatherland; *and specific locations*

fatherland: America as, 99, 113, 143, 232, 240; Germany as, 58, 76, 127
feminism. *See* women's rights
Ferslew, W. Eugene, 167, 168
Fessel, Christian, 31, 65
Fick, Heinrich, 153, 174
Finkler, Wilhelm, 51, 83
Fitch, Thomas, 80
Fletcher, Myla F., 141, 150, 210
Fogg, George G., 116, 136, 143, 171, 206
foreignization, 14, 17, 18
Forty-Eighters, 17. *See also* Revolutions of 1848–1849; *and specific names*
France, observations of, 224. *See also* Paris
Freemasons, 164, 165–68, 185
Freiligrath, Ferdinand, 23, 36
Frémont, John Charles, 146, 147, 205
French language: acquisition of, 27, 197, 220, 225–27, 228; instruction in, 233, 234; text in, 173; used, 81, 116, 228
Fröbel, Julius, 123

Garibaldi, Giuseppe, 55, 100, 101, 131, 150
Gartenlaube, 102
Geisterhaus in New-York, 28–29n39, 50n115, 52, 110; publication of, 112, 119, 203–4; response to, 229
German language: acquisition of, 26; literary club, 69–70; skills, 45, 74, 233. *See also* translation
Giesler, Elisabeth Hülswitt (mother), 3, 9n21, 21, 117, 119; Mary Booth on, 23–24, 74; correspondence with, mentioned, 81, 143, 158, 203, 228; letters to, 99–104, 118–21, 140–45, 165–66; separation from Mathilde Anneke, 76, 82, 117, 121, 199, 206, 220, 242; visits with Mathilde Anneke, 29, 32, 65, 76. *See also under* illness and injury
Giesler, Julius (brother), 118, 237
Giesler, Louise (sister-in-law), 99, 118, 237

Giessbach, Switzerland, 171, 172
gifts, 22, 84; for children, 74–76, 94, 95, 98, 114, 119, 144; mailed (to adults), 75–76, 85, 94, 145, 175, 238; monetary, 129, 136, 147. *See also* birthdays; Christmas; letters
Glover, Joshua, jailbreak, 3, 21, 24n16, 53n124, 62–63, 94n96
Goegg, Amand, 139
Grand Haven, Mich., 27, 36, 66, 69
Grand Rapids, Mich., 36, 50, 54
grief, 237, 243; at Mary Booth's death, 238, 239, 240, 244; at children's deaths, 57, 98, 124, 157, 161–62, 199. *See also* death
Gritzner, Maximillian, 107, 146, 147n60

Halberg, Emma Emilia, 161
Hammacher, Franziska Rollmann, 52n121, 98, 118, 141, 142; marriage of, 77
Hammacher, Friedrich, 77, 138, 141, 239–41
Hatzfeldt, Sophie Josepha Ernestine von, 116–17, 119, 120, 182, 218; gifts from, 128, 148; visits to, 164, 173, 176
health. *See* illness and injury; physicians
Heidelberg, 138n25, 141, 142, 210
Heine, Heinrich, 19, 23, 101n18, 116n69, 213n44; quotations from, 32, 42
Hepp, Johann Adam Philipp, 97, 123, 134, 146, 173, 201, 203; court martial of Fritz Anneke and, 191, 193; debt to, 201
Herwegh, Emma, 100–101, 116–19, 126, 128, 133; no longer friend, 154; piano playing of, 103
Herwegh, Georg, 58, 100–101, 116–18, 120, 125, 191
Hölzlhuber, Franz, 34, 50
home. *See* Europe, as home; fatherland; Milwaukee; rental property; United States; Zürich
Hottingen, Switzerland, 136n21, 200, 220
Hurlbut, Stephen Augustus, 184, 192

illness and injury: Christian Anneke, 43; Fritz Anneke, 111; Hertha Anneke, 33, 65, 97, 121, 137, 146, 152; Mathilde Anneke, general, 71–73, 132–34, 137, 143–44, 148, 169, 234, 237; Percy Anneke, 121, 149; bedsores, 152, 161; Mary Booth, general, 24, 46, 48, 52–53, 76, 136, 161, 171, 206–7; epilepsy, 211–12, 230–31; Elisabeth Giesler, 37, 78–79, 81, 86, 91, 204, 242; "gout" and liver problems, 33, 60, 82, 102–3, 151–52, 189, 219; headache and fever, 67, 123–24, 127; resort "cures" for, 128, 134, 148, 151–52, 173, 182, 209; Johanna ("Fanny") Störger, 94, 103, 231–32, 243; treatments for, 33, 38, 72, 130–31, 169, 230–31; tuberculosis, 24, 133, 202–3, 230–31. *See also* physicians
immigrants: in Milwaukee, 7; in Union army, 9
Indianapolis, 117, 141, 150, 192
Indians, American, 35, 64, 67, 69–70
Interlaken, Switzerland, 171, 173, 175, 195
Italy, 43, 63–64; peace in, 54–55, 57–58, 59; war in, 21, 44, 63, 100–101. *See also* Garibaldi, Giuseppe

Kapp, Cäcilie: letters to Mathilde, 214, 215, 219; in Paris, 220–21, 223, 225; plans for Milwaukee, 232, 234, 236, 242–44; relationship with Percy and Hertha Anneke, 220, 235–36; as teacher, 228, 233; visits to Mathilde Anneke and Mary Booth, 102, 131, 142, 144. *See also* romantic friendship
Kapp, Friedrich, 148, 216, 241
Kapp, Ottilie, 36, 100, 131, 159; family and, 102n26, 123, 126, 128, 131, 142
Karcher, Théodor, 84
Karlsbad, Baden, 33n52, 128
King, Rufus, 49n111
King, Susan, 80
Kinkel, Gottfried, 7, 36, 150, 210
Kinkel, Gottfried, Jr., 150
Knell, John, 177, 178
Know Nothing Party, 67n14, 120, 122, 205
Kriege, Mathilde, 238
Kurrentschrift, 14

La Chaux-de-Fonds, 170–72
Lachmund, Carl, 202, 206, 217; Civil War service of, 177, 187; friendship

with Fritz Anneke, 163n95, 169n10, 172, 174n29
Lansing, Mich., 199, 204, 205, 206n17, 213
Lassalle, Ferdinand, 3, 12, 116–18, 154n86, 181–82, 218
Lavater, Johann Kasper, 106, 136, 189n55
Le Havre, 91
lesbians, 10–11. *See also* romantic friendship
Leslie, Frank, 169; payment from, 34, 60; translation for, 28, 38, 50, 52
letters: cost of sending, 62, 64, 71, 73; to deployed troops, 123; flowers enclosed in, 39, 46, 47, 51, 64, 89; logistics of sending, 36, 44, 46–47, 91–92, 108–9; missing, 32, 44, 63, 71, 113, 119; pictures enclosed in, 76, 101, 119, 137, 169, 193; private, 104, 114–16; reading, 29–30, 46–47, 85
Lexow, Rudolph, 240, 241, 243; payment from, 34, 38, 48, 133, 202. See also *Criminal-Zeitung und Belletrisches Journal*
Limmat River, Switzerland, 194
Lincoln, Abraham, 88, 102, 152, 197, 205, 223
Linke, Thomas J., 112, 201, 240
Lipka, Bertha, 44
Lippincott, Joshua, 210, 229
Liszt, Franz, 103

Madison, Wis., 13, 24, 35, 79, 192
Märklin, Edmund, 47, 66, 75n36, 121, 144, 194
marksmen's festivals, 58, 59, 170–71
marriage: Fritz and Mathilde Anneke, 27, 30, 31, 63–64, 71–73, 104, 162, 213–14; Sherman and Mary Booth, 33–34, 49, 60–61, 114–16, 195–96; divorce, 4, 33; Friedrich and Franziska Hammacher, 77–78; Georg and Emma Herwegh, 101; Mathilde and Alfred von Tabouillot, 4. *See also* child and spousal support; parenting; romantic friendship
Marx, Karl, 6, 84, 94n97, 116n69; associates of, 23n10, 36n70, 42n93, 43n94, 60n147, 90n81, 139n29; cousin of, 42n93
Marxhausen, August, 84
Mazzini, Giuseppe, 33n51, 55
McClellan, George B., 150–52
McClernand, John A., 152, 166, 178, 187
medicine. *See* illness and injury; physicians
Messmore, Isaac E., 164–65, 178, 183–86, 190
Michigan, Lake, 7, 27, 32, 66n8, 232
Milan, Italy, 55, 63, 64
military: Prussian army, 6, 181; United States Colored Troops, 178–81. *See also* Baden; Civil War; court martial, of Fritz Anneke; Italy; Rüstow, Friedrich
Miller, Elizabeth Smith, 125, 134, 239
Milwaukee: excursions around, 32, 66, 68, 69, 91; as home, 232; observations of, 7; politics, 83
Milwaukee Atlas, 67; Fritz Anneke's work for, 41, 48, 50, 59, 67; payment from, 47–48, 60, 73
Milwaukee Daily Life, 113n60, 148n65, 176n30, 196; Mary Booth's work for, 148, 176, 196
Milwaukee Daily Sentinel, 47, 71; Fritz Anneke's work for, 41, 49, 50, 67; payment from, 73
Milwaukee Free Democrat, 27n32, 41, 45n98, 49, 80n51, 80n53, 85
Milwaukee Gradaus, 18, 47n105, 48
Milwaukee Herold, 51n119, 193, 195
Milwaukee Seebote, 29, 31
Milwaukee Volksblatt, 18, 48
Milwaukee Wisconsin Banner und Volksfreund, 29n42, 110n51, 112
Milwaukee Wisconsin Freeman, 8
money: expenses in Milwaukee, 40–41, 43, 45, 48, 64–65; expenses in Paris, 225, 229, 236; expenses in Zürich, 109, 111, 127, 136–37, 159–61, 170, 201; financial instruments, 44, 52, 53, 92, 153, 190, 206, 216, 221, 224, 239, 241; property sales to raise, 89; requested from Fritz Anneke, 72, 133–34, 151, 162, 225–26, 234, 238–40; transferring, 43–44, 52, 170, 173, 190. *See also* child

money (*continued*)
and spousal support; debt; poverty; rental property; *and specific publications, publishers, and editors*
Münster, 4, 6, 98, 218
music, 32, 45, 66–67, 69–70, 103; children and, 200, 203, 214, 221, 228, 239

National Woman Suffrage Association, 12
Native Americans, 35, 64, 67, 69–70
Neue Kölnische Zeitung, 6, 23n10
Newark, N.J.: Annekes in, 8, 23, 243; Johanna ("Fanny") Störger in, 91, 223, 230, 243
Newark New Jersey Freie Zeitung, 60, 73
New Haven, Conn., 8, 209n26
New Year's celebrations, 118–19
New-Yorker Demokrat, 37, 41, 46, 50n113, 191
New York Staats-Demokrat, 41n85, 50

Ottendorfer, Anna (Uhl), 91, 92, 94
Otterburg, Marcus, 47, 73

Paine, Hortensius, 53, 80n49
parenting, 96–97, 109, 118, 120, 203; marriage and, 30, 33; as reason to live, 126, 152, 163, 202; sense of responsibility and, 73, 122, 133–34, 220, 232–33; when separated from children, 64, 70, 99, 107–8, 133, 138, 202, 203. *See also* child and spousal support; romantic friendship; *and specific children's names*
Paris: excursions around, 235–36, 239; observations of, 235; politics in, 59; relocation to, 219–21, 224, 236
passports, 40, 41, 86, 92, 95
Pestalozzi, Karl, 137, 152, 153, 173, 221
Pfäfers, Switzerland, 138, 141
Pfeiffer, Ida, 23
physicians: bills from, 160, 161, 201; in Milwaukee, 24, 31, 56, 65, 78, 81; in New York, 209, 211–12, 230–31; in Zürich, 87, 128, 130–34, 137, 149, 151–52, 202–3. *See also* illness and injury
politics: election of 1860, 102; European, 126–27, 182, 198–99; U.S. antebellum, 25nn22–23, 67, 88, 102; U.S. Civil War, 146–47, 205–6, 223, 227, 231, 242–43. *See also* Democratic Party; Republican Party; *and specific politicians*
poverty: in Milwaukee, 49, 62, 63, 71–73; in Paris, 228–29, 238–39; in Zürich, 129, 153, 159–61, 201
Prussian army, 6, 181,
publishing books, 101n20, 112–13, 119, 210–11, 229
publishing in newspapers. *See specific publications, publishers, and editors*

rape, 53–54, 56. *See also* seduction trial
Rapperswil, Switzerland, 55, 56, 173
Rastatt, Baden, 138
Raster, Hermann, 112, 188, 189, 193, 198
realia, 18
Reitzenstein, Pauline von (sister), 103, 119, 144
rental property, 99–100, 102, 124, 136–37; lawsuit over, 137, 153, 174, 202
Republican Party, 67, 86, 89, 102, 146–47, 197, 223
Revolutions of 1848–1849, 5–7, 58, 117. *See also* Baden; *and specific participants*
Rhine River, 39n81, 41, 56
Richmond, James Cook, 23, 25, 53, 75, 128–29, 242; interest in German, 25, 69; as priest, 23n11, 53, 68, 70, 74
Ritzinger, Friedrich, 133, 141n43, 159, 173, 192
Ritzinger, Maria, 141, 150
Robinson, Solomon S., 168
Rollmann, Franziska. *See* Hammacher, Franziska Rollmann
Rollmann, Maria Christina Elisabeth, 142
romantic friendship, 10–12; love and admiration, discussed, 22–23, 24–25, 30, 35, 38, 65, 76, 104, 199, 238; love notes, 92–93, 155–56, 208; mutual support in Milwaukee, 24, 31, 33, 35, 46, 49, 53, 58, 78, 82, 84; mutual support in Zürich, 151, 160, 170, 202–3; parenting and, 29–30, 65–65, 74–75, 200; separation, 199–201, 206–7, 211. *See also* death; grief; Kapp, Cäcilie
Ross, Leonard F., 187
Ruppius, Otto, 47, 48n108, 51, 60, 129n113

Rüstow, Anna Katharina, 154
Rüstow, Friedrich, 96, 100–101, 114, 174; military career of, 114; writings of, 154, 182

Saint-Hilaire, Jules Barthélemy, 173
Sallet, Friedrich von, 23
Salomon, Edward, 158n91, 176, 177, 186
Sanne, Hertha Anneke. *See* Anneke, Hertha
Schabelitz, Jakob, 201
Scheffer, Louis, 103, 118
Schleiermacher, Friedrich, 17
Schmidtill, Emily, 217, 221
Schmidtill, Ida, 83n61, 217n55, 221, 241
Schmidtill, Sigmund, 83, 241
Schmitt, Carl, 138, 141, 210
Schmitt, Caroline, 141n44
Schnake, Friedrich, 217, 218, 221
Schöffler, Moritz, 124, 136, 140
Schurz, Carl, 74, 151; Mathilde Anneke's opinion of, 88, 125, 132, 139, 162, 193; in Baden 1848–1849, 7, 25, 139, 188; in Civil War, 125, 132, 139, 142; political career of, 67, 88, 102, 151
Schurz, Margarethe, 74, 102
Schwedler, Friedrich, 41, 46, 50n113, 84
Sclaven Auction, 122, 145
Second War for Italian Independence. *See* Italy
seduction trial, 34, 56, 58, 59, 60, 62; lawyers in, 45, 49; preparations for, 45–46, 48–49, 53–54
separation. *See* child and spousal support; marriage; romantic friendship; *and under* Anneke, Hertha; Anneke, Percy; Booth, Mary Ella; romantic friendship
Seward, William, 88, 151
sexual misconduct, 114–15; rape, 53–54, 56; suspected, 45. *See also* seduction trial
Sholes, Charles C., 80
sickness. *See* illness and injury
Sigel, Franz, 139, 146–48
sightseeing. *See specific locations*
skopos theory, 14, 17, 18
slavery, 125, 241

Smith, Gerrit, 3, 241; as character in *Sclaven Auction*, 122n89; correspondence with, 115, 125, 136, 144, 151, 209; family of, 125, 134, 151n75, 239; gift from, 136
Sobolewski, Johann, 66
Solferino, Battle of, 55, 59
Southampton, England, 37n75, 46, 55, 91, 97, 98; correspondence via, 37, 43, 44
Springfield, Ill., 138, 142, 147, 152
Stallo, J. B., 235
Stanton, Edwin, 151n75, 183, 196
Stanton, Elizabeth Cady, 12, 25, 122, 125, 151
St. Louis, Mo., 47, 91, 206, 233; Fritz Anneke in, 140n34, 216, 223, 241; Mathilde Anneke's opinion of, 232, 237; schools in, 233
St. Louis Anzeiger des Westens: Carl Dänzer and, 216, 244; as Democratic-leaning paper, 216, 223, 237, 242; as Republican paper, 41n86, 43n94, 51, 60n147. *See also St. Louis WestlicheBlätter*
St. Louis NeuerAnzeiger des Westens. See St. Louis Anzeiger des Westens
St. Louis WestlicheBlätter, 41, 47, 49, 51, 60
Störger, Johanna ("Fanny"; daughter), 4, 24, 237; correspondence with, 103–4, 121; separation from Mathilde Anneke, 76, 199, 243; visits with, 94–95, 113, 222–23, 231. *See also* illness and injury
Störger, Paul (son-in-law), 24n19, 243
Störger, Paula (granddaughter), 231
Strasbourg, 7, 39–41, 50, 57, 224
Streit, Feodor, 154
Struve, Amalie, 126
Sturmgeiger, 113, 119, 218
Szarvady, Frigyes, 228

Tabouillot, Alfred von, 4
Tamina Gorge, Switzerland, 138, 141
Tarasp, Switzerland, 120, 173, 181
Techow, Gustav Adolph, 139
TiefenBrunnen guesthouse, 39, 40, 43, 64, 91
Töchter-Institut, 12, 223, 228, 232–35, 242

translation, 14–20; Mathilde Anneke's, 28, 32, 34, 52
transportation: carriage, 42, 68, 98, 124; lake, 27, 50, 55, 66–67, 69; railroad, 41, 55–56, 224, 243–44; river, 97; sea, 50, 89–90, 97, 107–8, 240–41, 243
travel. *See* transportation; *and specific locations*
Turners, 48, 79

Ubstadt, Baden, 139
Uhl, Anna (Ottendorfer), 91, 92, 94
Uhland in Texas, 101n19, 203, 229
United States: criticism of, 42, 58, 77, 81, 84, 194–95, 204; criticism of Americans, 76, 90, 201; as home, 82, 146, 199, 202, 212, 236. *See also* fatherland: America as; *and specific locations*
United States Colored Troops, 178–81

Varnhagen, Karl August, 127, 128n112
Vicksburg, Miss., 152n77, 172, 174, 177, 192
Vogt, Karl, 83–84

Wagner, Richard, 103
Walen, Lake, 56
Waring, George E., 166, 168n8, 178, 179
Washburne, Elihu, 146

Weib im Conflict mit socialen Verhältnissen, Das, 4
weight gain and loss, 33, 91, 97
Weiskirch, Alma (niece), 61, 70, 78, 145
Weiskirch, Emil (brother-in-law), 27, 61, 161, 173, 244; correspondence with, 95, 140, 190, 204; money transferred by, 170, 173
Weiskirch, Ida (niece), 61, 70, 78, 145
Weiskirch, Johanna (sister), 21, 61, 70, 140, 244; correspondence with, 140, 232
Willich, August, 6, 90, 139n31, 187, 206, 235
Woman in Conflict with Society (*Das Weib im Conflict mit socialen Verhältnissen*), 4
women's rights, 4–5, 7–8, 25, 64, 223, 227
worry, 33, 78, 153, 158, 189, 207. *See also* death; depression; grief
Wüst, Theodore, 209n27, 231

Zeller, Susanna and Thomas, 107, 137, 148, 153, 174
Zündt, Ernst Anton, 38, 48, 61, 140
Zürich: excursions around, 55–56, 109, 123, 124–25, 194; as home, 224; observations of, 41, 58, 64, 99–100, 195. *See also* rental property
Züricher Zeitung, 190, 193

New Perspectives on the Civil War Era

Practical Strangers: The Courtship Correspondence of Nathaniel Dawson and Elodie Todd, Sister of Mary Todd Lincoln
EDITED BY STEPHEN BERRY AND ANGELA ESCO ELDER

The Greatest Trials I Ever Had: The Civil War Letters of Margaret and Thomas Cahill
EDITED BY RYAN W. KEATING

Prison Pens: Gender, Memory, and Imprisonment in the Writings of Mollie Scollay and Wash Nelson, 1863–1866
EDITED BY TIMOTHY J. WILLIAMS AND EVAN A. KUTZLER

William Gregg's Civil War: The Battle to Shape the History of Guerrilla Warfare
EDITED AND ANNOTATED BY JOSEPH M. BEILEIN JR.

Seen/Unseen: Hidden Lives in a Community of Enslaved Georgians
WRITTEN AND EDITED BY CHRISTOPHER R. LAWTON, LAURA E. NELSON, RANDY L. REID

Radical Relationships: The Civil War–Era Correspondence of Mathilde Franziska Anneke
TRANSLATED BY VICTORIJA BILIĆ
EDITED BY ALISON CLARK EFFORD AND VIKTORIJA BILIĆ